An Ulster slave-owner in the Revolutionary Atlantic

An Ulster slave-owner
in the Revolutionary Atlantic

The life and letters of John Black

Jonathan Jeffrey Wright

EDITOR

FOUR COURTS PRESS

Set in 10 on 12 point Ehrhardt for
FOUR COURTS PRESS LTD
7 Malpas Street, Dublin 8, Ireland
www.fourcourtspress.ie
and in North America for
FOUR COURTS PRESS
c/o IPG, 814 N. Franklin St, Chicago, IL 60622.

ISBN 978-1-84682-736-5

A catalogue record for this title
is available from the British Library.

Printed in England
by CPI Antony Rowe, Chippenham, Wilts.

Contents

Abbreviations

In addition to standard abbreviations – *BNL, PRONI, UJA* and so forth – the following list includes abbreviated references for sources cited in both the introduction and the annotations to the letters, or in the annotations for more than one letter. Where a source has been referred to in one section only – i.e., in the introduction, or in the annotations to just one letter – it is cited in full in the first instance, and shortened citations are given for any subsequent references within the section.

['A gentleman of the Island'], *Political account*	['A gentleman of the Island'], *A political account of the Island of Trinidad, from its conquest by Sir Ralph Abercrombie, in the year 1797, to the present time, in a letter to the his grace the duke of Portland* (London, 1807).
Adams, *Printed word*	J.R.R. Adams, *The printed word and the common man: popular culture in Ulster, 1700–1900* (Belfast, 1987).
Agnew, *Merchant families*	Jean Agnew, *Belfast merchant families in the seventeenth century* (Dublin, 1996).
AJR	*Anti-Jacobin Review and Magazine.*
[Anon.], 'Further extracts'	[Anon.], 'Further extracts from "The Barbadian" newspaper, 1836' in *The Journal of the Barbados Museum and Historical Society*, 6 (1939), 205–15.
Apperson, Manser and Curtis, *Proverbs*	George Latimer Apperson, Martin H. Manser and Stephen J. Curtis, *Dictionary of proverbs* (London, 2006).
Barnard, 'Educating'	T.C. Barnard, 'Educating eighteenth-century Ulster' in D.W. Hayton and Andrew R. Holmes (eds), *Ourselves alone? Religion, society and politics in eighteenth- and nineteenth-century Ireland: essays presented to S.J. Connolly* (Dublin, 2016), pp 104–25.
Benn, *Belfast*	George Benn, *A history of the town of Belfast from the earliest times to the close of the eighteenth century* (London, 1877).
Benn, *Belfast from 1799 till 1810*	George Benn, *A history of the town of Belfast from 1799 till 1810 together with some incidental notices on local topics and biographies of many well-known families* (London, 1880).

Black, 'Ballydrain'	Eileen Black, 'Ballydrain, Dunmurray – an estate through the ages' in *Lisburn Historical Society Journal*, 5 (1984), 17–28.
Black's	Bryan A. Garner (ed.) and Henry Campbell Black, *Black's law dictionary*, 8th ed. (St Paul's, MN, 2004).
BNL	*Belfast News-Letter.*
Brereton, *Modern Trinidad*	Bridget Brereton, *A history of modern Trinidad, 1783–1962* (Kingston, Port of Spain and London, 1981).
Burke, *Landed gentry*	Bernard Burke, *A genealogical and heraldic history of the landed gentry of Ireland*, new ed. (London, 1912).
Burkholder and Johnson, *Colonial Latin America*	Mark A. Burkholder and Lyman L. Johnson, *Colonial Latin America*, 4th ed. (New York, 2001).
Candlin, *Last Caribbean frontier*	Kit Candlin, *The last Caribbean frontier, 1795–1815* (Basingstoke, 2012).
Carmichael, *Trinidad and Tobago*	Gertrude Carmichael, *The history of the West Indian islands of Trinidad and Tobago, 1498–1900* (London, 1961).
Chambers, *Faces*	George Chambers, *Faces of change: the Belfast and Northern Ireland Chambers of Commerce and Industry, 1783–1983* (Belfast, n.d.).
CJB	*The correspondence of Joseph Black*, Robert G.W. Anderson and Jean Jones (eds) (2 vols, Farnham, 2012).
Coquelle, *Napoleon and England*	P. Coquelle, *Napoleon and England, 1803–1813: a study from unprinted documents* (London, 1904).
Cullen, *Anglo-Irish trade*	L.M. Cullen, *Anglo-Irish trade, 1660–1800* (Manchester, 1968).
Cullen, 'Irish merchant communities of Bordeaux, La Rochelle and Cognac'	L.M. Cullen, 'The Irish merchant communities of Bordeaux, La Rochelle and Cognac in the eighteenth century' in L.M. Cullen and P. Butel (eds), *Négoce et industrie en France et en Irlande aux xviiiᵉ et xixᵉ siècles: actes du colloque Franco-Irlandais d'histoire – Bordeaux – Mai 1978* (Paris, 1980), pp 51–63
Davis and Mintz, *Boisterous sea*	David Brion Davis and Steven Mintz, *The boisterous sea of liberty: a documentary history of America from discovery through the Civil War* (New York and Oxford, 1998).
de Verteuil, *Sylvester Devenish*	Anthony de Verteuil, *Sylvester Devenish and the Irish in nineteenth-century Trinidad* (Port of Spain, 1986).
Devine, 'Business élite'	T.M. Devine, 'An eighteenth-century business

élite: Glasgow-West India merchants, *c.*1750–1815' in *Scottish Historical Review*, 57 (1978), 40–67.

DIB — James Maguire and James Quinn (eds), *Dictionary of Irish biography: from the earliest times to the year 2002* (9 vols, Cambridge, 2004).

DML — *The Drennan–McTier Letters*, ed. Jean Agnew (3 vols, Dublin, 1998–9).

Drescher, *Econocide* — Seymour Drescher, *Econocide: British slavery in the era of abolition*, 2nd ed. (Chapel Hill, NC, 2010).

Dunn, *Sugar and slaves* — Richard S. Dunn, *Sugar and slaves: the rise of the planter class in the English West Indies, 1624–1713* (Chapel Hill, NC, 2000).

Eakin, *Latin America* — Marshall C. Eakin, *The history of Latin America: collision of cultures* (New York, 2007).

Epstein, *Scandal* — James Epstein, *Scandal of colonial rule: power and subversion in the British Atlantic during the Age of Revolution* (Cambridge, 2012).

Esdaile, *The Peninsular War* — Charles Esdaile, *The Peninsular War: a new history* (London, 2003).

Fraser, *Trinidad* — Lionel M. Fraser, *History of Trinidad* (2 vols, Port of Spain, 1891–6).

Gamble, 'Business community' — Norman E. Gamble, 'The business community and trade of Belfast, 1767–1800' (PhD thesis, Trinity College Dublin, 1978).

Gillespie, *Early Belfast* — Raymond Gillespie, *Early Belfast: the origins and growth of an Ulster town to 1750* (Belfast, 2007).

Gillespie and Royle, *Belfast* — Raymond Gillespie and Stephen A. Royle, *Irish historic towns atlas: Belfast: part 1, to 1840* (Dublin, 2003).

GM — *Gentleman's Magazine*.

Henige, *Colonial governors* — David P. Henige, *Colonial governors from the fifteenth century to the present: a comprehensive list* (Madison, 1970).

Hilton, *A mad, bad and dangerous people?* — Boyd Hilton, *A mad, bad and dangerous people? England, 1783–1846* (Oxford, 2006).

John, *Plantation slaves* — A. Meredith John, *The plantation slaves of Trinidad, 1783–1816: a mathematical and demographic enquiry* (Cambridge, 1988).

Johnston, 'Grenada, 1775–79' — E.M. Johnston, 'Grenada, 1775–79' in Peter Roebuck (ed.), *Macartney of Lisanoure, 1737–1806: essays in biography* (Belfast, 1983), pp 88–126.

Joseph, *Trinidad* — E.L. Joseph, *History of Trinidad* (London, 1838, repr. 1970).

Letterbook of Greg & Cunningham, ed. Truxes	*Letterbook of Greg & Cunningham 1756–57: merchants of New York and Belfast,* ed. Thomas M. Truxes (Oxford, 2001).
Letters of Decius	*Letters of Decius, in answer to the criticism upon the* Political account of Trinidad*; and upon the defence of the crimes of governor Picton, in the* Anti-Jacobin Review, *under the title of the 'Pictonian Prosecution'* (London, 1808).
Livesey, *Civil society*	James Livesey, *Civil society and empire: Ireland and Scotland in the eighteenth-century Atlantic world* (New Haven, 2009).
McBride, *Scripture politics*	I.R. McBride, *Scripture politics: Ulster Presbyterians and Irish radicalism in the late eighteenth century* (Oxford, 1998).
McCallum, *Travels*	Pierre McCallum, *Travels in Trinidad during the months of February, March, and April, 1803, in a series of letters, addressed to a member of the imperial parliament of Great Britain* (Liverpool, 1805).
McTear, 'Personal recollections'	Thomas McTear, 'Personal recollections of the beginning of the century' in *UJA,* second series, 5 (1989), 211–13.
Miller, Schrier, Boling and Doyle (eds), *Irish immigrants*	Kerby A. Miller, Arnold Schrier, Bruce D. Boling and David N. Doyle (eds), *Irish immigrants in the land of Canaan: letters and memoirs from Colonial and Revolutionary America, 1675–1815* (Oxford, 2003).
Millette, *Society and politics*	James Millette, *Society and politics in colonial Trinidad* (London, 1985).
Morgan, *Slavery and the British empire*	Kenneth Morgan, *Slavery and the British empire: from Africa to America* (Oxford, 2007).
Naipaul, *El Dorado*	V.S. Naipaul, *The loss of El Dorado* (London, 1970).
ODNB	*Oxford dictionary of national biography* (accessed online at http://www.oxforddnb.com).
Partners, ed. Robinson and McKie	*Partners in science: letters of James Watt and Joseph Black,* ed. Eric Robinson and Douglas McKie (London, 1970).
Pocock, *Out of the shadows*	Michael Rogers Pocock, *Out of the shadows of the past: the story of the 'Great House' of Champs Elysées, Maraval, and an account of the lives and times of the families who lived in it, 1780–1932* (Hastings, 1993).
Polasky, *Revolutions without borders*	Janet Polasky, *Revolutions without borders: the call to liberty in the Atlantic world* (New Haven, 2015).
PRONI	Public Records Office of Northern Ireland.

Register, ed. Gillespie and O'Keeffe   *Register of the parish of Shankill, Belfast, 1745–1761*, ed. Raymond Gillespie and Alison O'Keeffe (Dublin, 2006).

Riddell, 'Great chemist'   Henry Riddell, 'The great chemist, Joseph Black, his Belfast friends and family connections' in *Proceedings of the Belfast Natural History and Philosophical Society*, 3 (1919–20), 49–88.

RMC   *The royal military calendar, or army service and commission book*, 3rd edition (5 vols, London, 1820).

Rodgers, *Ireland, slavery and anti-slavery*   Nini Rodgers, *Ireland, slavery and anti-slavery, 1612–1865* (Basingstoke, 2009).

Roebuck (ed.), *Macartney*   Peter Roebuck (ed.), *Macartney of Lisanoure, 1737–1806: essays in biography* (Belfast, 1983).

Ryden, 'Sugar, spirits, and fodder'   David Beck Ryden, 'Sugar, spirits, and fodder: the London West India interest and the glut of 1807–15' in *Atlantic Studies*, 9 (2012), 41–64.

'Table talk'   'Table talk of an old campaigner. No. II', *United Service Journal and Naval and Military Magazine*, pt II (1836), 207–18.

TNA   The National Archives, Kew.

Town book, ed. Young   *The town book of the corporation of Belfast, 1613–1816*, ed. R.M. Young (Belfast, 1892).

Uglow, *In these times*   Jenny Uglow, *In these times: living in Britain through Napoleon's wars, 1793–1815* (London, 2014).

UJA   *Ulster Journal of Archaeology*.

Ward, 'Black family'   Isaac W. Ward, 'The Black family' in *UJA*, second series, 8 (1902), 176–88.

Watson, *George III*   J. Steven Watson, *The reign of George III, 1760–1815* (Oxford, 1960).

Whiting, *Early American proverbs*   Bartlett Jere Whiting, *Early American proverbs and proverbial phrases* (Cambridge, MA, 1977).

Winer, *Dictionary*   Lise Winer, *Dictionary of the English/creole of Trinidad and Tobago: on historical principles* (Montreal and Kingston, 2009).

Acknowledgments

Reinforcing a long-held belief that serendipity plays an important role in historical research, I first encountered the letters of John Black by accident, when searching in the Public Records Office of Northern Ireland for materials relating to Ulster's connections with Atlantic Canada. It is thus only fair that I should begin by expressing my thanks to Peter Ludlow, who encouraged me to undertake that line of research, and who later assisted me in tracing Black's Nova Scotian connections. Equally important was Raymond Gillespie, who first suggested that I consider publishing Black's letters, and who kindly read a draft of the introduction and offered invaluable assistance and advice as I worked on editing and annotating the collection. The standard proviso, of course, applies: any errors of fact and interpretation remain my responsibility. Arguments developed in the introduction of the present volume were first presented to audiences at Brockport College, New York, and Trinity College Dublin, and to several groups of second year students at Maynooth University, who have taken my module Slavery and Anti-slavery in the British World. I am grateful to all those students and audience members who have asked questions and assisted me in clarifying my thinking on Black and his world. Thanks are also due to Gerry O'Keeffe and Helen Walker, who tracked down sources on my behalf in the British Library; to Kenneth Dawson, Richard Fitzpatrick, Jimmy Kelly, JoAnne Mancini, Jennifer McLaren, David Murphy, Tom O'Connor and Ian Speller, who shared references and sources, and offered advice on various points; to Eamon Darcy and Sylvie Kleinman, who assisted in matters of translation; to Martin Fanning at Four Courts Press, who has dealt patiently with a tardy and, at times, distracted author; to my colleagues in the Department of History, Maynooth University, who have provided a congenial and supportive environment in which to pursue research; and to the Maynooth University Publications Fund and the Department of History Research Incentivisation Fund, which have provided generous support towards publication costs. Particular thanks – for friendship, camaraderie and the occasional coffee and lunch break – are also due to Eamon Darcy, Alison Fitzgerald, Raymond Gillespie, Michael Potterton and Jennifer Redmond. Above all, however, I wish to thank Rhiannon, George and Clara, who have with forbearance borne with a distracted and, yes, at times, irritable husband and father, and who will, I rather suspect, be glad to see the back of Black.

John Black's Atlantic: the worlds and words of an Ulster slave-owner

Belfast in the eighteenth and early nineteenth centuries was a town inextricably linked to the wider Atlantic world – a world born, in the words of David Armitage and Michael J. Braddick, of 'kaleidoscopic movements of people, goods, and ideas'.[1] Central to the town's Atlantic connections were the activities of what one visitor, writing in 1759, described as its 'many merchants and traders of substance'.[2] That Belfast's merchants traded extensively with Britain's North American colonies is well known; as Raymond Gillespie has noted, Belfast was 'the first town in the north of Ireland to enter into a two-way trade with mainland North America'.[3] Equally significant, however, was the town's trade with the West Indies. By the second half of the eighteenth century this was deep-rooted. Belfast's merchants had been supplying beef and herrings to the West Indies from as early as the 1660s and, as Norman E. Gamble has observed, '[m]any of the most important merchant families in Belfast during the first half of the eighteenth century were engaged in the West Indian trade.'[4] In the years that followed, the trade grew in importance: by the 1780s Belfast's merchants are known to have been catering to Jamaica's voracious market for provisions and commodities, and the significance of the town's connections with the West Indies became readily apparent to contemporaries.[5] 'Belfast', the duke of Rutland observed in the late 1780s, 'is a giant of a town, flourishing in everything ... Their trade is immense. They go to the West Indies, and to almost every quarter of the globe.'[6]

But who, exactly, were 'they'? And what is known of their world? The first of these questions may be answered easily enough. The ground-breaking work

1 David Armitage and Michael J. Braddick, 'Introduction' in David Armitage and Michael J. Braddick (eds), *The British Atlantic world, 1500–1800* (New York, 2002), pp 1–7 at 1. See also, for the Atlantic world and the development of Atlantic history, Bernard Bailyn, *Atlantic history: concept and contours* (Cambridge, MA, 2005). 2 *The letters of Lord Chief Baron Edward Willes to the earl of Warwick, 1752–1762: an account of Ireland in the mid-eighteenth century*, ed. James Kelly (Aberystwyth, 1990), p. 34. 3 Gillespie, *Early Belfast*, p. 159. See also, Gamble, 'Business community', pp 296–321 and Thomas M. Truxes, *Irish-American trade, 1660–1783* (Cambridge, 1988), pp 78–81. 4 Agnew, *Merchant families*, pp 41, 105–6, 110; Gamble, 'Business community', p. 269. 5 Gamble, 'Business community', pp 279–88. 6 *Historical Manuscripts Commission. Fourteenth report, appendix, part 1. The manuscripts of his grace the duke of Rutland, K.G. preserved at Belvoir Castle. Vol. III* (London, 1894), pp 420–1. See also *Pococke's tour in Ireland in 1752*, ed. George T. Stokes (Dublin, 1891), p. 20.

of scholars such as Gamble and Nini Rodgers reveals that Belfast – and, more broadly, Ulster – was linked to the West Indies not simply by merchants, but by a mobile, Atlantic community of ship captains, agents, merchant factors and West Indian sojourners.[7] The second question is, though, more problematic, for such figures have attracted little sustained attention. Existing scholarship on Ulster's Atlantic connections tends, indeed, to focus on North America, and much remains to be discovered about the experiences of those merchants, agents and sojourners whose activities connected the province to the West Indies.[8] One such figure was John Black, and it is with this lacunae in mind that his letters are presented and contextualized in the present volume.

* * *

A Belfast-born slave-owner and some-time slave-trader, who spent the bulk of his adult life in Trinidad, John Black is not, in an Irish context, well known.[9] The same cannot be said for his family. Large and reasonably well-docu-mented, the Blacks rank among the better-known merchant families of eigh-teenth-century Belfast. With branches present, at various points during the eighteenth and early nineteenth centuries, in France, Spain, England, Scotland, Ireland, the Isle of Man and the West Indies, they functioned as a quintessential Atlantic mercantile family.[10] Thus, in addition to antiquarians

7 Gamble, 'Business community', pp 274–6; Rodgers, *Ireland, slavery and anti-slavery*, pp 82–91.   8 Given the large numbers known to have left Ulster for the North American colonies over the course of the eighteenth century, the concentration on connections with America is understandable. See, R.J. Dickson, *Ulster emigration to colonial America, 1718–1775* (Belfast, 1966); Patrick Griffin, *The people with no name: Ireland's Ulster Scots, America's Scots Irish, and the creation of a British Atlantic world, 1689–1764* (Princeton, 2001); Miller, Schrier, Boling and Doyle (eds), *Irish immigrants*; Benjamin Bankhurst, *Ulster Presbyterians and the Scots Irish diaspora, 1750–1764* (Basingstoke, 2013). See for Irish sojourners in the West Indies more broadly, Mark S. Quintanilla, '"From a dear and worth land": Michael Keane and the Irish in the eighteenth-century West Indies' in *New Hibernia Review* 13 (2009), 59–76 and Orla Power, 'Friend, foe or family? Catholic creoles, French Huguenots, Scottish Dissenters: aspects of the Irish diaspora at St Croix, Danish West Indies, *c.*1760 in Niall Whelehan (ed.), *Transnational perspectives on modern Irish history* (Abingdon, 2015), pp 30–44.   9 In the discussion that follows I have preferred to use the term 'enslaved person', rather than 'slave'. I have, however, elected to use the term 'slave-owner' and here follow Catherine Hall, Nicholas Draper and Keith McClelland who have noted the 'investment by the original "planters" and "proprietors" in resisting the term "slave-owner"' and have worked to 'reinstate that term in British history-writing'. I have also elected to use the terms 'slave-trader' and 'slave trading', but have preferred 'trade in enslaved people' to 'slave trade'. See Catherine Hall, Nicholas Draper and Keith McClelland, 'Introduction' in Catherine Hall et al., *Legacies of British slave-ownership: colonial slavery and the formation of Victorian Britain* (Cambridge, 2014), pp 1–33 at 6 and, for discussion of the use of the terms 'slave' and 'enslaved', Lucy Feriss, 'The language of enslavement', available at https://www.chronicle.com/blogs/linguafranca/2017/10/12/the-language-of-enslavement/ (accessed, 25/10/2018).   10 Livesey, *Civil society*, pp 131–2.

and historians of Belfast, the Blacks have attracted the attentions of scholars of Irish trade and, in the work of James Livesey, those interested in charting the ways in which the changing British empire of the eighteenth century was experienced and its obstacles and opportunities negotiated.[11] Likewise, attention has been paid to the family by historians of science wishing to contextualize the career of John Black's uncle, Dr Joseph Black, professor of chemistry at Edinburgh University and, in the judgment of Robert G.W. Anderson, 'an outstanding figure of what has become known as the Scottish Enlightenment'.[12] John Black himself, however, remains little known. Born in 1753, he came of age in the final quarter of the eighteenth century, by which point the Black family's fortunes seem to have waned, and spent the majority of his life in the West Indies.[13] As a result, he appears as a peripheral figure in the literature relating to his family, and references to his life, where made, tend to be vague and imprecise.[14] From an Irish perspective, John Black appears to have been something of a 'nobody'.

Yet, if Black is approached from a West Indian perspective a very different figure emerges: in the historiography of Trinidad we encounter John Black as a prominent member of the plantocracy that dominated the island in the late eighteenth and early nineteenth centuries. Lionel M. Fraser's late nineteenth-century *History of Trinidad* (1891–96) provides a case in point. Discussing a series of deaths 'of persons long connected with the Colony' that occurred in 1836, Fraser identified Black as a man 'universally looked up to by all ranks' who died, in October of that year, 'respected and regretted by all who knew him'.[15] Likewise, in her mid-twentieth-century *History of the West Indian islands of Trinidad and Tobago* (1961) Gertrude Carmichael identified Black as a prominent figure in society who 'had in his way much to do with the creation of Trinidad and its fundamental shaping'.[16] More recently, Black's status as 'one of the most prominent inhabitants of the island' has been highlighted by Michael Rogers Pocock, and there are a series of scattered and suggestive references to his activities in V.S. Naipaul's *The loss of El Dorado* (1969) and James Epstein's *Scandal of colonial rule* (2012).[17] In the latter two books Black plays a supporting role in what

11 Benn, *Belfast*, pp 522–4; Ward, 'Black family'; Cullen, *Anglo-Irish trade*, pp 94, 148–9, 163; L.M. Cullen, 'The smuggling trade in Ireland in the eighteenth century' in *Proceedings of the Royal Irish Academy*, 67 (1968/9), 149–75 at 153–4; Gamble, 'Business community', passim; Cullen, 'Irish merchant communities of Bordeaux, La Rochelle and Cognac', pp 55, 58; Jean Agnew, *Merchant families*, pp 33, 40–1, 54, 66, 90, 134, 136, 169, 188–9, 191, 211–12; Livesey, *Civil society*, pp 128–53; *The Bordeaux–Dublin letters, 1757: correspondence of an Irish community abroad*, eds L.M. Cullen, John Shovlin and Thomas M. Truxes (Oxford, 2013), pp 54, 67–8, 75, 97–9. 12 *CJB*, i, ix. In addition to *CJB*, in which a significant tranche of the Black family's correspondence is published, see Riddell, 'Great chemist'; William Ramsay, *The life and letters of Joseph Black* (London, 1918); and *Partners*, ed. Robinson and McKie. 13 *Bordeaux–Dublin letters*, eds Cullen, Shovlin and Truxes, p. 54; Livesey, *Civil society*, pp 148–9. Black's birth and early life will be discussed in further detail below. 14 See, for example, Gamble, 'Business community', pp 273–7 and Livesay, *Civil society*, p. 150. 15 Fraser, *Trinidad*, ii, 339–40. 16 Carmichael, *Trinidad and Tobago*, p. 203. 17 Pocock, *Shadows*, pp

might be termed 'the Picton affair', a controversy provoked by revelations concerning abuses of power by Thomas Picton, the military officer appointed as the first British governor of Trinidad following the island's capture from Spain in 1797.[18] Black's name crops up in this affair as a result of his membership of a close-knit group of planters who advised Picton and, in Epstein's judgement, 'helped to shape his authoritarian style and to sanction his code of violence'.[19] Not merely a prominent figure, Black begins to appear, at this point, as a somewhat sinister one. At least one contemporary condemned him as complicit in 'injustice, terror, and oppression', and Naipaul later remarked that Black was 'impish, renowned for his meanness and admiringly feared for his crooked dealing ever since, as a Negro-shipper, he had landed and sold, at scarcity prices, a parcel of forty diseased Negroes, thirty-four of whom had died within three days.'[20] If all of this suggests that Black was not, as Fraser asserted, a man 'universally looked up to', it nevertheless serves to confirm the broader point that John Black, an Irish 'nobody', was a Trinidadian 'somebody'.

In John Black, then, we have an Ulsterman who occupied a prominent position in Trinidadian society, and whose reputation is by no means uncomplicated. But what of his letters? In all, just twenty letters penned by Black survive in the collections of the Black family, preserved in the Public Records Office of Northern Ireland. All are presented, with annotations, in the current volume. Written between March 1799 and June 1836, the letters are principally addressed to Black's younger brother, George Black Jr, who lived south of Belfast, at Stranmillis.[21] Letters three and eight are, however, addressed both to George Black Jr and to Black's sisters, Letitia and Esther, and it is likely that the other letters were shared within the Black family circle.[22] Black himself seems to have been well aware of this. While occasionally indicating that his comments are for his brother's eyes only, he appears generally to have been comfortable with the prospect of his correspondence being shared: 'You will consider this letter as wrote to you and to all the family', he noted on one occasion, 'for I really have not time to address one to each, and therefore this must be a circular'.[23] Addressees aside, all (bar one) of the letters were written in Trinidad, the exception here being letter two, which Black wrote on a 'pitching and heaving' ship while travelling to Nova Scotia for the sake of his

211–15 (211 for quote); Naipaul, *Loss of El Dorado*, pp 108, 212–13, 230–3, 257, 273; Epstein, *Scandal*, pp 107, 127, 133–5. See also de Verteuil, *Sylvester Devenish*, pp 13–14; Millette, *Society and politics*, pp 141–2, 151, 158 193–4, 199, 211, 213; and Candlin, *Last Caribbean frontier*, p. 85, though Black is here misidentified as English.   **18** This controversy is discussed in further detail below.   **19** Epstein, *Scandal*, p. 107.   **20** William Fullarton, *A statement, letters and documents, respecting the affairs of Trinidad: including a reply to colonel Picton's address to the council of that island: submitted to the consideration of the lords of his majesty's most honourable privy council.* (London, 1804), p. 28; Naipaul, *Loss of El Dorado*, p. 213.   **21** Ward, 'Black family', 188.   **22** 'Black family tree' (PRONI, D4457/363).   **23** Letter five: quotations from Black's letters are taken from the versions presented below and will be cited, as here, by letter number.

health in July 1799. Likewise, barring letter one, all of the letters have survived complete, though enclosures referred to within them are missing.

As with all sources, Black's letters are not without their shortcomings and must be approached with a degree of caution. Most obviously, with only twenty letters surviving for the thirty-seven-year period 1799–1836, the collection is fragmented and chronologically patchy: letters one to eighteen date from the period 1799–1810, while the two remaining letters date from 1836. Moreover, of the eighteen letters dating from the earlier period, nine date from the years 1803 (letters six, seven, eight and nine) and 1808 (letters eleven, twelve, thirteen, fourteen and fifteen), and no letters survive from the years 1801, 1804, 1805 or 1806. Internal evidence suggests that the letters originally formed part of a larger sequence that has not survived in full; indeed, early in the first of the letters presented below, Black makes reference to a previous missive, addressed to his sister Esther, which is not to be found in the family's papers.[24] What has survived is an irregular sequence of letters, and while it is possible to fill in some of the gaps with alternative sources – such as the group of five letters, penned by Black's daughter Adele between 1814 and 1817, that are presented here as an appendix – there are periods of Black's life, in particular the period 1810–36, concerning which relatively little is known.

Added to this, Black's letters are, in some respects, evasive. Black, a slave-owner, made frequent references to enslaved people, but said little about the violence underpinning their lives. Trinidad was an island on which the enslaved were whipped, mutilated, hung and burnt.[25] It was a former Spanish colony in which, during the early years of British rule, Spanish law continued to apply and torture was employed in investigating crimes.[26] Little of this found its way into the letters Black sent to Belfast. Yet omissions and prevarications can, in themselves, prove to be revealing, pointing, as they do, to what can and cannot be said, and highlighting the ways in which reputations are constructed. Evasive in some areas, Black's letters, when read carefully, can prove to be telling in others. They are, moreover, remarkably rich in detail, running to over 24,000 words of prose and addressing a wide range of concerns.[27] Political instability, ownership of the enslaved and plantation management; the dynamics of family life within the Atlantic world; debt and commercial reputation; transatlantic patronage networks and the political and

---

24 'Esther will show you my letter to her; comprehend it as if addressed to yourself and answer me in consequence.' Letter one.   25 Candlin, *Last Caribbean frontier*, p. 110.   26 Candlin, *Last Caribbean frontier*, pp 127–30, 132–6; Epstein, *Scandal*, pp 15–26.   27 While the shortest of Black's twenty surviving letters (letter nine) runs to just under 600 words, twelve of them (letters one, four, six, seven, eight, ten, eleven, thirteen, fourteen, sixteen, seventeen and eighteen) run to over 1,000 words. Four of these (letters four, six, eleven and seventeen) run to over 2,000 words, with the two longest letters being letters four and six, which run to around 3,430 words and 2,930 words respectively.

mercantile ties linking Ulster and the West Indies: all are subjects of comment in Black's letters. As such, and as the ensuing discussion will demonstrate, they provide us with a valuable means by which to explore in detail one Ulsterman's experience of the Atlantic world. In what follows an attempt will be made to do just this, but first a comment is required on the well-worn question of biographical representativeness.

John Black, it may be objected, was in no sense a 'typical' figure. Prominent in Trinidad's planter elite, he was representative neither of those who inhabited Trinidad in the late eighteenth and early nineteenth centuries, nor of that mobile community of merchants, seafarers and sojourners, referred to above, whose activities linked Belfast to the West Indies. Is his value as a focal point for historical investigation not, therefore, limited? One way of responding to such objections is by noting that they serve merely to prompt more fundamental questions revealing the futility of a search for representative figures. What, after all, *was* 'typical' within the context of an Atlantic world populated by slave-owners and the enslaved, soldiers and sojourners, migrants and merchants? Faced with such diversity, scruples regarding biographical representativeness can take us only so far.[28] Equally, it might be noted that, whatever may be said about representativeness or typicality, it remains the case, as James Van Horne Melton has observed, that 'global processes and structures ... cannot be understood in isolation from the lives of the people who participate in them'.[29] Whether Black was typical or not, his letters merit attention both insofar as they enable us to move beyond the abstract and explore one Ulsterman's lived experience of the Atlantic world, and insofar as they shed light on broader historiographical concerns – in particular, the working of the Atlantic family and the Irish involvement in slavery.

In Black, we encounter a man long absent and far removed from Ireland who sought to maintain familial bonds in the face of temporal and spatial distance. As such, his is a story which intersects with recent scholarship that has sought to shed light on the 'inner life of empires' and explore family dynamics within Atlantic and wider imperial contexts.[30] Equally, Black's letters bring

---

28 On diversity and variation within the Atlantic world more broadly, see Bailyn, *Atlantic history*, pp 61–2.   29 James Van Horn Melton, 'From Alpine miner to low-country yeoman: the transatlantic worlds of a Georgia Salzburger 1693–1761' in *Past & Present*, 201 (2008), 97–140 at 98. See also, for works illustrating the utility of individuals' stories in the exploration of transatlantic and global historical developments, Miles Ogborn, *Global lives: Britain and the world, 1550–1800* (Cambridge, 2008); Linda Colley, *The ordeal of Elizabeth Marsh: a woman in world history* (London, 2007); Maya Jasanoff, *Liberty's exiles: the loss of America and the remaking of the British empire* (London, 2011) and Polasky, *Revolutions without borders*.   30 Emma Rothschild, *The inner life of empires: an eighteenth-century history* (Princeton, 2011); Sarah M.S. Pearsall, *Atlantic families: lives and letters in the later eighteenth century* (Oxford, 2008); Margot Finn, 'Anglo-Indian lives in the later eighteenth and early nineteenth centuries' in *Journal for Eighteenth-century Studies*, 33 (2010), 49–65; Catherine Hall, *Macaulay and son: architects of imperial Britain* (New Haven and London,

us face to face to with an Irish slave-owner. In recent years, Irish connections with Atlantic slavery have come into sharper focus. Central here has been the work of Nini Rodgers, whose seminal *Ireland, slavery and anti-slavery: 1612– 1865* (2007) has demonstrated convincingly that 'black slavery had a dramatic impact both on the Irish who emigrated across the Atlantic and upon the economy at home.'[31] But if the contours of Ireland's relationship with slavery have become clearer, blind spots remain, and not least concerning those Irish men and women who owned enslaved people, whether as absentees or as resident planters; in short, Irish slave-owners remain shadowy figures. In this they may be said to have something in common with their British counterparts, for as Catherine Hall, Nicholas Draper and Keith McClelland have recently argued, '[s]lave-ownership is virtually invisible in British history. It has been elided by strategies of euphemism and evasion originally adopted by the slave-owners themselves and subsequently reproduced widely in British culture'.[32] Central to these 'strategies of euphemism and evasion' was the avoidance of the phrase 'slave-owner', and we need look no further than the literature on the Black family to discover an Irish instance of this obfuscating tendency: 'John [Black], born in 1753 in Belfast,' we read in Isaac W. Ward's early article on the Black family, published in the *Ulster Journal of Archaeology* in 1902, 'settled in Trinidad as a merchant, and held several posts under the local government ... and died there in 1836'.[33] As the following discussion will demonstrate, Black was a good deal more than a merchant. Focusing first on his worlds, before turning to his words, it will seek to make Black visible as an Irish slave-owner and to explore his particular Atlantic contexts, and the ways in which he thought about himself, his family and the enslaved people he owned.

JOHN BLACK'S WORLDS

As has been noted, John Black was a member of one of the better-known merchant families of eighteenth-century Belfast. In reconstructing his worlds, we may thus begin by situating him more precisely within these particular genealogical and social contexts.

Of Scottish origins, the Black family was first established in Ireland during the turmoil of the early seventeenth century: as Black's grandfather remarked

2012). See also Livesey, *Civil society*, pp 128–53, in which the Black family is explored within the context of Britain's changing mid-eighteenth-century Atlantic empire.   **31** Rodgers, *Ireland, slavery and anti-slavery*, p. 2. See also, for an equally ground-breaking study, Donald Harman Akenson, *If the Irish ran the world: Montserrat, 1630–1730* (Liverpool, 1997). Nini Rodgers, 'Ireland, slavery, anti-slavery, post-slavery and empire: an historiographical survey', in *Slavery and Revolution*, 37 (2016), 489–504 provides an overview of recent work.   **32** Hall, Draper and McClelland, 'Introduction', pp 1, 6.   **33** Ward, 'Black family', 188.

in 1754, they were 'invited over thence by King James the first to Colonize Ulster in Ireland which had been laid waste and depopulated by the wars amongst the chiefs and their clans'.[34] By the 1660s a John Black – John Black I, formerly 'a trooper against Cromwell' – had settled in Belfast. That this first John Black is said to have owned a ship suggests an early involvement in trade, an involvement that was sustained by his son, John Black II, who was born in 1647, and who pursued a successful career in what he termed 'merchandizinge' in the late seventeenth and early eighteenth centuries, establishing the Black family as a family of the Atlantic word.[35] During the course of his sixty-year mercantile career, John Black II was 'supercargoed in the West Indies, att Cadiz ... att Bordeaux, att Danzick, Holland, England, Rouen &c', and his sons were later to follow in his footsteps.[36] Writing in 1723, towards the end of his life, he noted that he had '5 sonns, and 2 Daughters, yet alive'. These included Robert, who was 'honr^d to be Kinge georgs Confull in Cadiz in Spain, where he enjoys both great honor and Riches'; Charles, 'a considerabl facto^r', also based in Cadiz; and John Black III, a successful merchant based in Bordeaux and, in the words of one recent historian, 'the central organizing figure in the family in the eighteenth century'.[37]

Born in 1681, John Black III was educated principally in Belfast, where he developed an affection for the town and its hinterland that he was to retain for the rest of his life, and an equally long-lasting knowledge of Latin.[38] He went on to serve an apprenticeship in Dublin with an uncle, John Eccles, following which he was sent to Bordeaux where, after a spell during which he was employed, by a relative, as a 'counting house servant', he established what Jean Agnew has described as 'one of the most successful and dynamic of the merchant houses in Bordeaux in the eighteenth century'.[39] There, too, he married and raised a large family. His wife, Margaret Black née Gordon, was the daughter of a prominent Scottish merchant based in Bordeaux, and in the twenty years that followed their wedding in 1716 fifteen children were born, thirteen of whom survived infancy. Included among their number was yet another John – John Black IV – who was born in 1717, and who was himself to father a son called John – John Black V – in 1754; Joseph Black, who was to earn renown as a chemist; and George Black, father of the John Black whose life concerns us here.[40]

---

34 Ward, 'Black family', 186.   35 Ward, 'Black family', 177, 186; Agnew, *Merchant families*, pp 211–12.   36 Ward, 'Black family', 177, 186; Agnew, *Merchant families*, p. 188.   37 Ward, 'Black family', 177; Agnew, *Merchant families*, p. 211; Livesey, *Civil society*, p. 130. 38 'Black family tree' (PRONI, D4457/363); Agnew, *Merchant families*, p. 211; Ward, 'Black family', 186; Barnard, 'Educating', p. 121; *Bordeaux–Dublin letters*, ed. Cullen, Shovlin and Truxes, pp 67, 98–9; Livesey, *Civil society*, p. 130.   39 Ward, 'Black family', 186–7; Agnew, *Merchant families*, pp 189, 211; Livesey, *Civil society*, p. 130. 40 'Black family tree' (PRONI, D4457/363); 'Births, marriages, deaths extracted from the Black family Bible' (PRONI, T1073/1); Ward, 'Black family', 186–7; Livesey, *Civil society*, p.

The sixth of John Black III's thirteen surviving children, and the third of eight surviving sons, George Black was born in 1725 and by 1748 had settled in Belfast and, with his father's encouragement, established a trading partnership with a Mr Hamilton.[41] Five years later, on 20 January 1753, he established a partnership of a different kind when he married Arminella Campbell, 'niece to Mr Hill Willson of Purdysburn', a prominent Co. Down gentleman.[42] The pair seem to have been much devoted to each other. Robert Black, George's brother, wrote shortly after their wedding of their 'long acquaintance & constant love', and on 1 November 1753 their first child, John Black, was born.[43] His birth was a complicated one; so complicated, indeed, that it was feared, at one point, that both mother and child would be lost.[44] Nevertheless, in the months that followed the young John Black flourished. Writing to her father, in April 1754, George Black's sister Priscilla reported that she had received word that 'little Jacky' – for 'Jacky' John Black soon became in the family's affectionate correspondence – was 'thriveing apace', and the following October George Black himself offered a report on his son's progress in which his fondness is readily apparent. 'Our Dear Jacky', he wrote, 'comes forw^d prosperously as we could wish & already is very dear to us'.[45]

Other pregnancies would end less happily for George and Arminella Black. Writing on 7 June 1754, less than a year after John Black's birth, another of George's sisters, Esther, reported that Arminella had recently miscarried, and further evidence of the misfortunes that befell Black's parents can be found in the Church of Ireland parish register for Belfast.[46] This records the baptism, on 11 October 1757, of Margaret Black, a daughter who appears not to have survived childhood, and the burial, on 10 September 1760, of a son and daughter – most likely infant or still born twins – named George and Arminella.[47] Like so many early modern parents, George and Arminella Black

130. John Black III's other surviving children were Isobel (b. 1718), Jane (b. 1719), Robert (b. 1721), Priscilla (b. 1722), Alexander (b. 1729), Samuel (b. 1730), Esther (b. 1732), James (b. 1733), Thomas (b. 1735) and Katharine (b. 1736). Margaret (b. 1720) died in 1722 and Charles (b. 1724) died in 1727.   41 'Black family tree' (PRONI, D4457/363); 'Births, marriages, deaths extracted from the Black family Bible' (PRONI, T1073/1); John Black to George Black, Apr. 1748 (PRONI, D1950/20).   42 John Black to Samuel Black, 20 Jan. 1753 (PRONI, D4457/72); 'Black family tree' (PRONI, D4457/363); 'Births, marriages, deaths extracted from the Black family Bible' (PRONI, T1073/1); *The antient and present state of the County of Down* (Dublin, 1757), pp 71–2; Arthur Knox, *A history of the County of Down, from the most remote period to the present day* (Dublin, 1875), p. 94.   43 Robert Black to George Black, 31 Jan. 1753 (PRONI, D4457/74).   44 George Black to John Black, 3 Nov. 1753 (PRONI, D4457/80).   45 Priscilla Black to John Black, 12 Apr. 1754 (PRONI, D4457/88); George Black to John Black, 18 Oct. 1754 (PRONI, D4457/94).   46 Esther Black to John Black, 7 June 1754 (PRONI, D4457/91).   47 *Register*, ed. Gillespie and O'Keeffe, pp 246, 289. The correspondence of the Black family also contains references to a child called Robert who appears not to have made it to adulthood. See, John Black to George Black, 15 Feb. 1759 (PRONI, D4457/145) and John Black to Robert Black, 14 Feb. 1760 (PRONI, D719/53).

thus experienced perinatal and infant mortality.[48] In the years following John
Black's birth, however, the couple did have three further, surviving children:
Letitia (b. 1756), Esther (whose date of birth is unknown) and George Black
Jr (b. 1763) – the future recipients of the letters presented in this volume.[49]

Turning from Black's immediate familial context, what can be said about
the broader social and cultural settings in which he spent his childhood?
Writing in October 1762, John Black III observed that 'My dear George & my
Jacky Black are by the Will of kind Providence the first & principal representatives of our name & family in my native Belfast', and it was Belfast that provided the chief backdrop to Black's childhood.[50] At the time of his birth,
Belfast was a close-knit port town on the verge of major growth.[51] During the
first half of the eighteenth century it had experienced an economic slump,
with its share of Irish shipping – the 'life blood of the town' – falling from 14
per cent in 1700 to 9 per cent in 1750.[52] Recovery was, however, underway by
the middle of the century. Belfast appeared to Edward Willes, in 1759, as 'the
London of the north of Ireland', and in the decades that followed it pros-
pered.[53] Its physical fabric, somewhat threadbare at the time of Black's birth,
was improved by the construction of new buildings, such as St Anne's parish
church, the poor house and the White Linen Hall, and its population
expanded significantly, rising from just 8,459 in 1757 to nearly 20,000 by
1800.[54] In short, the Belfast of John Black's childhood was a vibrant, growing
urban community. It was a town that was characterized, in the words of
Black's grandfather, by 'smoke, hurry, bustle and noise', and that was, as has
already been noted, very much a part of the wider Atlantic world.[55]

How conscious Black was, as a child, of the developments taking place in
Belfast is unknown, but as he passed into adolescence and young manhood he
would, no doubt, have been aware of the position his family occupied within
the town. Viewed one way, this was an entirely conventional one: the Black
family was a merchant family in a town whose prosperity derived largely from
trade.[56] But in two related regards the Black family can be seen to have occupied a somewhat more distinctive place within Belfast's wider social context.
First, as adherents of the Church of Ireland, the Blacks were members of a
religious minority in a town that was, in confessional terms, overwhelmingly
Presbyterian.[57] Second, and perhaps more significantly, the Black family occu-

48 Lawrence Stone, *The family, sex and marriage in England, 1500–1800* (London, 1979),
pp 50, 52, 55–7, 59, 65–6.   49 *Register*, eds Gillespie and O'Keeffe, p. 217; Ward, 'Black
family', 188; letter one notes two, three and six.   50 John Black to George Black, 21 Oct.
1762 (PRONI, D4457/184).   51 Gillespie *Early Belfast*, p. 167   52 Gillespie, *Early
Belfast*, pp 128–9.   53 *Letters of Lord Chief Baron Edward Willes*, ed. Kelly, p. 34;
Gillespie, *Early Belfast*, pp 156, 158–9, 171.   54 Gillespie and Royle, *Belfast*, p. 10;
Gillespie, *Early Belfast*, pp 161, 168–71. See also, for the development of Belfast during
this period, S.J. Connolly, 'Improving town, 1750–1820' in S.J. Connolly (ed.), *Belfast 400:
people, place and history* (Liverpool, 2012), pp 161–97.   55 Quoted in Gillespie, *Early
Belfast*, p. 168.   56 Gillespie, *Early Belfast*, p. 171.   57 Evidence of the Blacks' episco-

pied a distinctive position insofar as it became associated, in the final quarter of the eighteenth century, with the public life of Belfast. Black's father, George Black, and uncle, Samuel Black, were both members of Belfast's corporation: George Black from 1770 to 1801, and Samuel Black from 1774 to 1797. Likewise, both men served for several terms as sovereign of the town: George Black in 1774, 1775, 1776, 1782, 1783 and 1785; and Samuel Black in 1779, 1780, 1781, 1784 and 1789.[58] The family's adherence to the Church of Ireland was by no means incidental here. Despite being numerically and economically dominant, Belfast's Presbyterians were excluded from the formal offices of power in the town, and the corporation's membership was, as Gillespie has put it, 'drawn only from the narrow pool of members of the established church'. As such, the corporation was an unrepresentative body. Added to this, it was a body subservient to Belfast's landlords, the earls of Donegall.[59] By the 1770s, George and Samuel Black had thus become members of what might be considered as Belfast's establishment. Significantly, this appears to have been the culmination of a long-term process of socio-political manoeuvring by members of the family. Writing of the mid-eighteenth century, Livesey has suggested that the Black family tended towards an 'independent political line'.[60] This may have been true in a general sense, but by the mid-1760s John Black III was advocating the cultivation of links with the Donegall family and its representatives and, looking beyond Belfast, his son George appears, by the early 1770s, to have been working as an agent for George Macartney, the Co. Antrim landowner and colonial administrator whose family had long-standing connections with Belfast.[61] The young John Black, a figure who later associated himself with established political power in the West Indies, thus came of age in a family that valued links with representatives of landed power and authority in Ireland.

As a member of an established and increasingly well-connected merchant family, Black was raised in the fashionable and leisured milieu of Belfast's emergent middle classes.[62] He was later to refer in his correspondence to having attended Dick Lee's dancing school, and it is known that his father acquired a summer residence, south of Belfast at Stranmillis, at some point in

---

palianism can be seen in the appearance of records pertaining to the marriage and baptism of members of the family in the Church of Ireland parish register. *Register*, eds Gillespie and O'Keeffe, pp 26, 28, 30, 177, 189, 217, 246. For the confessional makeup of Belfast in the mid-eighteenth century see Raymond Gillespie, 'Preaching history, 1749: the Belfast sermons of Gilbert Kennedy and James Saurin' in Jacqueline Hill and Mary Ann Lyons (eds), *Representing Irish religious histories: historiography, ideology and practice* (Cham, 2017), pp 123–36 at 127. **58** *Town book*, ed. Young, p. 238; Benn, *Belfast*, p. 524. **59** Gillespie, *Early Belfast*, pp 152–3, 161; Gillespie, 'Preaching history', pp 127–8. **60** Livesey, *Civil society*, p. 140. **61** John Black to Alexander Black, 14 Mar. 1764 (PRONI, D719/72); John Black to George Black, 18 July 1765 (PRONI, D4457/214); George Black to George Macartney, 17 July 1771 (PRONI, MIC438/1); *DIB*, v, 705–6, 709–10. See, for Macartney's career, Roebuck (ed.), *Macartney*. **62** Gillespie, *Early Belfast*, p. 171.

the 1770s.[63] Black himself had most likely departed Ireland by the time the
family acquired this property, but his letters nevertheless reveal his familiarity with the families – the Stewarts and Kennedys – who lived nearby.[64] In
addition, they reveal him to have been a man who valued learning, and it
seems likely that he received a reasonably extensive education.[65] It is likely,
too, that he travelled as a youth. His father discussed the possibility of taking
him on a business trip to the Isle of Man as early as 1761, and Black's own
letters suggest that he spent some time in Bordeaux with his uncle, John Black
IV.[66] The evidence relating to this is unclear, but the fact that it is a possibility nevertheless illustrates the point that the world Black had access to, as a
member of the Black family, reached beyond the confines of Belfast.[67]

Closer to home, one place where Black definitely did spend time was
Ballintaggart in Co. Armagh, the property his grandfather John Black III
resided in following his retirement from Bordeaux in the late 1750s.[68]
Ballintaggart, indeed, left a deep and long-lasting impression upon him: writing in January 1803, he remarked that it 'was once I thought of all places the
most beautifully romantic and as youthful impressions are lasting so I retain
still the same high idea of it'. His subsequent reminiscences of the property's
grounds and gardens, its 'drawing room lined with Morocco leather' and its
'fish pond where my dear Aunt Kitty caught me with her fishing hook by the
finger' reveal it to have been, for Black, a site heavily invested with memories.[69] Above all, however, it was a site he associated with the memory of John
Black III. 'I have a sort of religious respect for that old mansion', Black noted,
in an earlier letter. 'My grandfather of sacred memory was much attached to
it and my respect for his virtues would naturally incite me not to let it be separated from the family.'[70] As his comments here suggest, Black held his grandfather in high regard, and it appears that the older man played an important
role in his early life. Certainly, he attempted to shape his grandson's spiritual
development and to inculcate a proper understanding of his duties vis-à-vis his
elders. Writing in July 1764, John Black III informed Black's father that he
had 'taken frequent opportunities to assure your dear Jacky Black that to be a
good boy & doe his duty to God & to obey his dear Papa & Mama would

63 Letter four; Ward, 'Black family', 87–8.   64 Letters one and four.   65 See, for
instance, letter sixteen, in which Black, while making arrangements for the return to
Trinidad of his daughter Adele, who had spent several years in Belfast, urged that she 'be
very alert in learning any thing she requires to know before she leaves Ireland', and
expressed regret that she had not 'met with an occasion to attend one or two sets of lectures on natural and experimental philosophy.'   66 George Black to John Black, 30 Oct.
1761 (PRONI, D4457/167); Cullen, *Anglo-Irish trade*, pp 148–9.   67 Black made reference
to having spent time in Bordeaux in January 1836, but did not specify when he had done
so. However, his reference in the same passage to his 'honoured Uncle' suggests that the
visit occurred at an early point in his life, the uncle in question, John Black IV, having died
in 1782. Letter nineteen; Ward, 'Black family', 187.   68 Ward, 'Black family', 187;
Livesey, *Civil society*, pp 132, 149.   69 Letter six.   70 Letter one.

bring down a blessing from heaven upon him & make him the happy comfort & staff of support to theirs & his old age which he has readily promised to Remember'.[71] Likewise, in November 1765, he sent a copy of a 'New Shorter Catechism' to George Black, recommending that it 'may be Seriously read & in memory retained by my dear Jacky & Letty & Betty & Peggy Black as it recommends the Love of God & to doe always to our Neighbour as we would he should – in Lyke case – doe unto us'.[72] Whether the catechism was read or not is unknown, but Black would later treasure a prayer book purchased for him by his grandfather, and his letters, with their references to providence, to hoping in God and, on one occasion, to the 'omnipotence of the creator', carry the stamp of a religious upbringing.[73]

John Black's early life was thus shaped by a variety of influences. The eldest son of George and Arminella Black, he was the member of a well-established Ulster merchant family, and appears to have come under the particular influence of its paterfamilias, John Black III. He was the product also, of a port town that was connected to the wider Atlantic world and that was, by the years of his adolescence, thriving. If the Blacks occupied a distinctive place within this town, as a family that adhered to the Church of Ireland and orientated itself toward landed authority, theirs was nevertheless the world of the town's prosperous merchant class. However, like so many young men from similar backgrounds within the Atlantic world – a 'world in motion', in which 'fractured families' were the norm – Black was to leave his home town and family circle: upon coming of age he struck out for the West Indies, and we may now turn to explore the world he came to occupy on the other side of the Atlantic.[74]

* * *

Black was to spend the majority of his West Indian life in Trinidad, but he first settled on the island of Grenada. The precise point at which he did so is unclear, though he is known to have visited the island as early as 1771, and was in residence by 1775, in November of which year his 'personal papers and books' were destroyed in a fire which consumed much of its capital, St George.[75] That he should have sought his fortune in the West Indies is by no means surprising. Black was, after all, the product of a merchant community that had long-standing links with the region; indeed, his father was involved in the trade with Barbados as a member of the Daniel Mussenden and Co. partnership in the 1760s.[76] Nor, moreover, is there any mystery as to why he

71 John Black to George Black, 26 July 1764 (PRONI, D4457/203).   72 John Black to George Black, 8 Nov. 1765 (PRONI, D4457/217).   73 See letters one, two, three, eight, nine, eleven and sixteen.   74 Bailyn, *Atlantic history*, pp 47–8, 61; Pearsall, *Atlantic families*, pp 13, 26.   75 George Black to George Macartney, 17 July 1771 (PRONI, MIC438/1); Gamble, 'Business community', p. 256; Johnston, 'Grenada, 1775–79', p. 97; letter one.   76 John Black to George Black, 16 Oct. 1762 (PRONI, D4457/183); John

should have settled in Grenada. Formerly a French island, Grenada had been ceded to Britain following the end of the Seven Years War in 1763. Under French rule its potential had not been fully exploited, but this was quickly to change. In the first ten years of British rule would-be planters flocked to Grenada and, in Mark Quintanilla's words, 'developed agricultural lands at a frantic pace'.[77] What emerged was, in some respects, a troubled colony, characterized by divisions – most notably between French planters and British planters, but also at various points between representatives of civil and military authority and between the island's governors and members of its assembly.[78] Yet if troubled, it was also a colony that flourished economically, quickly achieving 'a sustained growth that made it Britain's second leading West Indian colony'.[79] In simple terms, Grenada was an island on which an ambitious man could make a fortune.

Regrettably, evidence relating to the ways Black sought to make *his* fortune is limited. That said, it is known that he was involved in the sale of enslaved people. This is revealed by a deposition by Black, dated 25 April 1777, that relates to the capture by privateers of a ship named the *Swallow* – a ship that Black owned in partnership with a man named Francis Woolsey, and that had, when captured, been sailing with a consignment of '50 new Negroes for Tobago'.[80] As an Ulsterman involved in trading the enslaved, Black was far from unique, for a number of other Ulstermen are known to have participated in the trade in the second half of the eighteenth century. There is evidence to suggest that Waddell Cunningham, one of the best-known Belfast merchants of the second half of the eighteenth century, had purchased enslaved people in New York during the 1750s, and in 1784 he advocated the establishment of a slave trading company in Belfast. Further examples are provided by John Greg (brother of Cunningham's Belfast business partner, Thomas Greg), who was involved in the trade of the enslaved in Charleston, South Carolina in the 1760s; Valentine Jones, who traded the enslaved in Barbados and who appears, at one point, to have been involved in business with Black's father; and the Newry-born merchants James and Lambert Blair, who purchased enslaved people for clients in St Eustatius during the 1790s.[81]

Black to Alexander Black, 21 Oct. 1762 (PRONI, D719/62); *BNL*, 16 Mar. 1764; Gamble 'Business community', pp 255, 269.   77 Mark Quintanilla, 'The world of Alexander Campbell: an eighteenth-century Grenadian planter' in *Albion*, 35 (2003), 229–56 at 232–5 (233 for quote); Johnston, 'Grenada, 1775–79', pp 97–101; Rodgers, *Ireland, slavery and anti-slavery*, p. 64; Millette, *Society and politics*, p. 9.   78 Candlin, *Last Caribbean frontier*, p. 11; Johnston, 'Grenada, 1775–79', pp 97–101; Rothschild, *Inner life of empires*, pp 36–8; Pocock, *Shadows*, pp 14–15.   79 Quintanilla, 'The world of Alexander Campbell', 245.   80 'Copy deposition of John Black', 25 Apr. 177 (TNA, SP 78/303/31); Pocock, *Shadows*, p. 212. I am grateful for Jennifer McLaren for bringing Black's deposition to my attention, and for generously sharing a copy of the document with me.   81 *Letterbook of Greg & Cunningham*, ed. Truxes (Oxford, 2001), pp 38, 75; Nini Rodgers 'Belfast and the Black Atlantic' in Nicholas Allen and Aaron Kelly (eds), *Cities of Belfast* (Dublin, 2003), pp 27–

Moreover, if Ulstermen participated, as merchants, in the trade of the enslaved, they can also be placed on the ships that transported enslaved Africans across the Atlantic. Writing from Liverpool in August 1762, for instance, Andrew Irwin of Limavady, Co. Londonderry, informed his parents that he had 'agreed w[it]h a ship bound to the Coast of Guiney' and was promised '£4 a month [and] one shilling a head for each slave I bring safe to the West Indies.'[82] Named the *Charles*, the ship with whose captain Irwin had come to this agreement duly set sail on 14 October 1762 and made for Sierra Leone. There, 218 enslaved Africans were loaded. It then crossed the Atlantic, making land not in the West Indies, but at Charleston, South Carolina, where just 187 of the enslaved were disembarked, thirty-one having presumably perished during the middle passage.[83] Irwin himself survived the voyage, and the following year wrote to inform his parents that he had 'made an agreement to go to the coast of Africa once more'.[84] A second example dates from the early nineteenth century. Writing from Barbados in July 1802, James Watt of Ramelton, Co. Donegal, informed his brother that he had been 'tormented with a Ramelton man by the name of Sheales'. Sheales was 'blind of an Eye' and given to drunkenness, and in a letter penned the following November Watt revealed that he 'came from Africa in a ship that was there for Slaves.'[85]

There were, of course, others in late eighteenth-century Ulster who opposed the trade in enslaved people. Thus, Cunningham's attempt to establish a slave trading company in Belfast was frustrated by the opposition of the watchmaker and future United Irishman Thomas McCabe in a well-known set-piece commemorated by a plaque in Belfast's current City Hall.[86] Nevertheless, the examples presented here demonstrate that Black was the product of a world in which many viewed slavery as a legitimate form of commercial activity. Indeed, it appears to have been viewed as such within Black's own family, for in 1765 two of his uncles, James Black and Alexander Black, were considering a 'scheme ... of purchasing a good plantation on the Leeward Island of Grenada'. This scheme was eventually abandoned, but it is telling that Black's grandfather, John Black III, had considered it 'promising'.[87]

---

40 at 30, 31–2; Nini Rogers, 'Making history in Belfast: the tale of Francis Joseph Bigger, Samuel Shannon Millin and Waddell Cunningham' in Sabine Wichert (ed.), *From the United Irishmen to twentieth-century unionism: a* festschrift *for A.T.Q. Stewart* (Dublin, 2004), pp 24–34 esp. 29, 32; Rodgers, *Ireland, slavery and anti-slavery*, pp 144–58; John Black to George Black, 21 Oct. 1762 (D719/62); Gamble, 'Business community', pp 46–7.   **82** Andrew Irwin to 'Honored parents', 31 Aug. 1762 (PRONI, T3607/1).   **83** 'Voyage 91008, *Charles* (1763)', available at http://www.slavevoyages.org/voyage/91008/ variables (accessed 11/11/2018).   **84** Andrew Irwin to 'Honored parents', 10 Nov. 1763 (PRONI, T3607/2).   **85** Samuel Watt to James Watt, 6 July and 30 Nov. 1802 (PRONI, MIC 135).   **86** See Rodgers, 'Making history', pp 26, 28–9 and, for anti-slavery in Belfast more broadly, Nini Rodgers, 'Equiano in Belfast: a study of the anti-slavery ethos in a northern town' in *Slavery and Abolition*, 18 (1997), 73–89.   **87** John Black to Alexander

Here, it seems, was a family that viewed slavery as a fact of commercial life in the Atlantic world.

Contextualized thus, Black's participation in the trade of enslaved people appears far from remarkable. What is, however, noteworthy is the nature of his business practice. As has already been noted, Black achieved a degree of notoriety in a Trinidadian context as a consequence of his involvement in the sale of a consignment of the enslaved who were sick, and most of whom had died within a matter of days. That episode seems to have taken place in 1785, but was not the only controversial transaction in which Black was involved.[88] The previous year, in partnership with another Irishman, one Edward Barry, he appears to have defrauded the Liverpool slave trading partnership of Baker and Dawson, who had received a contract from the Spanish crown to supply enslaved Africans to South America.[89] Evidence for this is to be found in two documents: a 'Memorandum of Events' penned many years later by John Dawson, and a letter written in 1788 by Moses Young, a one-time business partner of Barry and Black. In his letter, Young complained that his partners had 'been doing one mad imprudent thing after another until they obliged Baker and Dawson of Liverpool ... to send out an Agent to sue Mr Barry for one of their cargoes of Slaves'.[90] This appears to relate to events, described by Dawson, which had occurred in 1784. 'A contract', Dawson wrote, 'was signed between H.E. Joseph, Count de Galvez, Minister for the Department of the Indies, and Messrs Baker & Dawson of Liverpool to supply slaves. The slaves were sent to Edward Barry of Messrs Barry, Black & Co who appropriated the funds. E. Barry took one half to America while J. Black brought the other half to Trinidad.'[91] While the ins and outs of this affair remain murky, one thing emerges clearly: by the mid-1780s Black's business affairs were characterized by more than a hint of irregularity.

The later irregularity of Black's dealings may well have been related to complications he had encountered in Grenada. Here, again, it must be noted that evidence is scarce. That being said, we can catch a suggestive glimpse of a young man running into trouble in a letter penned by Black's father on 1 December 1783. Addressed to his brother, Joseph Black, the letters details a plan he had made to travel to Grenada in order to investigate his son's affairs

Black, 12 Jan. 1765 (PRONI, D719/75); John Black to Alexander and James Black, 25 Feb. 1765 (PRONI, D719/76); John Black to James Black, May 1766 (PRONI, D719/77B).   88 Brereton, *Modern Trinidad*, p. 26.   89 Naipaul, *Loss of El Dorado*, p. 108; Pocock, *Shadows*, p. 213; Brereton, *Modern Trinidad*, p. 26; Alex Borucki, 'Trans-imperial history in the making of the slave trade to Venezuela, 1526–1811' in *Itinerario*, 36 (2012), 29–54 at 41.   90 *The papers of Henry Laurens: volume sixteen: September 1, 1782 – December 17, 1792*, ed. David R. Chesnutt and C. James Taylor (Columbia, SC, 2003), pp 752–3.   91 'Slave trade to Trinidad. John Dawson to the Secretary of State. 1802.' *The Historical Society of Trinidad and Tobago, publication no. 756* (N.D.), p. 1. See also ['A gentleman of the Island'], *Political account*, pp 18–19.

on behalf of an unnamed Belfast company that had become concerned with the way in which its business was being handled.[92] While this plan had, in the end, been abandoned, George Black conceded that his son had 'been hitherto shamefully remiss' in dealing with the company's business, and agreed with his brother's proposal that he should 'lay the state of his affairs confidentially before two persons of character & honour upon the spot, who would give a faithful report of them to the comp[an]y'.[93] Clearly, something had gone wrong for Black in Grenada. But what? In the absence of further documentation, the answer to this question must remain unclear. However, it is possible that Black's business affairs had suffered as a result of events in July 1779, when a French force led by Comte d'Estaing had invaded Grenada.[94] Certainly, Black is known to have been involved at the sharp end of these developments: as a member of the island's militia he participated in the defence of St George, and he later recalled that he had 'lost all my linen and clothing by the plunder of the French soldiery'.[95] Alternatively, Black's difficulties might have been related to his rapid rise to social prominence in Grenada in the period immediately preceding the French invasion – a rise that had been occasioned by the appointment of George Macartney as governor of the island in 1775.[96]

As has already been noted, Black's father had established a link with Macartney in Ireland in the early 1770s. Black quickly benefitted from this connection in the West Indian context. Within two years of his arrival in Grenada, Macartney had written to London to recommend that Black be appointed to the island's council, and by June 1779 word had reached Joseph Black that his nephew was 'in a very high way at Granada [*sic*]' and was considered 'the Governour's intimate Friend & companion'.[97] Fortuitous as these developments might seem, they were not without their complications. On an obvious level, intimacy with the governor was a distraction from the mundane realities of business. This was readily apparent to Joseph Black. While conceding that his nephew's relationship with Macartney might be 'attended with very great advantages in Business', he also pointed out that 'it may, & perhaps must, be difficult to enjoy this advantage & attend sufficiently to the Business at the same time'.[98] Added to this, membership of Grenada's council was expensive, and particularly so for a young man on the make. The council's members were typically drawn from the ranks of the island's 'wealthier inhab-

92 It is possible that the company in question was the Jones, Tomb, Joy and Co. partnership. See letter fourteen, note 17.   **93** George Black to Joseph Black, 1 Dec. 1783 (PRONI, D4457/240).   **94** Johnston, 'Grenada, 1775–79', pp 123–4; Quintanilla, 'The world of Alexander Campbell', 240–1.   **95** *BNL*, 28 Sept. 1779; letter one; Pocock, *Shadows*, p. 212. **96** Johnston, 'Grenada, 1775–79', p. 90.   **97** *Journal of the Commissioners for Trade and Plantations from January 1776 to May 1782: preserved in the Public Record Office* (London, 1938), p. 106; Johnston, 'Grenada, 1775–79', p. 105. *CJB*, i, 375; Pocock, *Shadows*, p. 15; Fraser, *Trinidad*, ii, 340.   **98** *CJB*, i, 375–6.

itants', and Black himself later made clear that his relationship with Macartney had been financially burdensome: 'my exertions to serve his interest in my younger days', he noted, in August 1802, 'laid the basis of my misfortune (this *entre nous*) by exposing me to a line of expense that my means no ways entitled me to support'.[99]

That Black wrote, in 1802, of his earlier activities having 'laid the basis' of subsequent 'misfortune' is telling, highlighting that his Grenadian difficulties, whatever their cause, had long-lasting repercussions. It is, indeed, by no means coincidental that debt and financial difficulty constitute recurrent themes in the letters he sent from Trinidad to Belfast in the early 1800s. He appears to have accrued heavy debts as a consequence of the years he spent in Grenada, and to have been making 'large payments to his creditors' long after his departure from the island.[100] Moreover, there is evidence to suggest that his troubled affairs served to damage his standing within his family. His uncle, Joseph Black, the wealthiest of John Black III's children, and the family member best-placed to have offered financial assistance, is known to have taken a very dim view of his nephew's dealings; so dim that in 1795 he carefully excluded him from his will.[101] Whether this was as a result of Black's activities in Grenada, his irregular dealing in the mid-1780s or, indeed, some other transgression, is unclear. But what is clear is that Joseph Black held his nephew culpable of wrongdoing, and considered him to be beyond the pale until amends had been made. 'He certainly was guilty in his youth of many follys & neglect of his dutys', he noted in August 1798, 'but he is now labouring to make reparation and I have no doubt he will do it, if his life be spared. In the mean time however nothing can be expected from him until he shall have paid up the borrowed money by the use of which he is endeavouring to make his fortune.'[102]

Overall, we are thus left with the impression that Black's early years in Grenada were a failure. In an Atlantic mercantile world in which trustworthiness and a 'good name' were essential, Black's name was besmirched and he was to spend much of the rest of his life seeking, as his uncle put it, 'to make reparation'.[103] He was to do so not, however, in Grenada, but on the nearby island of Trinidad.

* * *

Like Grenada in the 1760s and 70s, Trinidad in the 1780s was a hitherto undeveloped colony on the verge of rapid transformation. Located south of Grenada, and off the north-eastern coast of South America, it was a Spanish

99 Johnston, 'Grenada, 1775–79', pp 105; letter 4.   100 *CJB*, ii, 1344; *AJR*, 27 (1807), p. 17.   101 *CJB*, i, 53–4; ii, 1266–8, 1344, 1462.   102 *CJB*, ii, 1344.   103 Pearsall, *Atlantic families*, pp 113–18 (esp. 116); *CJB*, ii, 1344; Livesey, *Civil society*, p. 139.

colony that had been largely ignored since the late sixteenth century. Its population, both indigenous and non-indigenous, was notably small, numbering around 2,813 in the early-1780s, and it appeared, as Bridget Brereton has put it, 'as a "colonial slum" of the Spanish empire'.[104] Change, however, came rapidly. In the 1770s, attempts had been made to attract French Catholics to the island from Grenada, where they had found themselves under British rule, and in 1783, thanks in part to the lobbying in Madrid of one such settler, Roume St Laurent, the Spanish crown introduced a *cedula*, opening the island to Catholic settlers more widely.[105] In the years that followed, Trinidad's population quickly grew, reaching over 13,000 in 1789, and the influx of new settlers, who brought with them large numbers of enslaved people, radically altered the colony's character: the *cedula*, E.L. Joseph noted, in his *History of Trinidad*, published in 1838, 'brought a great number of inhabitants, good and bad, to this island, which soon ceased, in all but name, to be a Spanish possession'.[106]

One of those new inhabitants was John Black, who appears to have moved to Trinidad from Grenada in 1784.[107] This prompts two questions. First, how did he manage to do so? And second, why did he decide to move from Grenada to Trinidad? As an Irish Protestant, Black was technically ineligible to settle on Trinidad, for the first of the twenty-eight articles of the *cedula* of 1783 required that 'foreigners ... who are desirous of establishing themselves, or who are already settled in, the said Island of Trinidad, shall sufficiently prove to the Government thereof, that they are of the Roman Catholic persuasion, without which they shall not be allowed, to settle in the same'.[108] This obstacle was, however, far from insurmountable. The open-mindedness and 'tolerant spirit' of Don José Maria Chacon, the governor tasked with overseeing the implementation of the *cedula*, ensured that the religious requirement was 'little enforced', and in any case Black would have benefitted from a tendency to equate Irishness with Catholicism.[109] 'Natives of *Ireland* were received *without examination*', one commentator on the island's affairs later noted, 'the Catholic faith being in the Spanish idea, as inherent to that nation

104 Brereton, *Modern Trinidad*, pp 2, 4, 8; Candlin, *Last Caribbean frontier*, pp 51–4.   105 Brereton, *Modern Trinidad*, pp 11–12, 13–15; Carmichael, *Trinidad and Tobago*, pp 35–6; Candlin, *Last Caribbean frontier*, pp 56–7.   106 Candlin, *Last Caribbean frontier*, pp 54, 59; Joseph, *Trinidad*, p. 160; Brereton, *Modern Trinidad*, pp 22–7; Millette, *Society and politics*, p. 17.   107 Ward, 'Black family', 188.   108 Carmichael, *Trinidad and Tobago*, p. 363; Joseph, *Trinidad*, p. 161.   109 Joseph, *Trinidad*, p. 161; Candlin, *Last Caribbean frontier*, pp 56, 58–9. It was not simply within the context of the Spanish empire that Irish Protestants were able to overcome religious requirements of this nature. As Thomas O'Connor has recently demonstrated, Irish Protestant workers settled in Spain itself. Although 'reconciliation' to Catholicism was required, Irish Protestants benefitted from 'the Inquisition's legalistic understanding of religious loyalty, and its preoccupations with its external manifestations'. Thomas O'Connor, *Irish voices from the Spanish inquisition: migrants, converts and brokers in early modern Iberia* (Basingstoke, 2016), pp 171–4 (173 for quote).

as to their own.'[110] Religion aside, Black would have been required upon settling in Trinidad to swear an 'oath of fealty and submission' but this, as Kit
Candlin has observed, 'counted for very little on both sides amidst the late
eighteenth century's political and financial uncertainty'.[111] Whatever its nature
on paper, the *cedula* was, in practice, 'generous, flexible and open to interpretation', and while its provisions were principally exploited by French settlers,
who came from islands such as Grenada, Martinique and St Domingue,
bestowing upon Trinidad a distinctly 'French' character that it was to retain
until well into the nineteenth-century, it nevertheless provided opportunities
that non-French 'others', figures such as Black, were able to seize.[112]

Leaving aside the question as to *how* Black was able to settle in Trinidad,
what of that regarding his motivation? As with so much concerning his life
prior to 1799, the precise reason as to why Black moved from Grenada to
Trinidad is unclear. It is, however, known that Trinidad became a haven of
sorts for those whose financial affairs were, like Black's, troubled. Alongside
the *cedula* of 1783, Trinidad's governor introduced a 'regulation' which, in
effect, protected newcomers to the island from the consequences of earlier
financial misadventures, holding them 'exempt from the responsibility of any
debts contracted in the foreign colony or country they left, during the first
five years of their residence in Trinidad.'[113] This 'regulation', Joseph complained in the 1830s, had 'brought hither [i.e., to Trinidad] almost all the
bankrupts in this part of the world'.[114] Could it be that Black was included in
their number, and that he had fled to Trinidad from Grenada to escape his
creditors? In light of what is known of his financial affairs, this is by no means
implausible, though there were other reasons to settle in Trinidad. Under the
terms of the *cedula* of 1783, new settlers in the island were given access to
trade with the Spanish Main and Spain itself. Moreover, they were offered
grants of land, with the largest grants being given to those who brought with
them the largest numbers of enslaved people, a fact which perhaps helps
account for Black's involvement in the Baker and Dawson affair, referred to
above, during which he appears to have taken a group enslaved people to
Trinidad in controversial circumstances.[115] Given the fragmentary nature of
the evidence, perhaps is the operative word here, though the broader point –
that Trinidad was an island of opportunity – remains. Not simply a colony in
which a debtor could hide from a creditor, Trinidad was an island on which

110 ['A gentleman of the Island'], *Political account*, p. 80.   111 Carmichael, *Trinidad and
Tobago*, pp, 36, 363; Joseph, *Trinidad*, p. 161; Candlin, *Last Caribbean frontier*, p. 59.   112
Candlin, *Last Caribbean frontier*, pp 57–8, 60 (57 for quote); Joseph, *Trinidad*, pp 165–6;
Brereton, *Modern Trinidad*, pp 14, 22–3, 116–18; Epstein, *Scandal*, pp 97–9.   113 Joseph,
Trinidad, p. 165.   114 Joseph, *Trinidad*, p. 166.   115 Joseph, *Trinidad*, p. 162–3, 166;
Millette, *Society and politics*, p. 17; Brereton, *Modern Trinidad*, p. 13; Epstein, *Scandal*, p.
97; *Papers of Henry Laurens: volume sixteen*, ed. Chesnutt and Taylor, pp 752–3; 'Slave
trade to Trinidad. John Dawson to the Secretary of State. 1802.'

those who had failed elsewhere could start again, and later accounts, relating his attempts to repay his debts and make amends for earlier 'follys & neglect', suggest that this is what it became for Black.[116]

But if Trinidad was an island of opportunity, it was also an island on which Black would, once more, experience the vicissitudes of life in a region that, as Kenneth Morgan has put it, 'served as the cockpit of international rivalry'.[117] Having moved from Grenada, a former French colony that had been ceded to Britain in 1763 and occupied by France during the period 1779–83, Black found himself on a Spanish island that was heavily influenced by French settlers, and that would, in 1797, be captured by Britain.[118] Small wonder, then, that his later letters reveal a wry awareness of the provisional nature of life in the West Indies: 'I should not admire to become a Spaniard again', he quipped, in February 1807, when discussing Napoleon Bonaparte's desire to force 'England to deliver up all her conquests to their respective nations'.[119]

Likewise, Trinidad was an island on which Black would encounter the winds of revolution and counter-revolution that buffeted the Atlantic world of the late eighteenth century. By the 1790s, Trinidad had become home to refugees from St Domingue, who brought with them a horror of revolution and a particular suspicion of so-called 'free blacks', of whom there were many on Trinidad, and also to revolutionary fellow travellers and outright republicans.[120] Writing in 1803, Black characterized Trinidad as 'an island whose population is composed of the vagabonds of the revolution of all opinions'.[121] His judgment was no doubt informed by his experiences in the mid-1790s, for at one point in 1795 it was rumoured that letters had been discovered detailing a republican conspiracy in which a guillotine would be used 'to cut off the heads of all the principal Spaniards, loyal French and British inhabitants.' Joseph, who relates this episode, cautions that the rumours were 'doubtless exaggerated'. But he suggests also that they were too widespread to be without at least an element of truth.[122] And whatever about a guillotine, Trinidad is known to have had its *sans culottes*. Black knew this all too well: in May 1796 he was nearly killed during rioting in Trinidad's capital, Port of Spain – rioting during which '[e]very English and Irishman or woman was obliged to make their escape out of town, and conceal themselves for some weeks'.[123] While accounts of this episode inevitably vary, they nevertheless reveal Trinidad to have been, at times, an unstable place.[124] Indeed, it is perhaps best

116 *CJB*, ii, 1344; *AJR*, 27 (1807), p. 17. 117 Morgan, *Slavery and the British empire*, p. 49; See also, Johnston, 'Grenada, 1775–79', p. 92. 118 Johnston, 'Grenada, 1775–79', pp 92, 123–4; Carmichael, *Trinidad and Tobago*, pp 40–2; Henige, *Colonial governors*, pp 122, 183. 119 Letter ten. 120 Candlin, *Last Caribbean frontier*, pp 58, 60–1, 63, 100; Epstein, *Scandal*, pp 99–105; Millette, *Society and politics*, pp 32–4; Brereton, *Modern Trinidad*, pp 23–5. 121 Letter eight. 122 Joseph, *Trinidad*, p. 178. 123 Joseph, *Trinidad*, pp 179–84 (183 for quote); Candlin, *Last Caribbean frontier*, pp 61–2. 124 Compare, for instance, Joseph,

viewed, as Candlin has suggested, as part of a South Caribbean 'frontier world', a 'transcultural, transcolonial world' of emergent colonies, which also included Grenada and Demerara, and which was 'populated by people who did not fit (or would not fit) into any one particular empire'.[125]

Unstable as it was, this 'frontier world' was a world in which Black put down roots and rose to prominence. Under Spanish rule he is known to have served on the island's *cabildo* and by the time of Trinidad's capture by Britain in 1797, he ranked among its most noteworthy planters. Thus when Thomas Picton, the newly appointed British governor, was directed to establish a 'Council of Advice' he chose Black as one of its members, identifying him in a letter to the secretary of state for the colonies as one 'of the most respectable and opulent proprietors of the Colony'.[126] Black also served as a judge on the island, and as its master in chancery, but he was not simply a prominent planter and public figure; he was also a husband and father.[127] During, the eighteenth century, as Sarah E. Yeh has remarked, the West Indies was 'a realm of loose morals, broken families and genders turned upside down'.[128] That Trinidad was no exception is illustrated neatly by the domestic arrangements of Governor Picton, who openly cohabited with his mistress, Rosette Smith.[129] Black, in contrast, carved out a domestic life along more respectable lines. In 1784, he married Bonne Clothilde Mathews née Fournillier, a French creole[130] who he appears first to have encountered in Grenada, where she was 'well known' to the wife of his patron, George Macartney.[131] While she remains a somewhat shadowy figure, Bonne Clothilde appears to have been central to Black's rise to prominence in Trinidad: according to one source she was, at the time of their marriage, 'possessed of a sugar estate', and Black himself wrote, in March 1799, that '[i]f I possess anything I owe it to Mrs B'.[132] There was, however, more to Black's marriage than money. With Bonne

---

Trinidad, pp 183–4 with Fullarton, *A statement, letters and documents*, pp 168–9.   **125** Candlin, *Last Caribbean frontier*, xxi. For Trinidad as a frontier, see also Brereton, *Modern Trinidad*, p. 17 and Epstein, *Scandal*, pp 96–101.   **126** Carmichael, *Trinidad and Tobago*, pp 50, 383; Epstein, *Scandal*, p. 107.   **127** The *cabildo*, the council and the positions Black occupied in Trinidad are discussed in further detail in letter four, note 28.   **128** Sarah E. Yeh, '"A sink of all filthiness": gender, family, and identity in the British Atlantic, 1688–1763' in *The Historian*, 68 (2006), 66–88 at 67.   **129** Epstein, *Scandal*, pp 152–5; Candlin, *Last Caribbean frontier*, pp 138–56.   **130** The term creole is used here, and throughout, as it was by some contemporaries, to indicate only that the individual in question was West Indian born. The term does not necessarily carry racial connotations: creoles could be of European ancestry, African ancestry or both, and, likewise, both the enslaved and the free could be described as creoles. Christer Petley, '"Home" and "this country": Britishness and creole identity in the letters of a transatlantic slaveholder' in *Atlantic Studies*, 6 (2009), 43–61 at 47.   **131** 'Black family tree' (PRONI, D4457/363); letters two, four and five; *AJR*, 27 (1807), p. 17; Ward, 'Black family', 188.   **132** *AJR*, 27 (1807), p. 17; letter one. A handful of letters penned by Bonne Clothilde survive in the papers of the Black family, but these are limited in scope. See Bonne Clothilde Black to Ellen Black, 19 Apr. 1800, date

Clothilde, he raised five daughters – Julie, Mariquite, Josefine, Adele and Esther – and his letters show him to have been an affectionate husband and father, who worried about the health of his children, made arrangements for their education and fretted over their marriages.[133] In an unstable, disordered world, Black thus sought to live a life that was, in at least some respects, conventional. But how did he think about himself and the unstable world he inhabited? How did he understand the relationship between his family in Trinidad and his family in Belfast? And how, above all, did he think about the enslaved people whose labour he sought to profit from in Trinidad? We may answer these questions by turning from Black's worlds to his words.

JOHN BLACK'S WORDS

Prominent as he was in Trinidad, Black was also a failure. In an Atlantic world in which being seen '[t]o be a man of credit ... who had a good name and who had honor in the community' was vital, Black was a debtor living with the consequences of his earlier financial indiscretions.[134] His letters detail his attempts to resolve this situation; indeed, in his very first surviving letter, that dated 1 March 1799, Black is to be found enlisting the support of his younger brother, George Black Jr, in his attempts to come to an agreement with his creditors. Detailing his affairs and the problems he faced in attempting to pay his debts, Black requested that his brother 'consider all this, consult with your friends who should be also mine and acquaint me [of] the result'.[135] Here, we see a dynamic that would play out again and again in Black's correspondence, with Black seeking his brother's assistance in his attempts to resolve his financial affairs; and here, moreover, we see the consequences of financial failure. 'Ruin', Sarah M.S. Pearsall has noted, 'terrified men of credit because it could push them into a state of dependence. In that case, they might be not much better off than their wives, their children, or their servants.'[136] If Black was not necessarily ruined, he knew all too well that his financial difficulties placed him in a position of vulnerability and need in relation to his brother: 'my dependence', he informed George Black Jr, when seeking his assistance in 1799, 'is on you'.[137]

George Black Jr was not, however, the only figure in relation to whom Black occupied a position of dependence. Black's attempts to satisfy his creditors were linked to the fortunes of his sugar plantation, but during the late 1790s and early 1800s unexpected plantation costs combined with the cost of

unclear, 22 July 1807, Oct. 1808, 12 Mar. 1812 (PRONI, D4457/271, 280, 282, 285 and 300) and same to Mariquite Graves, 22 July 1807 (PRONI, D4457/281). **133** Letter three. See also, letters four, five, seven, eight, nine, thirteen, fourteen, sixteen, seventeen and eighteen. **134** Pearsall, *Atlantic families*, p. 116. **135** Letter one. **136** Pearsall, *Atlantic families*, p. 121. **137** Letter one.

living to create for Black a cash flow problem.[138] One way of addressing this
was by belt-tightening. This Black did, insofar as he found it possible, though
he was unwilling to deny his family what he considered to be 'the necessaries
of life' and writing in 1803 he remarked that 'my income for several years preceding 1802 barely kept pace with my expenses and we live as frugally as the
extent of my family and estate can possibly admit'.[139] Black needed, in short,
to earn more money, and his correspondence reveals his ongoing attempts to
do so by placing himself in a position of dependence to influential figures
who, he hoped, would leverage networks of patronage in order to secure him
a lucrative government position in Trinidad. That he should have done so is
scarcely surprising, for patronage was fundamental to the working of his
world.[140] Moreover, as has been demonstrated, Black was the product of a
family, which had, in the 1760s and 70s, orientated itself towards representatives of landed authority – potential patrons – in an Irish context. He himself
had benefitted from this, up to a point, in Grenada, when George Macartney
had appointed him to the colony's council, and he demonstrated a keen eye
for opportunity in Trinidad.

Given their prior relationship, Macartney inevitably played a prominent
role in Black's schemes. While his governorship of Grenada came to an end
with the French invasion of 1779, Macartney remained an influential and well-
connected figure.[141] He went on to hold positions in India, China and the
Cape of Good Hope and sat, as John McAleer has put it, 'at the heart of a
complex web of information and personal connections'.[142] The Black family
had, moreover, retained their connections to Macartney and he had demonstrated his continued willingness to assist them by using his influence to help
Black's brother, George Black Jr, in securing a position as a customs official
in Belfast.[143] Writing in March 1799, Black noted this development with
approval, but expressed his hope that he, too, might benefit from Macartney's
influence. Anticipating that Trinidad would remain a British colony, he noted
that 'there will be a number of employments to be disposed of here that he
[i.e., Macartney] might easily bring me in for'. These included the positions
of 'collector and comptroller of customs, commissaries for the sale or distribution of lands, provost marshal register, judge of admiralty, master in
chancery and a number of others', and he requested that his brother, when

---

138 Letters one, two, three, four, five, six and seven.   139 Letters one and six.   140 S.J.
Connolly, *Religion, law and power: the making of Protestant Ireland, 1660–1760* (Oxford,
1995), pp 87–8; A.P.W. Malcomson, *John Foster: the politics of the Anglo-Irish ascendancy*
(Oxford, 1978), pp 235–80; Bailyn, *Atlantic history*, pp 50–1.   141 Johnston, 'Grenada,
1775–79', pp 123–5.   142 John McAleer, 'This "*Ultima Thule*"': the Cape of Good Hope,
Ireland and global networks of empire, 1795–1815' in *Eighteenth-Century Ireland*, 29 (2014),
63–84 at 66. For Macartney's career after Grenada, see the essays in Roebuck (ed.),
Macartney.   143 George Black to George Macartney, 27 Jan. 1790 (PRONI, MIC438/5);
Riddell, 'Great chemist', 64–5; Ward, 'Black family', 188.

next in contact with Macartney, 'hint the places to be given'.[144] Three years later, in August 1802, Black returned to the subject of patronage, informing his brother that he wished to secure the position of 'commissioner for the sale of lands' and suggesting that he might, if a suitable opportunity arose, 'hint this subject to his lordship'.[145] Here, Black's language is telling, as, indeed, it was on other occasions. Seeking a letter of recommendation from Macartney in January 1803, he noted that 'it should not appear ... sought for'; securing patronage was a delicate business, requiring nudges and hints, and Black knew well the rules of the game.[146]

But if the search for position required tact, it also required vigilance and initiative. By August 1802, Trinidad's governor, Thomas Picton, had appointed Black as master in chancery, a potentially lucrative legal position that Black estimated would 'be worth from £1,200 to £1,500 sterling a year when the court is once fairly a going'. Black was, however, all too aware that he held the position 'only under Governor Picton's commission', and suggested that Macartney might 'get me confirmed from the lord chancellor in whose province it immediately lies'.[147] A later letter, dated 1 August 1808, reveals that Macartney, steered by George Black Jr, had obliged Black in this instance. 'Lord Macartney readily undertook the office', Black wrote, 'and I received a very handsome letter from him acquainting me of his having applied to Lord Hobart, then secretary of state for this department, who promised I should have the appointment under his majesty's commission whenever a change of the laws here should take place, which was the earliest period at which I could use it.' Viewed one way, this serves as a neat example of patronage at work: Black's brother contacted Macartney on his behalf, and Macartney, in turn, made representation to the lord chancellor. But it also illustrates the provisional and uncertain nature of such affairs, for Black went on to explain that, with Macartney dead and Hobart removed from office, he 'consider[ed] all that arrangement as null as if it had never taken place'.[148]

Disappointed in regard to the position of master in chancery, Black looked elsewhere. Indeed, in the same letter in which he detailed the worthlessness of the master in chancery arrangement, he elaborated a more ambitious scheme, centring on a cousin, Francis Turnly, who had earlier been employed in the East India Company and who, he believed, had enjoyed the patronage of Lord Castlereagh.[149] Having learnt that the position of collector would likely become vacant, Black suggested that Turnly might intercede on his behalf, though he held back from suggesting that he might be appointed to the position outright. Still more lucrative than that of master in chancery, the positon of collector was, Black estimated, 'worth £5,000 currency a year'. This, he knew, was a significant gift, and he did not expect that Castlereagh should bestow it upon an unknown. Rather, he suggested that 'it might suit Lord Castlereagh to

144 Letter one.   145 Letter four.   146 Letter six.   147 Letter four.   148 Letter eleven.
149 See for Turnly and Castlereagh letter eleven, note 19.

confer the appointment on some of his noble relatives who might condescend to give me the deputation, finding proper security for the discharge of the trust and allowing him a half of the revenues.'[150] Convoluted as this might seem – here Black was suggesting that his brother request that their cousin contact his patron and suggest that he appoint a relative to a lucrative position, and that that relative would, in effect, employ Black as a deputy – it was nevertheless a scheme in which Black invested much hope. In a letter written on 15 August 1808 he returned to it, detailing it at length for a second time, and adding a second strand by indicating that if the position of collector went to a 'better interest' he could be appointed as treasurer.[151] Likewise, he raised the matter in October 1808, noting that he was 'in want of something of that nature to help me out', and in December 1808 declared himself 'impatient to know if my cousin F.T. is inclined to assist me'.[152] By the following April, however, he had received word that nothing could be done. 'What cannot be cured must be endured', he noted ruefully. 'If the Turnlys can't serve me, I must be content to struggle through as well as I can, the journey is almost over and the worst part of the road past, at least I hope so.'[153]

Beyond offering further illustration of the state of dependence that his financial affairs placed him in, two further points emerge from Black's attempts to leverage the influence of men such as Macartney and Castlereagh. That he believed that these schemes could work demonstrates, first, his understanding of the realities of the Atlantic world. 'Office holding in the British Atlantic colonies', Bernard Bailyn has observed, 'was a direct part of the patronage system at the heart of eighteenth-century British politics.'[154] Black well knew this, and his story illustrates neatly the interconnectedness of Britain and its colonies; Trinidad might have been geographically distant from Britain, but it was nevertheless linked intimately to wider networks of power and influence. More particularly, Black's attempts to leverage patronage illustrate something of how he saw himself. When faced with the prospect of others seeking patronage, he responded with tight-lipped disapproval. In August 1808, detailing the frustration of his attempts to secure the position of master in chancery and the likely vacancy of the collectorship he noted that the former would 'be filled by some more fortunate but I'll venture to say less meritorious aspirant or supplicant' and complained that there would 'be Scotch pretenders enough' for the latter.[155] At first glance, this might appear as a straightforward expression of self-interest; keen to secure patronage for himself, Black was invariably less sympathetic to the claims of others. However, it is clear that, self-interest aside, Black believed firmly that he was, according to the rules of the society he inhabited, a genuinely 'meritorious aspirant'. He held, for instance, that Macartney was in *his* debt as a consequence of his 'exertions to serve his interests' in Grenada. This was compli-

150 Letter eleven.   151 Letter twelve.   152 Letters thirteen and fifteen.   153 Letter sixteen.   154 Bailyn, *Atlantic history*, p. 50.   155 Letter eleven.

cated somewhat by Macartney's having assisted George Black Jr to secure a position in Belfast. Black believed that that had 'in some measure cancelled any claim I might have had on him for protection', but nevertheless felt that he had a residual claim on Macartney's favour.[156] 'He owes me a good turn,' he wrote, in September 1802, 'and he ought to discharge the debt when he can.'[157] Added to this, Black felt, too, that he was owed a position as a consequence of the earlier willingness he had shown to undertake public service 'without fee or reward' in Grenada and Trinidad. 'I stand in need of some assistance from government,' he wrote, in August 1808, 'and I will make bold to say how much I am a creditor to that assistance by my long and gratuitous services.'[158] A dependent debtor Black might have been, but he nevertheless contrived to conceive of himself as a creditor.

* * *

Financial difficulty and the search for patronage are not the only recurrent themes that we encounter in Black's letters. Equally striking are the themes of exile and family. Writing in March 1799, Black introduced what was to become a leitmotif in his correspondence when he observed that it was his 'ambition ... to re-visit my native soil'.[159] He would return to this dream – and dream it was – on a number of subsequent occasions. The following July, while travelling to Nova Scotia, where he hoped to recover his health, which had suffered 'by too long a residence among the evergreen forests of the West Indies', he wrote of his intention to settle in 'some more healthful climate', noting that he would 'prefer however my own to every other country provided I can attain that retreat without making sacrifices unjustifiable towards Mrs B and my children'.[160] In August 1802, likewise, he declared that 'my ambition has one great and desirable object, that of placing Mrs Black and my children under the guardianship of my relatives and of ending my days where I so happily began them', and in January 1803 he lamented that 'my desire leads me home and I see myself bound here faster than ever'.[161] Telling, here, is the use of the word 'bound'; in his own mind, Black considered himself to be an exile, trapped in the West Indies by financial circumstance.[162]

As was the case for so many planters, then, the West Indies were not home for Black.[163] Home was Ireland, to which he longed to return. Yet his letters also reveal an inner tension, foregrounding his awareness that what he

---

156 Letter four.   **157** Letter five.   **158** Letter eleven. See also letter four, in which Black suggested he was 'well entitled from my rank in the island of chief magistrate, president of the council and of the corporation and also master in chancery to take place under the new constitution being already in possession of the appointment'.   **159** Letter one.   **160** Letter two.   **161** Letters four and six.   **162** See, for Black's use of the term 'exile' in relation to himself, letters one and four.   **163** James Walvin, *Black ivory: slavery in the British empire*, 2nd ed. (Oxford, 2001), pp 65–6; Michael Craton, 'Reluctant creoles: the planters' world in

described in 1799 as a '25 years West India existence' had changed him and
accustomed him to a set of social norms very different from those he had been
used to in Ireland.[164] This emerges most clearly in his letter dated 1 August
1802, in which he inquired after Ballintaggart, his late grandfather's home in
Co. Armagh. While Black had formerly been 'very partial' to the property, he
had, by the time of writing, been 'long exposed to a very active life and a sea
port situation' and conceded that he would ultimately find a 'retreat' such as
Ballintaggart 'wearisome'. Moreover, he was well aware that a return to
Europe would entail difficult readjustments, observing that:

> it's a general observation that when a man has passed upwards of 10
> years in the West Indies he can never brook living anywhere else and I
> have invariably seen it turn out so, with all the old stagers I have seen
> attempt to stay at home. They all soon became disgusted with the
> European formalities and returned to our good West India hospitality
> in which all formality and ceremony had been long abolished.[165]

Here, Black's use of language reflects a bifurcated identity. While 'old stagers'
who left the West Indies returned 'home', the possessive reference to 'our
good West India hospitality' gestures to a self-identification as West Indian –
a self-identification illustrated elsewhere by Black's description of himself as
'a pretty old West Indian'.[166]

Further evidence of Black's awareness of cultural differences can be found
in his references to his daughters. Black was, it is clear, a proud and affectionate father: his daughter Mariquite he described as 'a very fine woman',
while Josefine was 'the best of all God's creatures' and Adele and Esther, his
youngest daughters, were 'two charming children, sensible to an astonishing
degree'.[167] However, like their mother, Bonne Clothilde, Black's daughters
were West Indian-born creoles, and his letters also hint at a degree of unease
regarding the cultural differences they embodied. Writing in September 1802,
for instance, he informed George Black Jr that his daughters were 'a very fine
family for creoles as you will allow when you see them'.[168] 'For creoles': that
slight, insecure qualification is revealing, reflecting Black's understanding that
his daughters may appear somewhat differently in an Irish context and his

the British West Indies' in Bernard Bailyn and Philip D. Morgan (eds), *Strangers within the
realm: cultural margins of the first British empire* (Chapel Hill, NC, 1991), pp 314–62 at 346–
7. See also, Petley, '"Home" and "this country"', though the subject of this discussion, the
Jamaican slave-owner Simon Taylor, while retaining connections to Britain and considering himself to be 'British', was Jamaican-born and favoured Jamaican life to British life (see
46, 48–9). **164** Letter one. **165** Letter four. **166** Letter three. **167** Black's fifth daughter, Julie, was 'subject to a momentary convulsion, that has something [of] the appearance
of epilepsy'. She is mentioned less often in Black's correspondence than her sisters, and it
is possible she was, as a consequence of her health, a source of worry. Letters three, four
and five. **168** Letter five.

desire that they be judged on their own terms. A similar insecurity is evident in Black's letter of 3 March 1803, in which he noted that his daughter Mariquite was 'a child of nature, bred in the woods of this country, but whom civilized life and polished society will make an amiable woman of'.[169] Much is left unsaid here, though the implications are clear: Trinidad was neither civilized nor polished, its norms might not be acceptable in an Irish context and Mariquite would be required to change.

Cultural differences mattered to Black because he hoped, ultimately, to settle in Ireland with his family. Foregrounding the distinctiveness of his daughters was thus necessary in order to prepare his Irish siblings for an encounter with his Trinidadian children. In the end, however, the longed-for return to Ireland was not to occur – or rather, not in the way that Black had hoped. Writing in August 1802, Black informed George Black Jr that he had planned 'to have sent Mrs Black and the children home this year and to have given her united with you full powers of attorney to arrange my affairs in such a manner as would soon have permitted my following her'. Circumstances having prevented this, he was forced to alter the arrangements and explained that 'it is my serious intention that they shall embark on or before the 20 June next [i.e., by mid-1803] either direct for Belfast or via Glasgow'.[170] By the following March, arrangements had changed again: 'my inviolable determination', Black declared, 'is to send you Mrs Black next year [i.e., in 1804]'.[171] The plan appears, eventually, to have been abandoned entirely, but two of Black's daughters – Mariquite and Adele – did travel to Ireland in March 1803. The previous October, Mariquite had married Captain James Graves, a military officer stationed in Trinidad whose father, Thomas Graves, was the dean of Connor and rector of Carrickfergus.[172] Graves' regiment was recalled to Britain early in 1803, and Mariquite travelled with him, taking with her Adele, who was to proceed to Belfast, where Black intended that she would live with George Black Jr and his wife and 'be improved, by every species of qualification that education can procure her'.[173] Just 9 years old in 1803, Adele would spend the next six years with her uncle's family, before returning to Trinidad in 1809.[174] Meanwhile, her sister Esther spent several years in New York with Madame de Malleveault, a French Royalist from Martinique who appears to have acted as a governess of sorts, while Mariquite, living the peripatetic life of a military officer's wife, returned to the West Indies in 1808, stopping briefly in Trinidad before travelling on to Curaçao.[175] Far from seeing his family settled in Ireland, Black thus saw it become scattered and divided.

---

169 Letter seven. **170** Letter four. **171** Letter eight. **172** Letters five and six. For Graves and his father see letter five, note 2. **173** Letters seven, eight and nine. **174** Black gave Adele's age as 8 in August 1802, but her precise date of birth is unknown. See letters four and, for her return to Trinidad, eighteen. **175** Letters eleven, thirteen, fourteen, seventeen and eighteen. For Madame de Malleveault see letter thirteen, note 15.

That Black's family should have become separated in this way is not in itself remarkable. Separation was a feature of Atlantic life and the marriage of daughters was, of course, considered desirable.[176] In addition, many West Indian planters chose to send to their children to Britain for education. Indeed, so common was the practice that West Indian children, freed from direct parental constraints, came, in Britain, to acquire a reputation for unruly behaviour.[177] What is, however, significant is the fact that Black felt he could, in 1803, consign his 9-year-old daughter to the care of a brother he had not himself seen in nearly thirty years. Requesting George Black Jr's assistance in financial matters and the search for patronage was one thing, but entrusting him with the care of a child was quite another. That Black felt he could do so illustrates his belief that family ties and bonds of affection and duty had been sustained despite his long absence from home.

Adele's sojourn in Belfast served to reinforce these ties. While living with George Black Jr and his family she represented a physical link between Belfast and Trinidad, her presence ensuring that Black and his family could not be forgotten. For the most part, though, it was through the writing of letters that family connections were maintained and 'the demons of distance and disloca-tion' overcome.[178] Following the example of earlier generations of the Black family, who had 'managed ... dispersion, and sustained the emotional bonds necessary for a successful family network, by writing', Black used his letters to shore up family relationships.[179] In a very obvious way, the act of writing served to draw Black to the mind of his siblings in Ireland: as Christer Petley has noted, 'reading letters made it necessary to imagine the invisible others who sent them'. But such recollection was not left to chance: 'distant letter writers', Petley continues, 'sought to manipulate their self-image as well as evoking a world that was amenable to the imaginations of their readers'.[180]

Black's letters conform to this pattern, and he deployed a number of strategies to reinforce familial ties. One such strategy involved the use of names – or rather the lack thereof. In his earlier surviving letters, for instance, Black used the phrase 'your sister' when referring to his wife, Bonne Clothilde; in so doing, he impressed upon his siblings the fact of their rela-tionship with their sister-in-law, a woman they had never, in fact, met.[181] Likewise, in the years following George Black Jr's marriage in 1801, Black made reference to *his* sister-in-law, Ellen Black née Stewart, as 'my sister' and 'my dear sister', signalling that she was not simply his brother's wife, but an individual with whom he considered that he had a relationship, albeit a rela-tionship conducted on the page.[182]

---

176 Pearsall, *Atlantic families*, pp 13, 23, 26–8.   **177** Yeh, '"Sink of all filthiness"', 75. **178** Pearsall, *Atlantic families*, pp 7–9 (7 for quote); Rebecca Earle, 'Introduction: letters, writers and the historian' in Rebecca Earle (ed.), *Epistolary selves: letters and letter-writers, 1600–1945* (Aldershot, 1999), pp 1–12 at 2.   **179** Livesey, *Civil society*, pp 132–3.   **180** Petley, '"Home" and "this country"', 45.   **181** Letters one and two.   **182** Riddell, 'Great

Naming strategies aside, Black also inquired assiduously as to the well-being and whereabouts of friends and family members, and participated in the exchange of family news. His letter of 1 August 1802 provides a case in point. In this, the longest of his surviving letters, Black discussed the pregnancy of his daughter Josefine and provided updates on Mariquite, Julie, Adele and Esther; reminisced about the family of his sister-in-law, whose mother he had known as a youth; thanked his brother for an earlier 'detailed account' he had provided of 'the happiness of all around you and also of Mrs Bagenal, my old aunt Turnly and the Bordeaux family'; requested further information on relatives he had not received news of; and expressed his 'tender love and affection to our dear mother, sisters, aunts, cousins, *cousines*, and friends of all descriptions'.[183] In short, Black sought, in writing, to situate himself, and his Trinidadian family, within an extended web of relationships and connections.

One other method of reinforcing family relationships in the face of distance, as Pearsall has recently demonstrated, was by 'sentimentalizing' the family and 'writing with feeling' – that is, by adopting the epistolary rhetoric of sensibility, with its 'invocations of tender feelings and the attachments of the heart'.[184] Earlier members of the Black family had employed such rhetoric in the context of the mid-eighteenth century and – unsurprisingly in the light of this familial precedent – it is to be found in Black's letters dating from the early nineteenth century.[185] Reminiscing about Ballintaggart in January 1803 he adopted a distinctly sentimental tone – 'these were the delights of my soul at that time' – and in August 1802, as we have seen, he expressed his 'tender love and affection' for his relatives and friends.[186] These are no isolated examples. Sentimental turns of phrase – 'inviolable affection', 'brotherly tenderness', 'tender affections', 'I love her tenderly', 'Your brother who loves you', 'affectionate brother' – are scattered throughout Black's letters, and he leant heavily on the rhetoric of sensibility at times of high emotion.[187] Upon learning of the death of his mother, for instance, he sought in writing to 'join' with his brother and sisters in their 'natural affliction' and ruminated, with not a little self-pity, on his feelings. Noting that 'the loss must have been sensible' for his siblings, he reflected that 'I unfortunate I, who have been estranged from everything consanguinely dear to me for nearly 30 years, the period I may say of a man's life, I feel it with probably less poignant sorrow, but perhaps more lasting impression'.[188]

As might be expected, the departure from Trinidad of Black's daughters Mariquite and Adele in March 1803 produced similar expressions of sensibility. 'The day of parting with our dear children is arrived', Black wrote on 20 March 1803:

chemist', 64; letters seven, eight, ten, eleven, sixteen and twenty.   **183** Letter four.   **184** Pearsall, *Atlantic families*, pp 7, 89, 109.   **185** Livesey, *Civil society*, pp 133–4.   **186** Letters four and six.   **187** See letters two, three, five, six, seven, eight, nine, ten, eleven, twelve and fifteen.   **188** Letter six.

and with resignation I commit them to the protection of providence and yours. They have ever experienced from us the most tender affections and I trust sympathy in the breast of you my brother will prevent their perceiving the want of us. Our feelings at this trying moment can be better conceived than described; their poor mother is in the most poignant affliction, she knows not where or to whom they are going, and I who do am not insensible to their situation ... Let God's will be done and let us with confidence in it hope for the best.[189]

The following morning, having suffered what he described as 'a night of affliction', Black again picked up his pen and described the scene of departure:

the *Excellent* is now under way gradually removing from us what is most dear, soon to be seen no more. It is impossible to describe our sufferings, the whole family and neighbourhood, with floods of tears, keep their eyes on the ship so long as a sail can be perceived above the horizon. Mrs Black is in despair and Mariquite's acute feelings, if losing sight of the land don't assuage them, give me everything to apprehend for her life in her critical situation. To that providence which has hitherto preserved her I must commit her and I trust it will afford her strength of body to support the anguish of her mind.[190]

The use of language in these passages is striking. 'Poignant affliction'; 'sufferings'; 'despair'; 'anguish of mind'; 'acute feelings'; 'floods of tears': here, Black appears as a quintessential 'man of feeling'.[191] But equally striking is the manner in which such rhetoric jostles alongside references to providence and the will of God. We need see no contradiction here, for the language of sensibility, although increasingly prominent in Atlantic epistolary practice by the late eighteenth century, did not displace religious rhetoric entirely.[192] Nor, of course, should it be viewed as surprising that Black, who had been raised as a Protestant, should have invoked providence and the will of God in this way: such references reflect the ongoing influence of his upbringing. But Black's attitude to religion was not untouched by his West Indian residence. Quite the reverse, as comments he made when making preparation for Adele's education and upbringing in Belfast reveal, he adopted a decidedly ecumenical approach to religion in Trinidad. 'As to her religion', he wrote of Adele

189 Letter eight. 190 Letter nine. 191 Thomas Dixon, *Weeping Britannia: portrait of a nation in tears* (Oxford, 2015), pp 96–107. 192 Religious and sentimental rhetoric could, indeed, intersect. As Thomas Dixon has noted, biblical precedents for the expression of emotion were embraced over the course of the eighteenth century, and there emerged in Britain 'a consensus that the tears of Jesus ... were marks of tenderness and compassion which should be seen as a divine pattern for those who would imitate Christ'. Pearsall, *Atlantic families*, pp 96–7; Dixon, *Weeping Britannia*, pp 106–7.

provided she has one well instilled I am almost indifferent whether it be Protestant or Romish. The want of an established church here has always occasioned the children to follow their mother to mass and me too till lately; but Adele will now go with you to our own mode of worship and adopt it in future as her faith …[193]

Here, again, Black can be seen dealing with cultural difference. Although willing to accommodate himself to Trinidadian confessional realities, Black was aware that Irish realities were different. Thus Adele, a creole child, raised in Trinidad as a Catholic, would be required in Ireland to embrace Protestantism and to adopt what Black still considered, despite his Trinidadian ecumenism, as '*our* … mode of worship'.

Overall, the picture that emerges from Black's discussion of his family and of his desire to return home is that of a man caught between two worlds. Long absent from Ireland, Black sought in his letters to reinforce connections with his family and to overcome both geographical and cultural distances and prepare his siblings for encounters with his children – children who were, he recognized, different. At the same time, however, Black's letters also reveal the extent to which he himself became acclimatized to Trinidadian cultural norms: the husband of a creole wife and father of five creole daughters, Black became, in his own description, 'West Indian', and might be said to bear out Petley's observation that 'Creole status could … be earned by propinquity'.[194] Indeed, while he professed a longing to return to Ireland in his earlier letters, Black appears, ultimately, to have become reconciled to the fact that this would not occur and to have accepted, albeit reluctantly, that Trinidad had, in the end, become 'home'. 'It would be to me the perfection of happiness,' he informed his brother, shortly after his daughter Adele's return to Trinidad in 1809, 'to conduct her back to you, never more to be separated; but alas!, where the goat is tied, there he must browse, thanks to Mr Wilberforce and his proselytes, he has consigned all the poor West Indians to live at home.'[195] Self-pity aside, what is revealing here is Black's use of a proverb suggesting compulsion and constraint: 'where the goat is *tied*, there he *must* browse'.[196] As was the case in January 1803, when he had described himself as 'bound here faster than ever', Black, one of Trinidad's most prominent slave-owners, presented himself as unfree.

✳ ✳ ✳

That Black, a slave-owner, could portray himself as unfree might be taken to indicate that he lacked a sense of irony. But what do his letters tell us about his plantation and the enslaved workforce for whom it was home? They tell us, first, that Black's plantation was named Barataria.[197] Although Black him-

193 Letter eight.   194 Letter three; Petley, '"Home" and "this country"', 47.   195 Letter eighteen.   196 See, for this proverb, letter eighteen, note 12.   197 Letter six.

self makes no comment on the meaning of this name, its resonances are intriguing. Deriving ultimately from Cervantes' *Don Quixote*, Barataria was employed as a synonym for Ireland in political pamphlets produced during the viceroyalty of Lord Townshend and it is tempting, given Black's sense of himself as an exile and his desire to return to Ireland, to conclude that he named his estate carefully, with the Hibernian resonances of Barataria in mind.[198] This is certainly possible. In a study of Trinidadian place-names R.W. Thompson has identified Barataria as pre-British, and Black, as we have seen, settled on the island under Spanish rule and could therefore have been responsible for the naming of the estate.[199] Could is, however, the central word here, for there is, in fact, no evidence to the effect that he did so, and the name is known to have been in use elsewhere on the fringes of the Atlantic world.[200]

Whatever might be said about the associations of its name, it is clear that Barataria, which was located in the north-west of Trinidad, close to Port of Spain, was a source of pride for Black.[201] 'Barataria was never in such high condition,' he wrote in January 1803, 'it is the admiration of all travellers'.[202] Here, of course, some allowances must be made for proprietorial bias. Yet, even making such allowances, it is clear from Black's letters that Barataria was, during the late 1790s and early 1800s, a substantial concern. Discussing unexpected costs in March 1799, for instance, Black informed his brother that

> our revenues the present year will in gross reach £6,000 sterling, but I have had my wind mill stripped of her vanes in a squall, the cane cylinder dismounted, a new set of sugar boilers in copper to mount and all my negro houses to the number of 31 destroyed by fire and here is an unexpected expense of £2,000 sterling extraordinary besides our current expenses, so that you see the revenues of sugar although apparently immense are reduced to a small sum when expenses are deducted.[203]

Likewise, in July 1799 Black noted that he was required to 'increase ... our gang of slaves by 15 or 20 and our other stock in proportion' and remarked that the 'expenses will be considerable', while in August 1802 he explained that he had 'laid out a large sum of money in slaves and lands within these

198 Rashauna Johnson, *Slavery's metropolis: unfree labour in New Orleans during the age of revolutions* (Cambridge, 2016), p. 191; Thomas MacNevin and Thornton MacMahon, *The history of the Volunteers of 1782; and the casket of Irish pearls* (Dublin, 1848), p. 51; Thomas Bartlett, 'The Townshend viceroyalty, 1767–72' in Thomas Bartlett and D.W. Hayton (eds), *Penal era and golden age: essays in Irish history, 1690–1800* (Belfast, 1979), pp 88–112 at 94. 199 R.W. Thompson, 'Pre-British place-names in Trinidad' in *De West-Indische Gids*, 39ste Jaarg., no. 2/4 (1959), 137–65 at 153. 200 In Louisiana, Barataria Bay was a centre of piracy. Johnson, *Slavery's metropolis*, p. 191. 201 Johnson, *Slavery's metropolis*, p. 191. 202 Letter six. 203 Letter one.

two years, say nearly £8,000 sterling'.[204] By this point, Barataria was equipped with '60 mules, two complete sets [of] sugar boilers with a clarifier of 600 gallons, 2 3,000 gallon stills with 28 300 gallon vats for liquor and ... a wind and mule mill on the most approved construction'. It was, moreover, home to 180 enslaved people, or, as Black accounted them, 'prime slaves'.[205] Elsewhere in the West Indies, a plantation population of this size would not necessarily have appeared as significant. 'By 1774', James Walvin has noted, 'the medium-sized Jamaican plantation was 600 acres, worked by 200 slaves.'[206] In Trinidad, however, things were different. As A. Meredith John has demonstrated, in 1813 the average size of enslaved population on Trinidadian sugar plantations was just fifty-six, while the average population of *all* Trinidadian plantations (cocoa, coffee, cotton, provisions and sugar) was smaller still, numbering just twenty-six.[207] In a Trinidadian context, Black was thus a major planter and while he may, at times, have struggled to realize profits from Barataria, it is small wonder that Governor Picton viewed him as an 'opulent proprietor'.[208]

If, however, Barataria was a substantial plantation in the Trinidadian context, it was also a plantation in decline. This is made clear by the fullest account we have of its enslaved population, which is to be found not in Black's letters, but in Trinidad's 'slave registration' ledgers. Although it was not until 1820 that registration became widespread in the British West Indies, it was introduced in Trinidad – a crown colony, and thus a colony where there was no legislative assembly to oppose the measure – in 1813.[209] In that year, the enslaved workforce of Barataria numbered just ninety-seven, a marked decline from 1802, when Black had estimated that he possessed '180 prime slaves'.[210] What accounts for this decline? That Black was a man whose earlier business dealings had been somewhat irregular raises the possibility that he under-reported the number of enslaved people he owned in 1813, though this is unlikely, for the consequences of under-reporting were potentially severe. Those found to have made returns that were 'false or fraudulent' were held 'liable to all such pains and penalties as ought by the laws in force within the said island [i.e., Trinidad] ... to be inflicted upon persons convicted of forging or fraudulently altering public judicial records', and any enslaved that were unregistered would, if discovered, be 'deemed and taken to be free'.[211] A

---

204 Letters two and four.   **205** Letter four.   **206** Walvin, *Black ivory*, p. 65.   **207** John, *Plantation slaves*, pp 54–5; B.W. Higman, *Slave populations of the British Caribbean, 1807–1834* (Kingston, 1995), pp 105–6.   **208** Epstein, *Scandal*, p. 107.   **209** Morgan, *Slavery and the British empire*, pp 176–7; A. Meredith John, 'Plantation slave mortality in Trinidad', *Population Studies*, 42 (1988), 161–82 at 165–5; Higman, *Slave populations*, pp 6–9. See also John, *Plantation slaves*, pp 20–36.   **210** 'Register of plantation slaves', 1813 (TNA, T71/501 at 191/203–194/208), consulted online via the 'Slave Registers of former British Colonial Dependencies, 1813–1834' database, available at https://search.ancestry.co.uk/search/ db.aspx?htx=List&dbid=1129&offerid=0%3a7858%3a0 (accessed 01/10/2018). Henceforth cited as 'Register of plantation slaves', 1813 (TNA, T71/501).   **211** John, *Plantation slaves*, pp 66, 232–3.

more plausible explanation for the decline in Barataria's enslaved population can, however, be found in what Philip D. Morgan has described as Trinidad's 'exceptionally high' rate of mortality among the enslaved.[212] Black himself offered an indication as to just how high this was when he informed George Black Jr, in January 1803, that he had 'buried 36 slaves since 1 day of June last' and noted that there were 'properties where the mortality has exceeded 100 or 260 and there are many, many of 60 and 80.'[213] Losses on such a scale, if ongoing, would have been sufficient to account for the virtual halving of Barataria's population between 1802 and 1813, particularly given the difficulties involved in acquiring enslaved labour after the abolition of the trade in enslaved people in 1807.[214]

High mortality among the enslaved was not the only difficulty that Black faced as a planter. He also faced the problems of market fluctuations – writing in August 1800 he noted 'the very discouraging state of the sugar market' – and of climactic irregularities.[215] The problem in April 1800 was drought: as a consequence of the 'dry weather' the sugar crop fell 'an half short', and Black fretted about the following year's possibilities, noting gloomily that 'the sources of vegetation are dried up.'[216] In January 1803, the issue was downpour: 'the season', Black wrote, 'has been hitherto worse than I have ever before known it, nothing but deluge of rain'.[217] Rain was equally problematic in the early months of 1809. Black grumbled on 26 April that 'we have not had 8 days dry weather successively since Christmas', and by the end of May the adverse weather combined with a discouraging market to drive him to self-pity and despair. 'We are literally submerged', he wrote. 'It has rained since the 3 April incessantly. Our crop is lost. Our roads impassable. Our rivers flooded and the sugar market at home from the capture of Martinique and the Swedish revolution reduced to its former ebb. When and where will the miseries of we poor sugar makers end?'[218]

But to focus only on the problems that confronted Black is to elide the fact that he remained, in the Trinidadian context, a substantial slave-owner. Indeed, he was a man with an entire community at his disposal. From Trinidad's 'slave registers' we know that the ninety-seven enslaved people living on Barataria in 1813 ranged in age from just a few weeks old to 59 years old, with the average

212 Philip D. Morgan, 'The Black experience in the British empire' in P.J. Marshall (ed.), *The Oxford history of the British empire: volume ii, the eighteenth century* (Oxford, 1998), pp 465–86 at 469. See also, Brereton, *Modern Trinidad*, pp 26–7; Candlin, *Last Caribbean frontier*, xxiv; John, *Plantation slaves*, pp 162–3; Gelien Matthews, 'Trinidad: a model colony for British slave trade abolition' in *Parliamentary History*, 26, s1 (2007), 84–96 at 91. 213 Letter six. 214 Attempts to limit the importation of the enslaved to Trinidad had, in fact, been made as early as 1799, in which year, Gelien Matthews notes, 'the British government, under abolitionist pressure … approved a policy which outlawed the practice in the colonies of transferring enslaved labourers from one island to another'. This was, however, widely flouted. Matthews, 'Trinidad: a model colony', 93, 95. 215 Letter four. 216 Letter three. 217 Letter six. 218 Letters sixteen and seventeen.

age being approximately 27.[219] Over half of Barataria's enslaved – 54 of the 97 – appeared as unattached males in the so-called 'General List of Male Slaves', while just 14 were listed in the 'General List of Female Slaves'. The remaining 29 fell within one of nine family groups: the Winds, Roughs, Laws, Clarkes, Pierres, Monros, Tongos, Smiths and Lacostes. A significant majority of the plantation's enslaved population (68 of 97) were of African birth, with just 29 being identified as creoles; of these, 21 were Trinidadian creoles, while 8 had been born elsewhere in the West Indies. In many ways, what emerges from these figures is a picture of a typical Trinidadian plantation population, for in 1813 the island's plantation population was 'overwhelmingly male' and was 'composed largely of young adults', among whom the African-born predominated.[220] Typical, too, was the varied nature of Barataria's workforce, which included sixty-one labourers, a cattle boy, two carters, five mule boys and a handful of skilled workers, including two carpenters, two coopers, three distillers, two boilers and a blacksmith.[221] Mixed workforces of this nature were to be found on sugar plantations throughout the West Indies, their compositions reflecting the fact that work was 'dictated as much by the routines of the sugar factory as it was by the natural pace of agricultural growth and harvesting.'[222]

If, however, it serves to illustrate wider patterns and norms, it must also be remembered that the Barataria's enslaved population was made up of individuals for whom enslavement was a personal, lived experience. The plantation's sixty-eight African-born enslaved had each experienced the squalor and trauma of the middle passage, and its eight non-Trinidadian creoles had been drawn, who knows how, from colonies including St Lucia, Grenada, Barbados, Dominica and Martinique.[223] Its cattle boy was a child of just 9 years old, and its mule boys ranged in age from 9 to 14 years old. It was home to three 'infirm' women – Mary Tongo and Peggy Wales, both aged 50, and Margaret Cramp, aged 59 – and to children without parents, and parents who knew the pain of infant mortality. Raymond and Justine Rough, both African-born and both labourers, provide a case in point: in 1813 they had an infant daughter, named Charlotte; within two years she was dead.[224] The Roughs and their infant daughter were as much a part of Black's world as were his family, his fellow slave-owners and the grandees whose patronage he sought. Slavery was, in short, integral to his world. How, then, did Black think about the enslaved people he owned?

As was the case with planters throughout the West Indies, Black viewed the enslaved with fear and suspicion.[225] This is illustrated by his letter of 20

---

219 The data presented here has been extracted from 'Register of plantation slaves', 1813 (TNA, T71/501 at 191/203–194/208). **220** John, *Plantation slaves*, pp 56, 58. See also Matthews, 'Trinidad: a model colony', 93. **221** 'Register of plantation slaves', 1813 (TNA, T71/501 at 191/203–194/208). **222** Walvin, *Black ivory*, p. 68. See also Morgan, *Slavery and the British empire*, pp 107–10 and Dunn, *Sugar and slaves*, pp 189–201. **223** For the middle passage, see Walvin, *Black ivory*, pp 34–51. **224** 'Register of plantation slaves', 1813 (TNA, T71/501 at 191/203–194/208). **225** Walvin, *Black ivory*, pp 223–4; Candlin, *Last*

March 1803, in which he observed that Trinidad's 'population is composed of the vagabonds of the revolution of all opinions to a very great number of which, above 5,000, are mulattoes that would not fail to cut our throats and enrage the slaves if occasion offered'.[226] The reference here to 'mulattoes' reflects the Trinidadian planters' particular dislike of the island's so-called 'free coloured' population, a dislike informed by the belief that such people had sparked unrest in St Domingue and Grenada.[227] However, what is particularly significant is Black's assumption that Trinidad's enslaved population *could* be enraged: here, we see the slave-owner's ever-present fear of rebellion.[228] But the enslaved were not simply a source of fear. It is clear, too, that Black derived a certain satisfaction from the sight of his enslaved workforce labouring in the fields. In a striking passage in his letter dated 19 January 1803, Black recalled an earlier visit to Nova Scotia, and reflected on the different agricultural practices to be found there and in Trinidad. 'When I landed in Nova Scotia in August '99', he noted, 'they were in the midst of harvest, mowing and reaping':

> It is impossible to conceive or describe the pleasure I felt on seeing those delightful labours ... but it soon wore off. It was the lure of novelty and winter no sooner began to show her dreary head by the fall of the leaf than my heart yearned again for West India luxuriant, eternal verdure and the attendant activity in our species of industry. To see one lonely man mowing a field of several acres of hay or to see 100 negroes holing a piece of cane land to a chosen song led by one of the number is wonderful odds to an active mind, and this last I have been so long inured to that I can't conceive how a large farm can be cultivated with so few hands or how farmers contrive to live by it.[229]

Here, in just a few short words – '100 negroes holing a piece of cane land to a chosen song led by one of the number' – Black conjures up the sights and sounds of what must have been an everyday scene in Barataria, though the depiction is, of course, a partial one. Missing here, as it is throughout Black's correspondence, is any reference to the overseer and his whip.

If punishment is not mentioned by Black, the provision he made for the welfare of his enslaved workforce is. In the same letter in which he described the labour of the enslaved, he remarked that he had 'an hospital at Barataria well-ordered and attended', and insisted that 'no estate in this country offers a more healthful situation for slaves'.[230] At first glance, this might appear to suggest that in Black we are dealing with a planter who shared the paternalistic outlook that scholars have identified among slave-owners elsewhere in the Atlantic world, particularly when we consider the rhetoric of sensibility he

Caribbean frontier, pp 101–2.   **226** Letter eight.   **227** Candlin, *Last Caribbean frontier*, pp 63, 100.   **228** Walvin, *Black ivory*, pp 223–4.   **229** Letter six.   **230** Letter six.

employed in his correspondence when discussing his family.[231] It was, however, entirely possible for inhabitants of the West Indies to engage with the culture of sensibility while, at the same time, remaining unmoved by the plight of the enslaved, and the concept of paternalism is not required to account for Black's provision of medical treatment for the enslaved workforce of Barataria.[232] The establishment of estate hospitals, 'proportioned to the number of ... slaves', was in fact mandated by a 'slave code' introduced by Governor Picton in 1800.[233] Moreover, even had this not been the case, in a Trinidadian context, where the enslaved were in short supply relative to demand and prices were high, the establishment of a hospital would not have been a sign of paternalism, but of commercial calculation – and it was commercial calculation which above all characterized Black's attitude to the enslaved.[234]

Black's account of his loss of thirty-six of his enslaved workers between June 1802 and January 1803 neatly illustrates the point. 'I have buried 36 slaves since 1 day of June last,' he wrote, 'many of them my very best and most valuable people, refiners, distillers and mill boatswains, and when I estimate the intrinsic value of those people (together with 27 mules and 5 draft oxen) without calculating the inconvenience that must necessarily arise by the want of my leading people at £4,000 sterling Park will tell you I do not exaggerate.'[235] Here, the enslaved are listed as resources alongside mules and oxen. Viewed by Black as little more than livestock, their value for him lay not in their humanity, but in their skills. Refiners, distillers and mill boatswains were valuable people, but not valuable *as* people. For Black, the enslaved were stock. This, indeed, is precisely the language he used in relation to them. Earlier in his letter of January 1803 he remarked upon 'the mortality with which we have been afflicted in our slaves and stock' and, likewise, when he had written of his need to acquire more enslaved workers in July 1799, he had noted that it was necessary to 'increase ... our gang of slaves by 15 or 20 and our other stock in proportion'.[236]

Black was, of course, far from unique in viewing the enslaved in this way. As Christer Petley has demonstrated, the Jamaican planter Simon Taylor, 'one of the wealthiest and most politically powerful slaveholders to have lived in the British Caribbean', wrote of his enslaved workforce in a similar manner: like Black, Taylor viewed the enslaved as 'a resource ... a plantation input to be bought, worked and kept alive'.[237] In addition, Taylor 'frequently referred to workers in collective terms, avoiding any reference to individuals'.[238] Here, too, similarities can be identified, for Black's references to individual enslaved people are tellingly rare: in over 24,000 words of prose, he made clear refer-

---

231 Morgan, *Slavery and the British empire* pp 115–16; Yeh, '"A sink of all filthiness"', 86
232 Yeh, '"A sink of all filthiness"', 82.　　233 John, *Plantation slaves*, p. 215.　　234
Matthews, 'Trinidad: a model colony', 93–4; John, *Plantation slaves*, pp 44–5.　　235 Letter
six.　　236 Letters two and six.　　237 Petley, '"Home" and "this country"', 45, 51.　　238
Petley, '"Home" and "this country"', 51.

ences of this nature on just two occasions, and what he wrote is equally telling, reinforcing the impression that he was, above all, a calculating planter, indifferent to the humanity of the enslaved. Thus, in January 1803, he made reference to an enslaved person while complaining about the unprecedentedly wet weather being experienced in the West Indies:

> the season has been hitherto worse that I have ever before known it, nothing but deluge of rain in all those Windward Islands (insomuch that a flood was down a few days ago in the River Ricagua near Barataria by which one of my best negroes was carried away and drowned) and our accounts of the prospect of sugar advancing are worse and worse.[239]

One of Black's 'best negroes' this individual might have been, but here they are not even named; their story is placed in parenthesis – the symbolism is neat – and forms a mere illustrative aside in a complaint about the prospects of the sugar crop – a complaint which lays Black's priorities bare.

Two months later, Black singled out a second enslaved person for comment when making preparations for the departure of his daughters Mariquite and Adele for Europe. What concerned him was a third member of the party, a 'servant' called Fanny. 'As Mariquite carries a negress with her who has been for many years her servant,' he wrote, 'I fear Adele will be an encumbrance (as will Fanny) in the long journey they have to make by land ... Mariquite is not aware of the encumbrance of a negro servant in such a route, nor have we been able to dissuade her from carrying her; on this as for everything else that may tend to their ease or satisfaction I commit them to you and to providence.'[240] Fanny, it seems reasonable to conclude, was no mere 'servant', for had she been so there would surely have been no problem in Mariquite taking her to Britain. However, in the aftermath of Lord Chief Justice Mansfield's 1772 ruling in the Somerset case, carrying an enslaved person to Britain could prove to be problematic. Mansfield's judgment did not secure the freedom of enslaved people in Britain, but many believed that it did, including, it seems, Black's uncle, Joseph Black.[241] 'If M^rs. Black comes to Europe', he warned, in a letter written in November 1799, 'she must not bring Negro servants that are Slaves the law does not admit of slavery in Britain and such servants generally run away from their master or mistress who have no power by law to force them to remain in their Service or to return to a state

239 Letter six. 240 Letter seven. 241 Walvin, *Black ivory*, p. 14. For further discussion on Mansfield's judgement, see Douglas A. Lorimer, 'Black resistance to slavery and racism in eighteenth century England' in Jagdish S. Gundara and Ian Duffield (eds), *Essays on the history of Blacks in Britain: from Roman times to the mid-twentieth century* (Aldershot, 1992), pp 58–80 at 64–9; and Kathleen Chater, *Untold histories: Black people in England and Wales during the period of the British slave trade, c.1660–1807* (Manchester, 2009), pp 89–92.

of slavery.'[242] While it is doubtful that Black received this letter, his comments concerning Fanny nevertheless suggest that he, too, was aware of the difficulties that might be entailed in bringing an enslaved person into Britain.[243] More than an 'encumbrance', Fanny was a potential source of legal trouble and Black thus sought 'to dissuade' Mariquite from taking her to Britain. Needless to say, no consideration was given to Fanny's feelings in any of this. Her ultimate fate is unknown, though the fact that Black made no subsequent reference to her in his letters may suggest that his attempts at dissuasion were successful and that Mariquite did not, in the end, 'carry' her to Britain.[244]

Further evidence of Black's attitudes towards the enslaved can be found in his reflections on the abolition of the trade in enslaved people. As a planter, for whom the enslaved were, above all, a resource, Black was, of course, appalled by abolition. Writing in October 1808 he decried what he regarded as 'the ridiculous Philanthropy of Mr Wilberforce', and predicted that it would 'terminate by consigning thousands of whites to beggary, for the sake of a country of savages who are 10 thousand times happier with us as slaves, than at home free, if a man can be called free whose life and property (if he has any) is always at the disposal of his king.'[245] The duality Black here established between 'whites' and 'savages' (that is, Africans), highlights neatly the racism that lay at the heart of slavery and of Black's own worldview: in simple terms, the black African mattered less to him than did the white European.

Such views were by no means uncommon among slave-owners and defenders of slavery.[246] Nor, for that matter, was the pro-slavery argument – that Africans were better off enslaved than free – that Black developed here. This was, in Nini Rodgers' words, one of the 'traditional arguments which the abolitionists had worked so hard to displace'.[247] Yet if unoriginal, it is worth pausing to consider the implications of Black's defence of slavery. In the first instance, it is significant that Black felt he *could*, without any qualification or equivocation, articulate a pro-slavery argument when writing to his brother. This suggests that he was confident that George Black Jr shared his outlook, a conclusion reinforced by his open discussion of his plantation and the attempts he made to solicit his brother's assistance in sourcing cheap provisions with which to feed his enslaved labourers.[248] Clearly, Black was not a man who anticipated censure in the letters he received in response. Equally

---

242 *CJB*, ii, 1380. **243** Robert G.W. Anderson and Jean Jones, editors of Joseph Black's correspondence assert that '[i]t is not likely that this letter was passed on to John Black', noting that it 'seems to have survived with other family correspondence in Belfast.' *CJB*, ii, 1380. **244** In addition to the two examples given here, it is possible that a third example of the discussion of an individual enslaved person is to be found in letter ten, where Black refers to the death of a 'Mademoiselle Matthieu' who 'left Adele her blessing, which is all she had to give'; the identity of Matthieu is, however, unclear. **245** Letter thirteen. **246** Catherine Hall, *Civilising subjects: metropole and colony in the English imagination, 1830–1867* (Cambridge, 2002), pp 108, 110. **247** Rodgers, *Ireland, slavery and anti-slavery*, p. 86. **248** Letter four.

significant, however, is the fact that Black was not the only Ulsterman resident in the West Indies to develop pro-slavery arguments in his correspondence. Writing to his family in Ramelton, Co. Donegal, from Barbados, in 1804, Samuel Watt maintained that the institution of slavery saved the lives of Africans who would otherwise have been killed, arguing that:

> it is a well known fact that all the negroes that are imported from Africa, have either been slaves to their Lords & Masters or prisoners taken in their Country wars who would be put to death if there was not a prospect left them of selling them to the European trader thus in this instance alone do we save the lives of many of these wretched creatures ...

Watt insisted also that the enslaved in the West Indies were 'much more comfortable than in their native country, and ... much happier than the Labourers and lower order of people in our part of Ireland'.[249] This was an argument that another Ulsterman, Robert Tennent, had developed when writing to his family from Jamaica over a decade earlier. People in Britain, Tennent complained:

> suffered the soft sentiments of mercy and humanity, to transport them to (to them) an unknown Country, & interest them in the imaginary welfare of a people, whose situation compared with the labouring poor in Europe, appears not only comfortable, but desirable being tenderly treated & encouraged in health; & in sickness nursed, cherished & comforted with a deal more solicitude, than the poor unbefriended Whites, with all their boasted superiority.[250]

The appearance of such arguments in the letters Ulstermen sent home from the West Indies is noteworthy insofar as it points to the hitherto-unacknowledged complexity of the debate over slavery in Ulster. While it is known that anti-slavery emerged as a popular cause in Ulster (and especially in Belfast) in the late 1780s and early 1790s, opposition to abolition, and the pro-slavery networks and lobbies that supported the trade in enslaved people, have been left largely unexplored in the Irish context.[251] In the letters of men such as Watt, Black and Tennent, we see slavery being defended, justified and brought 'home' in a way that challenged abolitionist narratives, or at least sought to do so.[252] What the wider impact of these pro-slavery counter nar-

249 Samuel Watt to James Watt Jr, 30 Sept. 1804 (PRONI, MIC135/1). See, for Watt, Rodgers, *Ireland, slavery and anti-slavery*, pp 82–91 (esp. 86). **250** Robert Tennent to William Tennent, 1 July 1792 (PRONI, D1748/B/1/319/2). For the Tennent family, see Jonathan Jeffrey Wright, *The natural leaders and their world: politics, culture and society in Belfast, 1801–1832* (Liverpool, 2012), pp 13–48. **251** See for anti-slavery in Belfast, Rodgers, 'Equiano in Belfast'. **252** For the concepts of 'home' and 'away' within the wider

ratives was, in the Ulster context, is a question that requires further research, but such letters nevertheless offer further evidence of the fact of Ulster's connections with slavery – connections that were not kept safely overseas.

But perhaps above all, Black's articulation of the well-worn argument that Africans were better off enslaved than free is significant in demonstrating how completely immersed he was in the planting culture of Trinidad.[253] As has already been noted, Trinidad was an island on which mortality rates among the enslaved were high. Likewise, it was an island on which the enslaved could be treated with savage violence. Black might not have mentioned this in his letters, but it is inconceivable that he was unaware of it. That he served as a judge on the island has already been referred to, but here we might also note that he was, in his own words, 'intimate' with the prominent planter St Hillaire Begorrat.[254] In 1801, Begorrat had headed a commission that investigated claims that the high mortality rate among the enslaved was, in fact, the work of the enslaved themselves. The island's planters had conceived the idea that deaths on their plantations evidenced 'a widespread poisoning conspiracy' and as the commission went about its work, Trinidad was 'quickly reduced to … gruesome spectacles', as suspects were tortured, mutilated and, in at least one instance, clad in a sulphur-filled shirt and burnt alive.[255] This was the world Black inhabited. That he could, while inhabiting this world, maintain that Africans were better off enslaved than free, speaks powerfully of how completely he had absorbed the world-view of the planters and become acclimatized to the depraved norms of an island on which, as Epstein has put it, a 'macabre theatre of cruelty registered the violence central to maintaining the slave owners' power and authority'.[256]

* * *

That Black's letters should have neglected the violence underpinning his life in Trinidad is scarcely surprising. They were, after all, letters that focused on *his* problems, and that sought to sustain family connections and overcome cultural differences. Yet Trinidadian realities could not be obscured entirely, for between 1803 and 1808 the colony obtruded on metropolitan attention as a result of the controversy concerning the rule of its then former governor, Thomas Picton. Analysed in forensic detail by Epstein, this complex multi-layered affair may be sketched here in brief.[257] In 1802, the British govern-

imperial context see Catherine Hall and Sonya Rose, 'Introduction: being at home with the empire' in Catherine Hall and Sonya O. Rose (eds), *At home with the empire: metropolitan culture and the imperial world* (Cambridge, 2006), pp 1–31 esp. 20–1. **253** My interpretation here is informed by Rodgers' analysis of Samuel Watt's pro-slavery views, for which see Rodgers, *Ireland, slavery and anti-slavery*, p. 86. **254** Letter eighteen; Candlin, *Last Caribbean frontier*, pp 75–6, 80–2; Epstein, *Scandal*, pp 104–6. **255** Candlin, *Last Caribbean frontier*, pp 96, 102–7 (102 and 104 for quotes). See also Epstein, *Scandal*, pp 245–55. **256** Epstein, *Scandal*, p. 252. **257** These comments, and those which follow,

ment made arrangements to alter the administration of Trinidad, and Picton
was supplanted as governor by a commission, comprising the Scottish politician William Fullarton, Picton and the naval officer Samuel Hood. Prior to
the commission's appointment, Picton had ruled the colony with a decidedly
heavy hand: during his governorship a gallows was constructed, thirty-five
executions took place and a 'code of violence founded on expediency and
excess' was adopted.[258] By 1802 such authoritarianism had provoked opposition in Trinidad, and when Fullarton arrived in the island in January 1803
Picton's critics seized the opportunity to make known his wrongdoings.
Within weeks, the commission fell apart in a welter of acrimony and ill-feel-
ing and Fullarton returned to Britain, taking with him details of the misdeeds
of Picton, whose governorship came under intense scrutiny. Between 1803
and 1807, the privy council investigated allegations that Picton had author-
ized unlawful executions. These charges were eventually dropped, but Picton
was tried for having sanctioned the torture by picquet of Luisa Calderon,
a free Trinidadian of mixed-race who had been accused of theft in 1801.
The case came before the Court of King's Bench twice – in 1806 and 1808 –
and resulted in the legal fudge of a 'special verdict', which held '[t]hat by the
law of Spain torture existed in the island of Trinidad at the time of the
cession to Great Britain, and that no malice existed in the mind of the
defendant [i.e., Picton] against Luisa Calderon independent of the illegality
of the act.'[259]

Arguably more significant than the verdict in the Picton case, however, was
the broader scandal and discourse that surrounded it. As Epstein has noted,
'the chaos of the Caribbean, and rivalries born there, spread to the imperial
core' and the controversy 'produced a minor pamphlet war', during which 'the
rivalling parties put a vast colonial archive before the British reading public'.[260]
Black, a judge and a member of Picton's council, inevitably appears in the
polemics produced during the controversy.[261] As early as 1804, for instance,
Fullarton publicly attacked Black in his *Statement, letters and documents,
respecting the affairs of Trinidad* (1804), claiming that 'Mr Black in the hand of
B.G. Picton, became one of the chief instruments of injustice, terror and
oppression'.[262] Worse was to come in 1805, when the radical journalist Pierre
McCallum, who had spent several months in Trinidad in 1803, published his
account of his West Indian experiences, *Travels in Trinidad* (1805).[263] As por-
trayed by McCallum, Black was a debtor who 'ran away from one of the

draw on Epstein, *Scandal*, pp 15–26, 88–9, 90, 94–5, 112–15, 121–9, 130–1, 136 and
ODNB (Thomas Picton). See also Naipaul, *Loss of El Dorado*, pp 131–312 and Candlin,
Last Caribbean frontier, pp xvi–xx, 75–95, 118–37.   **258** Epstein, *Scandal*, p. 114.   **259**
Quoted in *ODNB* (Thomas Picton).   **260** Epstein, *Scandal*, pp 18, 132.   **261** Epstein,
Scandal, pp 107, 133.   **262** Fullarton, *A statement, letters and documents*, p. 28.   **263** For
McCallum, see Epstein, *Scandal*, pp 156–83.

British West India islands, and took shelter in this [Trinidad]' and whose dishonesty extended to his own son-in-law, who he had threatened to shoot in order to secure the return of exchange bills given as a marriage portion.[264] Added to this, McCallum discussed Black's actions as a judge, revealing that under the governorship of Picton's successor, Thomas Hislop, he had also sanctioned torture, the victim being 'a Mulatto of the name of Modest', who appears to have been accused of having poisoned a black woman who had refused his sexual advances.[265] According to McCallum, Modest was tortured twice and 'afterwards banished to the Spanish Main', while Black, aware that the affair had become known in London, 'absconded to America'.[266] While it is unclear how accurate this account is, it is known that Black spent some time in New York prior to 1807, and McCallum's is not the only account that makes reference to the torture of Modest.[267] Edward Alured Draper, a Picton supporter, who judged Black as 'one of the ablest, and most experienced, the most wealthy Magistrate in the colony', referred openly to Modest's treatment in his *Address to the British public* (1806), insisting – in an argument deriving from a belief that torture was permitted in Spanish law, which continued to apply in Trinidad following Britain's capture of the island in 1797 – that Black, like Picton, had acted as he believed he had a legal 'right' to act.[268] Likewise, the pseudonymously authored *A political account of the island of Trinidad* (1807) identified Black, in a list of Trinidad's council, as the man 'who *ordered* the torture of Modeste'. Like McCallum, the author of this account also cast aspersions on Black's financial probity, implying, in a note, that Black well knew that Trinidad was 'a place of refuge for fraudulent debtors and public delinquents'.[269] This, in turn, prompted a writer to defend Black's integrity in the columns of the *Anti-Jacobin Review* and thus, against the backdrop of the Picton controversy, Black himself became a subject of public polemic and debate.[270]

---

264 McCallum, *Travels*, p. 178.   **265** McCallum, *Travels*, p. 272; ['A gentleman of the Island'], *Political account*, pp 48, 157; Naipaul, *Loss of El Dorado*, pp 233–4; Epstein, *Scandal*, pp 1–2, 104; Millette, *Society and politics*, p. 194.   **266** McCallum, *Travels*, p. 272. **267** Black himself made reference to time spent in America in a letter penned in May 1809, and a surviving letter from Bonne Clothilde Black to her sister-in-law, Ellen Black, carries the address New York. Its date is unclear, but Black and Bonne Clothilde had returned to Trinidad by 1807, for in February of that month Black wrote to George Black Jr from the island. Bonne Clothilde Black to Ellen Black, date unclear (PRONI, D4457/280); letters ten and seventeen.   **268** Edward Alured Draper, *An address to the British public, on the case of Brigadier-General Picton, late governor and captain-general of the island of Trinidad; with observations on the conduct of William Fullarton, Esq. F.R.S. and the right honourable John Sullivan* (London, 1806), pp 257–9; Epstein, *Scandal*, pp 24–5, 92.   **269** ['A gentleman of the Island'], *Political account*, pp 21, 157.   **270** *AJR*, 27 (1807), p. 17. See also *Letters of Decius*, p. 20, which responds to the *Anti-Jacobin Review*'s defence of Black by raising further questions about his affairs.

The extent to which Black's family in Belfast was aware of this debate concerning his character and conduct is unknown. They would, however, have been aware of the wider controversy concerning Picton's governorship, for details were reported, at various points, in the *Belfast News-Letter* and Black himself had offered an insider's view of the emerging quarrel between Fullarton and Picton in the cluster of letters he penned early in 1803.[271] Having made reference to the appointment of Fullarton as 'first commissioner' – 'a sort of phenomenon I don't yet well comprehend' – in September 1802, Black reported on his arrival in the colony the following January, highlighting his own role in a carefully choreographed set piece, during which Fullarton was welcomed and the governing commission formerly 'opened'.[272] 'Colonel Fullarton and his *suitte* arrived here 15 days ago in the *Ulysses*', Black wrote, on 19 January 1803:

> It fell to my lot as senior member of the council to board the *Ulysses* long before she anchored, to be the mouth piece of General Picton's congratulations on his safe arrival and to take the proper arrangements with him for the style we had agreed on for his landing and reception. This took place the ensuing morning, with all the honours due his rank and the street completely lined by three regiments from the wharf to council chamber and here it again fell to my lot to receive him on the wharf and conduct him up. The commission was <u>there</u> immediately opened under a discharge of 21 guns and in presence of council and a great concourse of the first personages civil and military. It was read by the clerk and he and General Picton sworn as two of the three commissioners for executing the office of Governor of Trinidad. Since then little has been done but visiting and scraping, but we are summoned for council tomorrow to enter on business and then will see how the administration of Trinidad is to be managed.[273]

Here we see Black, not as debtor, patronage seeker, family man or slave-owner, but as 'senior member of the council' – a prominent public figure. As such, he would become privy to the squabbles and dissensions to follow.

Matters proceeded smoothly in the fortnight immediately following Fullarton's arrival, with Black noting that 'the most perfect harmony subsists between the <u>consuls</u>', but such concord proved short-lived.[274] In the weeks that followed, relations between Picton and Fullarton quickly deteriorated; as Epstein has put it, the pair 'clashed violently over matters of colonial governance and the administration of justice'.[275] Thus, on 20 March Black reported that 'we are all at loggerheads' and complained 'that administration could not possibly have chosen a man more unfit for the purposes he was sent out than

---

271 See, for instance, *BNL*, 14 June 1803, 11 May 1804 and 4 Mar. 1806. 272 Letter five. 273 Letter six. 274 Letter six. 275 Epstein, *Scandal*, pp 17–18, 130–1.

Colonel Fullarton'. By this point, Black had clearly taken sides: 'when such a character is attempted to be blended with the high ingenuous and honourable proceedings of two such men as Brigadier General Picton and Commodore Hood', he wrote of Fullarton, 'you may suppose a little what discord such a composition must produce but nothing equal to the reality.'[276] The 'reality' was a round of controversy and intrigue in which Black himself played a role. Indeed, just eight days after he had reported on the 'discord' prevailing in Trinidad, conflict was played out in Black's own home when Fullarton discovered that Black was, in his capacity as a judge, lodging Trinidad's *escribano*, Francisco de Castro, who had been arrested in a bid to frustrate Fullarton's attempts to secure copies of potentially compromising legal records. Upon discovering this, Fullarton called at Black's home with a sword and made an unsuccessful attempt to release de Castro, during which he threated to hang Black. Or so, at any rate, Black claimed. As with so much concerning events in Trinidad during the early months of 1803, accounts of the episode vary and Fullarton himself would later condemn the 'unqualified fallacies' and 'disreputable fabrications' of Black's version of events.[277]

While it is, however, clear that Black sided with Picton over Fullarton, his letters also afford a glimpse at more complicated relationships with the two men. In his recent study Candlin has offered an intriguing exploration of Picton's association with St Hillaire Begorrat, a prominent planter and, as we have seen, a friend of Black. Men such as Begorrat, Candlin suggests, saw an opportunity in Picton's arrival in Trinidad in 1797. Capitalizing on his 'lack of social power and gubernatorial inexperience', they came to control him, shaping his views regarding slavery and exploiting his power.[278] Black's relationships with Fullarton and Picton do not match this pattern in every respect, but his letters nevertheless suggest that a similar dynamic was at play, with Black seeking to capitalize on opportunities that presented themselves and responding to developments as best suited his interest. Thus while he came to view Fullarton as 'a most dangerous man', Black initially saw him as a potential patron. Indeed, upon learning of his appointment as a commissioner in 1802, he sought a 'recommendation' from George Macartney, with whom Fullarton had earlier served in India.[279] This arrived on 1 March 1803, by which point Black was, as he put it, 'familiarly acquainted' with Fullarton.[280] Early in January 1803, as we have seen, Black was charged with welcoming Fullarton to the colony, and the pair soon discovered mutual connections. Fullarton was not only known to Macartney, 'for whom he entertains

276 Letter eight.   **277** Epstein, *Scandal*, pp 132–3; Naipaul, *Loss of El Dorado*, pp 211–13; Archibald Gloster, *A letter to the right honourable the Earl of Buckinghamshire, late secretary of the colonial department, respecting affairs in Trinidad in 1803, and in answer to William Fullarton, Esq.* (London, 1807), pp 102–10; Fullarton, *A statement, letters and documents*, pp 16–17, 29.   **278** Candlin, *Last Caribbean frontier*, pp 75–95 (esp. 75–6).   **279** Letters five and eight.   **280** Letter seven.

the most inviolable attachment', but had known Black's late uncle, Dr Joseph Back, 'whom he speaks of in terms of admiration and of as having been one of his dearest friends'. From Black's perspective, this all bade well. 'Those circumstances, my situation in the colony and the preference given me by General Picton to carry him his congratulations and receive his orders,' he wrote, 'have given me it would appear more than a common title to his favour for on all occasions public and private he has been particularly attentive to me and I hope I shall continue to deserve it.'[281] Thus matters stood on 19 January 1803. But by the time Macartney's letter of recommendation had arrived, things looked rather different. On the one hand, it had become clear to Black that there were others with claims on Fullarton's patronage: 'Fullarton', he complained, 'has here the whole of Renfrew and Caithness shires well recommended to him and we old standers will all be kicked out to make way for them'.[282] On the other, quarrels within the commission had emerged and Fullarton considered himself unable to act on Black's behalf, though he blamed this on the latter's own partisan attitude. 'Unfortunately', he noted, in a letter to Macartney dated 3 April 1803, 'in the present state of Trinidad Discussions have gone so far between Br General Picton and me, that those who are Connected with him by Habits and Cooperation as Mr Black has been, cannot fail to feel a proportional alienation from me.'[283]

Thus as the conflict between Picton and Fullarton had developed, Black's relationship with Fullarton had deteriorated. But what of Black's relationship with Picton? Writing in August 1808, long after Picton's departure from Trinidad, Black claimed to be 'in habits of intimacy' with the former governor.[284] Likewise, in the spring of 1809, while making arrangements for his daughter Adele's return to Trinidad, Black broached the possibility of her staying in London, were she would encounter Picton, for whom 'she is or was a great favourite'.[285] Such comments appear to bear out Fullarton's claim that Black was bound to Picton 'by Habits and Cooperation', but what is striking in Black's early surviving letters is the brevity of his references to Picton. Writing on 1 August 1802, Black noted that he held the position of master in chancery 'only under Governor Picton's commission' and in January 1803 he made reference to 'passing the night with the family at a crowded ball given by Governor Picton in celebration of the anniversary of the Queen's birth'.[286] It was not, however, until his letter dated 20 March 1803, by which point conflict had broken out, that he made any substantial reference to Picton, though on this occasion he referred to both Picton *and* Hood, comparing the pair favourably to Fullarton, and it is not, in fact, until we reach his letter dated 13 November 1808 that we find him writing at length about Picton.[287] In short, Black's early letters contain little evidence of intimacy with Picton.

281 Letter six.   282 Letter seven.   283 William Fullarton to George Macartney, 3 Apr. 1803 (PRONI, MIC438/3).   284 Letter twelve.   285 Letters sixteen and seventeen.   286 Letters four and six.   287 Letters eight and fourteen. But see also letter eleven, dated 1 August 1808,

It would, of course, be unwise to draw firm conclusions from what is, essentially, an absence of evidence. Nevertheless, the paucity of references to Picton in Black's early surviving letters is suggestive, and prompts questions as to the precise nature of their relationship. Black was, admittedly, a member of Picton's council, but were the two as closely allied as Fullarton suspected? That Black appears, initially, to have been well disposed towards Fullarton would suggest not, for with the establishment of the commission Picton was reduced. Had Black been a die-hard supporter of Picton we might expect him, under such circumstances, to have viewed Fullarton with hostility from the outset, and it is possible that his later 'habits of intimacy' with Picton were the result of a relationship forged by the conflict between Fullarton and Picton, and by the subsequent controversy in which Fullarton's revelations concerning Trinidad threatened their reputations.

Whatever the precise nature of their relationship in Trinidad, it is clear that Black had come to associate himself firmly with Picton by 1808, for writing in November of that year he revealed that he was in contact with the former governor, and sought to defend his reputation.

> I have a letter from General Picton at Harrogate. He says he has become acquainted with my sister Younghusband … He expresses himself much pleased with her and the girls; I hope they were equally so with him and that his agreeable manners and interesting conversation will have removed any prejudices with which their minds might have been impressed by the injurious reports his enemies had disseminated. General Picton is an honourable man, humane in his prejudices and sincere in his friendships; any acts committed by him during his government in this country were the acts of necessity to prevent greater evils and without which we should have experienced catastrophes similar to those which happened in the neighbouring islands during the frenzy of the French revolutionary doctrine.[288]

Those 'neighbouring islands' included Grenada, where, in 1795, a republican rebellion led by Julien Fédon had taken place, and no doubt, too, Black had Haiti in mind.[289] Certainly he was aware of developments in the latter island.[290] But there is more going on in these comments from November 1808 than a slave-owner's articulation of counter-revolutionary conservatism, though that there certainly is. By 1808 the controversy surrounding Picton's governorship had, of course, been playing out in the metropolitan context for several years and Black's comments appear as particularly significant when viewed against this backdrop, for it was not simply Picton who faced the circulation of 'inju-

---

in which Black describes himself as 'having been one of his [i.e., Picton's] best friends and firmest supporters'. **288** Letter fourteen. **289** Candlin, *Last Caribbean frontier*, pp 1–23. **290** See, for instance, his comments at the end of letter four: 'We have very unpleasant intelligence from St Domingo. The business is not at an end there yet.'

rious reports'. As we have seen, Black's own actions and character had become the subject of public debate. In defending Picton and justifying his actions, Black was thus, in fact, defending himself. Moreover, there is within this passage a tacit admission that Picton had overstepped the mark – or, at any rate, that he might appear, in a metropolitan context, to have done so. Implicit in Black's assertion that 'any acts committed by him during his government in this country were the acts of necessity to prevent greater evils' is an acceptance that 'acts' *had* happened, and that Trinidad's violent realities – realities diligently ignored elsewhere in his letters – had become known 'at home', and had to be explained.[291]

* * *

Contextualized and read closely, the letters of John Black, an Ulster slave-owner in the revolutionary Atlantic, thus prove to be revealing documents. Not only do they enable us to place Black in the West Indies and identify him *as* a slave-owner, they offer insights as to how he thought about the enslaved and the institution of slavery – that he sought to communicate his thoughts in his letters home is, as we have seen, significant, raising questions as to the ways in which such letters might have shaped opinion in Ulster. Slavery aside, Black's letters also offer an intriguing 'behind the scenes' glimpse of the development, and outworking, of the controversy concerning Thomas Picton's governorship of Trinidad and, on a personal level, reveal a failing merchant and plantation owner, dealing with the consequences of early financial misadventure, and a man, many years absent from Ireland, struggling to maintain connections with his family. In many ways Black emerges from his correspondence as a contradictory and confused character. In financial terms a failure, he believed himself a creditor who had a reasonable claim on government patronage; a major Trinidadian slave-owner, he presented himself, absurdly, as an unfree man, trapped by circumstance; and although anxious to return to Ireland, his letters show him to have been transformed, and ultimately creolized, by his years in the West Indies. A product of mid-eighteenth-century Belfast, Black sought his fortune in a very different context, and while it is clear that his early upbringing and family background left an impress upon him, he appears also to have been shaped and remade by the West Indian environments he inhabited. Thus, while willing to use the language of providence, he cared little for confessional distinctions, and while orientating himself, as his family had done in Ulster, to established figures of authority, he was equally willing to engage in dubious commercial practices – practices not strictly compatible with a reputation for probity and respectability. An at times unpleasant and self-pitying figure, Black appears, ultimately, as a man who was simply trying to 'make it' in the chaotic and

291 Hall and Rose, 'Introduction', pp 20–1.

volatile context of the Atlantic, a world that encompassed both Ulster and Trinidad, and that was characterized, in the late eighteenth and early nineteenth centuries, by revolution, war and political instability.

But how does Black's story end? We may address this question in closing, though it is possible to do so only in brief for sources relating to the later years of Black's life are limited. Black remained a prominent public figure in Trinidad in the early 1810s: as a member of the island's council he appears to have been privy to the politicking that led chief justice George Smith to leave the colony in 1811, and he is known also to have chaired the committee established, following a destructive fire in March 1808, to oversee reconstruction in Port of Spain.[292] By the mid-1810s, however, his influence was clearly declining. Writing in June 1814, Black's daughter Adele expressed her concern that Trinidad's newly appointed governor, Sir Ralph Woodford, 'is not my poor father's friend', and by the following February her apprehensions had been born out.[293] 'Our Governor', she wrote sadly, 'is far, far from being his friend and it is greatly to be feared he will make his time most disagreeable to him, poor old man.'[294] At around the same time, uncomfortable questions were asked about the Port of Spain building committee's use of funds and Governor Woodford dismissed Trinidad's council of advice, seemingly ending Black's longstanding involvement in the government of the island.[295] Turning from Black's public life to his plantation life, we see further decline. As has already been noted, the enslaved population of Barataria fell from around 180 in 1802 to ninety-seven in 1813. In the years to follow it continued to drop – falling to eighty in 1819 – and by 1828 Barataria had passed from Black's hands.[296] Of Black's life in the 1820s and 30s we know little, for from the late-1810s onwards he recedes, in an archival sense, from view. Two later surviving letters do, though, offer a glimpse of Black in 1836, the year of his death. Read one way, these outliers in his surviving correspondence are the letters of an old man, replete with references to his health – on the whole good, though a 'deranged' head caused occasional difficulties – children (all now adults) and grandchildren.[297] But viewed another way, Black's final letters offer further evidence of a man, long separated from his relatives, writing himself into his family's consciousness and maintaining his web of familial connection. 'Assure my sister of my tender regards', he wrote, at the end of his letter dated 5 June 1836, 'and if you have any stock at home married or unmarried I embrace them.'[298] Four months later, on 6 October 1836, Black died.[299]

---

292 Carmichael, *Trinidad and Tobago*, pp 86–93, 94–5, 114; Pocock, *Shadows*, pp 177–81. **293** Appendix, letter two.   **294** Appendix, letter four.   **295** Carmichael, *Trinidad and Tobago*, pp 106–7, 114; Pocock, *Shadows*, p. 215.   **296** 'Barataria (Trinidad/Cimaronero)', available at https://www.ucl.ac.uk/lbs/estate/view/8503 (accessed, 29/11/2018).   **297** Letters nineteen and twenty.   **298** Letter twenty.   **299** *BNL*, 23 Dec. 1836.

Editorial Conventions

John Black was a lively writer whose letters are detailed and engaging, if at times given to self-pity. In editing his letters, I have sought to produce an accurate and accessible text, and to let Black 'speak' for himself. Certain editorial interventions have, however, been required. Throughout, Black's erratic and frequently unnecessary capitalization has been standardized and the spelling has been modernized: 'shew' is replaced with 'show', 'domestick' with 'domestic' and so forth. The spelling of place names has also been modernized – 'Stranmillis' for 'Strandmillis', to give just one example – and Black's occasionally inconsistent spelling of names has been standardized. Thus while the name of his daughter Mariquite is spelled as 'Mariquite', 'Mariquita' and, on one occasion, 'Marie Quite' in the original letters, I have elected here to spell it as Mariquite throughout. Likewise, I have favoured 'Josefine' over 'Josephine' for a second of Black's daughters, though both spellings appear in the originals. Spelling aside, Black's '&' has been replaced with 'and', his '&c' with 'etc.' and punctuation has been modernized, the dashes with which Black typically ends sentences being replaced with full stops. In some instances, it has been necessary to add or remove punctuation and modify Black's sentence structure, but care has been taken to ensure there is no alteration to the original meaning. Obvious errors and misspellings have been silently corrected and repeated words deleted. Similarly, obvious contractions and abbreviations have been silently expanded, though Black's references to his wife as 'Mrs B' have been left unchanged and on those occasions where there is room for doubt as to the identity of a contracted word additions have been placed in square brackets. Square brackets have also been employed on those occasions – thankfully rare – where Black's writing is illegible or damage to the original letter has rendered words unreadable. Superscript letters, employed inconsistently by Black, have been removed from dates, but retained, and employed consistently, when referring to military regiments. Lastly, the text of each letter has been prefaced with an editorial gloss, summarizing its contents and locating it within the sequence of letters, and notes have been added, identifying, where possible, people, places and events mentioned in the text.

Manuscript References

Manuscript originals of the letters presented here, and in the appendix, are held at PRONI in two separate collections of Black family correspondence with the references D4457 and D1950.* The individual references for each letter are as follows:

Letter one	D4457/284
Letter two	D4457/284
Letter three	D4457/271 and D4457/285
Letter four	D4457/286
Letter five	D4457/287
Letter six	D4457/291
Letter seven	D4457/290
Letter eight	D4457/288
Letter nine	D4457/289
Letter ten	D4457/283
Letter eleven	D4457/292
Letter twelve	D4457/293
Letter thirteen	D4457/294
Letter fourteen	D4457/295
Letter fifteen	D4457/296
Letter sixteen	D4457/297
Letter seventeen	D4457/298
Letter eighteen	D4457/299
Letter nineteen	D1950/37
Letter twenty	D1950/38

Appendix

Letter one	D4457/302
Letter two	D4457/303
Letter three	D4457/304
Letter four	D4457/305
Letter five	D4457/308

*Typed copies of letters one and four are also held in PRONI in the Stewart family's papers. See D1401/9 (letter one) and D1401/11 (letter four), but note that the former also contains a misattributed passage from letter six. These versions are available online via the PRONI catalogue.

Letter One

Black's first surviving letter was penned in March 1799, by which point he had been resident in the West Indies for nearly thirty years. He opens with a complaint about his health and declares himself unable to write at length, but the letter is far from perfunctory and introduces a number of themes that recur in his correspondence. These include Black's troubled financial affairs, his management of his sugar plantation, his attempts to secure the patronage of Lord Macartney and his desire to return home. The letter, which survives incomplete, concludes with a series of references to members of the extended Black family, and it is clear from Black's assumption of his brother's familiarity with his affairs and his acknowledgment of the receipt of an earlier letter that it formed part of a long-running correspondence between the two.

---

1 March 1799, by the *Minerva*[1] to Glasgow.

My dear George[2]

You must excuse my writing you a long letter, neither my head or hand will permit it; I am a valetudinarian and likely to be so for some time.

Esther[3] will show you my letter to her; comprehend it as if addressed to yourself and answer me in consequence.

My ambition is to re-visit my native soil and it is the dearest and nearest wish of your sister's[4] heart to be presented to our dear parents,[5] my sisters[6]

---

1 The *Minerva* was evidently a Scottish ship involved in the Trinidad trade; the previous September it was reported that it had reached the Clyde from Trinidad, under the command of a Captain Kerr. *BNL*, 28 Sept. 1798. 2 George Black Jr (1763–1837), Black's younger brother, to whom the bulk of Black's surviving letters are addressed, letters three and eight, which are addressed to George Black Jr and Black's sisters (see notes three and six), being the exception. Ward, 'Black family', 188. 3 Esther Black (d. 1839), one of John and George's two sisters. On 1 January 1802, she married James Pettigrew of Mullavilla. 'Black family tree' (PRONI, D4457/363); *BNL*, 5 Jan. 1802. 4 Black is referring here to his wife, Bonne Clothilde/Clotilda Black. Like Black himself, Bonne Clothilde had been resident in Grenada before settling in Trinidad. Her maiden name was Fournillier and she was probably related to the Marie and Peter Fournillier who owned the Bacolet estate in Grenada. Prior to her marriage to Black in 1784 she had been married to a man named Mathews. Letter four; 'Black family tree' (PRONI, D4457/363); 'Register of plantation slaves', 1813 (TNA, T71/501 at 191/203), consulted online via the 'Slave Registers of former British Colonial Dependencies, 1813-1834' database, available at https://search. ancestry.co.uk/search/db.aspx?htx=List&dbid=1129&offerid=0%3a7858%3a0 (accessed 1/10/2018); Ward, 'Black family', 188; Susanne Seymour and Sherryllynne Haggerty, 'Slavery connections of Brodsworth Hall (1600–*c*.1800)', pp 41, 42, report for English

and yourself. For this inestimable blessing my dependence is on you; I am ready to make every sacrifice my means can justify and if my creditors will not accept of such terms as I can offer, I must forget Ireland and turn my thoughts to some other country, but this would be painful indeed.

Let them consider 25 years[7] exile in a country where I have buried thrice over all my contemporaries. This alone should expiate a world of follies; enemies I have no doubt among them, but if they consider a moment their interest impartially, they will not be inexorable. Some years past when I thought I had a perspective of doing well I made propositions of accommodation and they offered to emancipate me for £3,000 Irish. It was treble what, on a settlement of accounts, I should fall in their debt, because they were my partners and therefore bound to support a share of considerable losses which I alone have made good, but I pass over all that and now wish to know for what sum payable in what time I can obtain a discharge. I say in what time because it is impossible for me to pay down any considerable sum. It must be by instalments. A sugar estate no doubt yields a considerable revenue but the expenses are also immense and we are exposed to such a number of accidents that any sum of liquid revenue is never to be depended on. For instance, our revenues the present year will in gross reach £6,000 sterling, but I have had my wind mill stripped of her vanes in a squall, the cane cylinder dismounted, a new set of sugar boilers in copper to mount and all my negro houses to the number of 31 destroyed by fire and here is an unexpected expense of £2,000 sterling extraordinary besides our current expenses, so that you see the revenues of sugar although apparently immense are reduced to a small sum when expenses are deducted. You will consider all this, consult with your friends who should be also mine and acquaint me [of] the result.

Another object to be considered is my annual domestic expenses. I will enter into no contract that might tend to deprive them of a decent support as

Heritage, 2010, available at https://historicengland.org.uk/images-books/publications/slavery-connections-brodsworth-hall/ (accessed 16/11/2018). 5 Black's parents were George Black (1725–1800) and Arminella Black (d. 1802). The two were married in January 1753, though Arminella appears to have been previously married to a man named Campbell. John Black to Samuel Black, 20 Jan. 1753 and 'Black family tree' (PRONI, D4457/72 and 363); Ward, 'Black family', 187; Riddell, 'Great chemist', 64. 6 Esther Black (see note three) and Letitia Black (1756–1833). Letitia's death notice in the *Belfast News-Letter* records that she died, on 17 September 1833, 'in her 80th year'. This suggests she was born in 1753, but a later family tree (corroborated by baptism records) gives her year of birth as 1756, and records that she was married twice: first to a Mr Harrison, with whom she had two children (Letitia and Margaret); and later to John Younghusband, with whom she had a third child (Martha). John Younghusband died on 10 April 1843 at the age of 90. 'Black family tree' (PRONI, D4457/363); *BNL*, 24 Sept. 1833 and 14 Apr. 1843; *Register*, eds Gillespie and O'Keeffe, p. 217. 7 This suggests Black had been *resident* in the West Indies since 1774, though he had first visited Barbados and Grenada in 1771. George Black to George Macartney, 17 July 1771 (PRONI, MIC438/1).

well in the necessaries of life as the education of my children. If I possess anything I owe it to Mrs B and it would in me be an injustifiable act to embarrass her in her circumstances. With respect to myself my ambition is satisfied; if I could find a retreat where I could pass the remainder of my days, as far from thunder as from Jupiter,[8] my desires would be satisfied.

Your letter of 12 October came to hand through Mr Gordon's[9] *entremise*[10] at St Pierre's and to say it afforded me much pleasure is to express a faint idea of the delicious sensations it procured me. The infirm health of our dear father and mother was however a bitter alloy to my feelings.[11] I hope in God the spring of the year would revive their spirits and that the annual and tranquil moments to be passed at Stranmillis[12] would set all to rights again. This also is a forcible reason to hasten my return home and if those persons on whom it depends have any remains of feeling for me I shall not be disappointed.

You will see what I say to Esther about the old family seat Ballintaggart.[13] I have a sort of religious respect for that old mansion that incites me to pur-

---

8 A reference to Roger L'Estrange's *Fables of Aesop*. Reflecting on Fable XI, 'A City Mouse and a Country Mouse', which 'set forth the Advantages of a Private Life, above Those of a Publick', L'Estrange gave the saying in the following form: '*Far from Jupiter (says the Adage) far from the Thunder*'. Roger L'Estrange, *Fables of Aesop and other eminent mythologists: with morals and reflections* (London, 1692), pp 10–11; Apperson, Manser and Curtis, *Proverbs*, p. 192. 9 Most likely John Gordon who had served in St Vincent as a factor for Belfast merchants, and whose former business partner in St Vincent, Samuel Cunningham, was briefly active in St Pierre in Martinique in the mid-1790s. John Gordon to Messrs Cheap and Loughnan, May 1797 (PRONI, D1108/A/20); Gamble, 'Business community', pp 275–6. 10 i.e., intervention. 11 Black's parents were, by 1799, approaching the end of their lives. William Bristow, Vicar of Belfast, and James McDonnell, a well-known Belfast physician, testified in December 1799 that his father 'for a long time past has laboured under a paralytic affection'. He died shortly thereafter on 6 March 1800, while Black's mother died two years later in 1802. *CJB*, ii, 1459; 'List of children' (PRONI, D4457/329); Ward, 'Black family', 187. 12 Stranmillis was one of a number of plantation-era properties located in Belfast's southern hinterland. Encompassed within the estate of the Donegall family, the property was developed as a 'deerpark' in the late seventeenth century, but was split, by the 1770s, into a demesne farm and a number of smaller holdings. The former was acquired by George Black, who used it as a summer residence, and whose brother, Thomas, described it, in 1795, as a 'sweet little farm … most Charmingly situated on a little hill from which there is a Commanding views of all the Country round about'. The property was subsequently occupied by Black's brother, George Black Jr, who, it is said, 'rebuilt Stranmillis in 1801'. Thomas Black to Joseph Black, 30 Sept. 1795 (PRONI, D4457/251); Ward, 'Black family', 187–8; Trevor Carleton, 'Aspects of local history in Malone' in *UJA*, third series, 39 (1976), 62–7 esp. 63–4. 13 Ballintaggart was the Co. Armagh farm to which Black's grandfather, John Black III (1681–1767), had retired, upon leaving Bordeaux, where he had been a successful merchant in the late 1750s. The property was acquired by the family in 1749 and Black's grandfather, discovering that the meaning of Ballintaggart was 'the priest's land', renamed the property Blamont. This was a name he had previously used for his property in Bordeaux and appears to have been created by merging the Black family name with the name of the Lamont family of Scotland,

chase it even were I never more to see it, and I request you will inform amply on the subject. My grandfather[14] of sacred memory was much attached to it and my respect for his virtues would naturally incite me not to let it be separated from the family. It was in the year 1768 (I think) or '69 he gave me a common prayer book bought at John Hays the bookseller in Bridge Street for 2:2.[15] He wrote in the title page – John Black – thus and then gave it me. How it has happened or why it has happened God only knows, but without any particular care on my part it has followed me ever since and is at this moment under my left hand while I write you and I have a sort of superstitious religious confidence in this book and his name, that I consider myself shielded and protected from all accidents so long as I have faith in it and keep it in my possession which I hope will be so long as I live. In November 1776 I lost all my personal papers and books in the fire at Grenada.[16] In 1779 I lost all my linen and clothing by the plunder of the French soldiery[17] and in all of the vicissitudes of life to which 25 years West India existence has exposed me still this little book has preserved itself and followed me, and I confess my confidence in it is unbounded, inspired no doubt by the religious respect in which I hold the memory of him who gave it me.

It rejoices me infinitely that you yourself are at length in so independent a situation and that you owe it to our friend Lord Macartney.[18] He was in some

to whom the Black family were distantly connected; as Joseph McMinn has noted, the new name 'never seems to have acquired official acceptance'. John Black III to Alexander and James Black, 2 Aug. 1766 (PRONI, D719/78); Livesey, *Civil society*, p. 132; Joseph McMinn, 'An engraving of Blamount, County Armagh', in *Seanchas Ardmhacha*, 17 (1996–7), 89–94 (90 for quote); Ward, 'Black family', 187.   14 i.e., John Black III.   15 John Hay was one of a number of printer-booksellers operating in Belfast's Bridge Street and High Street, printing and bookselling going hand-in-hand in the eighteenth century. In 1768, his stock included, amongst other titles, the *Critical Review*, Samuel Johnstone's *Dictionary of the English language* and Adam Ferguson's *Essay on the history of civil society*. *BNL*, 12 Aug. and 22 Nov. 1768; Adams, *Printed word*, p. 23; Gillespie, *Early Belfast*, pp 141–3; McBride, *Scripture politics*, p. 36.   16 On 1 November 1775 (not 1776), a fire broke out in the town of St George's in Grenada and 'in the space of three hours ... the whole town was in one continued blaze'. This was the second such fire to have occurred within five years, an earlier conflagration having devastated the town in December 1771. *The Universal Magazine*, 58 (1776), p. 162; Johnston, 'Grenada, 1775–79', p. 97.   17 Having been ceded to Britain by France following the Seven Years War, Grenada was re-taken by the French in July 1779 and held until 1783. Johnston, 'Grenada, 1775–79', pp 92, 123–4; Henige, *Colonial governors*, p. 122.   18 Thanks, in part, to the patronage of George Macartney (1737–1806), an Ulster landowner and colonial administrator with whom the Black family had a long-standing connection, Black's brother, George Black Jr, had recently secured a position as a customs official in Belfast. Black's father, George Black Sr, had helped manage Macartney's estate (as, in due course, would George Black Jr), and Macartney had served as governor of Grenada in the 1770s, when John Black was resident on the island. George Black to George Macartney, 17 July 1771, 12 Jan. 1789 and 17 Jan.

measure bound to do something for some one of the family and if he has in effect any regard for me (and he should have) he will have it soon in his power to show it. The probability is that this colony will not return to Spain,[19] and there will be a number of employments to be disposed of here that he might easily bring me in for some of. There will be a collector and comptroller of customs, commissaries for the sale or distribution of lands, provost marshal register, judge of admiralty, master in chancery and a number of others that he knows well are lucrative places and that my experience teaches me to fill. If he should come to Ballymoney[20] and you see him, pray remember me to him and hint the places to be given in Trinidad. I shall myself write him as soon as I hear of his arrival in England from the Cape.[21]

I have a thousand other things to say to you but really by debility will not admit of my saying much more at present; remember me affectionately to Jemmy Kennedy[22] (what is become of his sister Betty who was of so pleasing a disposition) and to Charles Brett[23] and our name sake his spouse (what Black

1790, and George Black Jr to George Macartney, 27 Sept. 1802 (PRONI, MIC438/1 and 5); Riddell, 'Great chemist', 64–5; Ward, 'Black family', 188; *ODNB* (George Macartney, Earl Macartney). See, also, for the fullest account of Macartney's career as an ambassador and imperial administrator, Roebuck (ed.), *Macartney*.   **19** The Spanish governor of Trinidad, José Maria Chacon, had capitulated to the British two years earlier, in February 1797; the island was formally ceded to Britain in 1802, under the terms of the Treaty of Amiens, and remained a British colony until the twentieth century. Carmichael, *Trinidad and Tobago*, pp 36, 40–2, 52; Henige, *Colonial governors*, p. 182.   **20** The bulk of the Macartney family's estate, inherited by George Macartney in 1759, was located near the town of Ballymoney in Co. Antrim, though the family also owned land in Co. Down. Ballymoney was described in 1818 as an 'inconsiderable' town, albeit one that boasted 'at least two Presbyterian places of worship'. John Gamble, *Society and manners in early nineteenth-century Ireland*, ed. Breandán Mac Suibhne (Dublin, 2011), p. 627; Peter Roebuck, 'Early years, 1737–64' in Roebuck (ed.), *Macartney*, pp 1–22 at 6, 14–15.   **21** Between 1796 and 1798, Macartney served as governor of the Cape colony, which the British had occupied for strategic reasons in 1795, following the French invasion, the previous year, of the Dutch United Provinces. He left the colony in November 1798. J.L. McCracken, 'The Cape of Good Hope, 1796–98' in Roebuck (ed.), *Macartney*, pp 266–77 at 266, 276; Henige, *Colonial governors*, p. 106.   **22** 'Jemmy' Kennedy was James Trail Kennedy (1751–1832), son of Revd Gilbert Kennedy (1706–73), minister of Second Belfast Presbyterian Church, and Elizabeth Kennedy, née Trail. A successful merchant, Kennedy lived at Annadale, close to George Black Jr's home at Stranmillis, though on the other side of the River Lagan. In the opinion of the nineteenth-century historian George Benn, Kennedy 'was of the roll of merchants that raised Belfast to a high mercantile standard, and was justly esteemed as one of the best of merchants'. He had three sisters, Mary, Margaret and Elizabeth, the latter presumably being the 'Betty ... of so pleasing a disposition' that Black goes on to refer to. Benn, *Belfast*, p. 409; Benn, *Belfast from 1799 till 1810*, pp 195, 197–8; J. Carmichael-Ferrall, 'Note on the Kennedy and Bailie pedigrees' in *Journal of the Royal Historical and Archaeological Association of Ireland*, fourth series, 7 (1885), 30–6 at 34–5; S. Shannon Millin, *History of the Second Congregation of Protestant Dissenters in Belfast* (Belfast, 1900), pp 27–30, 111.   **23** Charles Brett (1752–1829) was the son of a lawyer of Killough, Co. Down, also Charles Brett, and his wife Molly Brett, née Carr, a

is she, one of the Dromore family I suppose), to our good brother-in-law John Younghusband and his and her little ones, I have some to match them; John has forgot me but I have not forgot him, he is as fresh in my memory as the last day I saw him in the lapping room off the parlour at Ballydrain.[24] Nay I remember his brother Isaac at whose death and sepulture I was present. He died at a lady's in Warren Street[25] whose name I forget.

I received this day from Glasgow by a ship of the Cork convoy a profile in plate of our uncle the doctor taken in 1788 which bears a strong resemblance, but I observe by your letter he is now very old and infirm.[26] Esther[27] gives me a dazzling account of her tour through Scotland to Harrogate[28] and speaks

merchant's daughter. Following an early flirtation with the linen trade, he established himself as a merchant in Belfast and played a prominent role in the life of the town; in the opinion of his descendant, the lawyer and architectural historian C.E.B. Brett, he 'was one of the first of the new Whig merchant class that sprang up in Ireland in the second half of the eighteenth century'. A supporter, in County Down politics, of the Downshire family's interest, Brett was appointed, at Lord Downshire's prompting, as barrack master of Belfast in 1797. Two years earlier, in 1795, he had married Matilda Black, of Armagh. C.E.B. Brett, *Long shadows cast before: nine lives in Ulster, 1625–1977* (Edinburgh, 1978), pp 36–40, 48–59 (49 for quote).   **24** Located close to Stranmillis, in what is today Malone, Ballydrain was the home of the Stewarts, who were closely connected to the Black and Younghusband families. In 1801, Black's brother, George Black Jr, married Ellinor Stewart of Ballydrain (see letter four, note 19), whose aunt, Martha Stewart, had earlier married Israel Younghusband and whose children included John Younghusband, the second husband of Letitia Black (see note 6). Martha Younghusband was, moreover, the daughter of Jane Stewart née Legg, who was the niece of Jane Black née Eccles, the wife of Black's great-grandfather, John Black II. Benn, *Belfast from 1799 till 1810*, pp 164–6; Riddell, 'Great chemist', 64, 67–71; Black, 'Ballydrain', 17–28.   **25** Most likely a reference to Waring Street in Belfast, a commercial street known also, at various points during the second half of the eighteenth century, as Broad Street, Waren Street, Warren Street, Warring Street and Wern Street. The identity of the lady referred to is unknown. See Gillespie and Royle, *Belfast*, pp 3–4, 19; Gillespie, *Early Belfast*, pp 93–9, 136–43.   **26** Born three years after Black's father, Joseph Black (1728–99) was the ninth of fifteen children of John Black III and Margaret Black née Gordon (1692–1747). A chemist of international renown, he was, from 1766 to 1799, professor of chemistry at the University of Edinburgh. His friends and acquaintances included James Watt (with whom he collaborated), James Hutton, Adam Smith, David Hume and Adam Ferguson; the latter two are known to have consulted him as a physician. The profile image to which John Black refers here was presumably the medallion in glass paste produced in 1788 by James Tassie (1735–99), a Scottish-born sculptor of portrait miniatures. 'Black family tree' (PRONI, D4457/363); Riddell, 'Great chemist', 82–8; Ward, 'Black family', 187–8; *ODNB* (Joseph Black), (James Tassie); 'Joseph Black', available at https://www.npg.org.uk/collections/search/ portrait/mw00596/Joseph-Black?LinkID=mp07619&role=art&rNo=5 (accessed 26/8/2018).   **27** i.e., Esther Black, Black's sister.   **28** A spa town in Yorkshire. Esther Black appears to have visited in 1796, but it is possible that Black is referring here to a subsequent visit. *CJB*, ii, 1293–4; Phyllis Hembry, *The English spa, 1560–1815: a social history* (London, 1990), pp 50, 95–7, 202–9.

much of the doctor and a surgeon Russell's attention.[29] Who is Colonel Burnet from India? A brother of John, Bob and James of the Aberdeen family, I suppose [...][30]

29 Most likely the prominent Edinburgh surgeon and later holder of the University of Edinburgh's professorship of clinical surgery, James Russell (1754–1836). Russell's father, also James Russell, who died in 1773, had succeeded Adam Ferguson (1723–1816) as professor of natural philosophy at Edinburgh in 1764, and had been related to Joseph Black, his mother being a sister of Black's mother. Ferguson was also a cousin of Black, and the two had, at one point, lived in a house owned by Russell. Riddell, 'Great chemist', 83–4; *ODNB* (James Russell), (Adam Ferguson); Andrew Dalzel, *History of the University of Edinburgh from its foundation*, 2 vols (Edinburgh, 1862), ii, 434; David Allan, *Adam Ferguson* (Aberdeen, 2006), pp 12–13. 30 The Aberdeen family referred to here was that of Joseph Black's sister Isobel (1718–81) who had married James Burnet of Aberdeen in August 1741. The couple's ten children included Katharine, who was reputedly the 'favourite niece' of Joseph Black and who married Adam Ferguson in 1766; John, Robert and James, who are referred to here; and Joseph Burnet (1752–1833), who is known to have served in Bengal and to have risen to the rank of lieutenant-colonel by the time of his retirement in 1798, and who was, most likely, the 'colonel Burnet from India' that Black here enquires about. 'Births, marriages, deaths extracted from the Black family Bible' (PRONI, T1073/1); *CJB*, ii, 1388–90, 1437–8; *Partners*, ed. Robinson and McKie, pp 317, 340, 365; *ODNB* (Adam Ferguson); Riddell, 'Great chemist', 83–4; T.E. Thorpe, 'Joseph Black and Belfast' in *Nature*, 30 Sept. 1920, p. 165.

Letter Two

Between March and July 1799, the ill-health Black referred to at the outset of his first letter worsened, and he wrote his second letter while travelling to Nova Scotia, where he hoped to mend his constitution. The chief purpose of the letter, composed on a 'pitching and heaving' ship, was to inform his brother of his movements: following 'a couple of months' in Halifax, Nova Scotia, he planned to travel southward through the United States, visiting the major cities of the north-eastern seaboard, before returning to Trinidad in early 1800. The letter makes reference to a plan, ultimately abandoned, to resettle permanently in 'some more healthful climate', and there is also a brief allusion to Irish affairs, Black having been given a 'miserable account' of the country by one of the Park brothers of Belfast, figures who appear frequently in his letters.

Brig *Commerce* at sea in company with the homeward bound
Windward Island Convoy 132 sail escorted by the *Santa
Margarita* and *Matilda* frigates. Friday 5 July 1799.
Latitude 25.15 north. Longitude 64.40 west.

A ship from Antigua for Dublin[1] in company affords me an opportunity my dear brother of acquainting you that I am this far on my way to Halifax in Nova Scotia for the recovery of my health which has been gradually declining since the month of February last, notwithstanding all my endeavours to restore it that either medical assistance or changes of air among our islands could procure; my constitution has fairly given way to the climate and as a last resource I have been obliged to cut and run in hopes that the hoary rocks of Nova Scotia will remedy the evils produced by too long a residence among the evergreen forests of the West Indies. Thank God I already find myself so much better, that I have every reason to hope my voyage will be attended with perfect success and that I shall be able to return to Mrs Black and the children[2] (who I left all in perfect health this day 3 weeks but much afflicted

1 Dublin had long-standing connections with Antigua. The Delap family, who were involved in the Bordeaux–Dublin wine trade, acquired a plantation on the island in the 1760s and by the later 1810s it was said that there were, 'belonging to the port of Dublin, two vessels which trade to Jamaica, [and] ten which trade to Barbadoes, Antigua, and Trinidad'. J. Warburton, J. Whitelaw and Robert Walsh, *History of the city of Dublin, from the earliest accounts to the present time* (2 vols, London, 1818), ii, 989; Rodgers, *Ireland, slavery and anti-slavery*, p. 159.   2 Black had five daughters: Adele, Esther, Julie, Josefine and Mariquite. See letter three.

at this our first separation since 15 years)[3] early in spring so as to be at home in time for crop. My intentions are to stay at Halifax a couple of months, then get to Boston, to New York and Philadelphia and so on to Baltimore or Norfolk and embark there early in January for the islands. I hope my letters to you and Esther dated in March last and dispatched via Glasgow will have reached you.[4] Your answers to those letters which I expect to find with your sister on my return will determine my future residence, because from what has happened it is evident I can exist no longer in the West Indies and my intentions are to abandon them for some more healthful climate, before this time twelve months with the family. I shall now have an opportunity of seeing the northern provinces of the U.S. and judging how far that country will suit my inclinations; I would prefer however my own to every other country provided I can attain that retreat without making sacrifices unjustifiable towards Mrs B and my children, who are growing up very fast and Josefine in particular is now as tall as her mother.

I made a crop this year of £6,000 sterling, our next will exceed 8,000 but I must increase for that purpose our gang of slaves by 15 or 20 and our other stock in proportion, so that the expenses will be considerable. I have been obliged also to lengthen our manufacture 40 feet to admit another set of coppers,[5] at which the masons and carpenters were employed when I left home.

We have been detained collecting the ships from all the other islands and although we are 3 weeks from Trinidad, we are only 5 days from Tortola.[6] We go on very well however with fair weather and as we propose taking advantage of the first spurt of variable wind (which we expect in a few days) to make the best of our way, I hope to be in Halifax in about 15 days.

---

3 According to a family tree in the papers of the Black family, John Black and Bonne Clothilde Matthews née Fournillier were married in 1784. Thus Black is here suggesting that they have not been separated since marriage. 'Black family tree' (PRONI, D4457/363). 4 See letter one.   5 Copper kettles, decreasing in size, were central to the process whereby sugar cane juice was transformed into sugar. 'Within the boiling house', Richard S. Dunn has explained, 'a battery of four or five great copper kettles hung over a furnace. These coppers were carefully scaled in size ... It was the job of the boiler, the most valued laborer on the plantation staff, to ladle freshly extracted juice from a cistern into the first copper, skim off the impurities that rose to the surface, and ladle the remaining liquid into the second copper. As the juice passed into progressively smaller, hotter coppers, with constant skimming and evaporation it began to turn thick, ropey, and dark brown in color ... The final, smallest copper had the thickest bottom and hottest fire. The boiler "tempered" the bubbling syrup with lime to promote granulation, and when he thought it on the point of crystallization he made his "strike" – dampened the fire and ladled the sugar into a cooling cistern. The boiler had to be something of an artist, for there was no sure way of telling whether the sugar had been tempered enough or too much, or when it was ready to strike.' Dunn, *Sugar and slaves*, p. 194.   6 Formerly a Dutch colony, Tortola had become a British possession in 1672 and was administered under the Leeward Islands government. Henige, *Colonial governors*, p. 102.

I have an old acquaintance there, a Jonas Fawson[7] who commands a brig of war on the station[8] and is married into a respectable family.[9] He is from the Isle of Man and was placed in his younger days by our good father a midshipman on board the old *Hind* man of war with McCleverty.[10] It was in the year 1768 or '69 and I have not seen him since.[11]

It blows fresh and we have a nasty head sea which renders writing very inconvenient, I must therefore cut short; you shall hear from me from every part of the continent I may be at and you will receive long letters from your sister[12] and the children.

I hope in God our aged and honoured parents continue to enjoy their health, assure them of my inviolable affection as you will also Letty and

7 Jonas or Jones Fawson (1751–1833), an officer in the navy, was present in Nova Scotia in the late 1770s and later became high sheriff of Halifax County. George Mullane, 'The privateers of Nova Scotia, 1756–1783' in *Collections of the Nova Scotia Historical Society*, 20 (1921), 17–42 at 39; 'Ancestry.co.uk, Fawson Message Board', available at https://www. ancestry.co.uk/boards/localities.britisles.england.nth.general/358.440.1/mb.ashx, (accessed 4/9/2018).   8 Halifax, Nova Scotia had been established as a station for Britain's North American squadron in the mid-eighteenth century, but was somewhat neglected during the Revolutionary and Napoleonic Wars. A full-strength squadron was not present until 1806 and the North Atlantic was considered less important than other naval theatres. 'Even the Indian Ocean', Julian Gwyn has noted, 'held more importance for Britain in its war with France and her allies than the Halifax station.' Julian Gwyn, *Frigates and foremasts: the North American squadron in Nova Scotia waters, 1745–1815* (Vancouver, 2003), pp xi, 89, 102.   9 In 1784, Fawson had married Dorothea Morris, a relative of Nova Scotia's surveyor general, Charles Morris (1731–1802). In 1805, Fawson's daughter, Dorothea, married equally well, her husband being Crofton Uniacke, son of Thomas Uniacke, Nova Scotia's Irish-born attorney general and, in the words of one biographer, 'the most influential Nova Scotian of his time'. 'Dorothea Morris and Jones Fawson Esq. marriage bond 1784', available at https://www.novascotiagenealogy.com/ItemView.aspx?ImageFile=1700-501&Event =marriage&ID=191595 (accessed 16/11/2018); Donald F. Chard, 'Morris, Charles', Dictionary of Canadian Biography, available at http://www.biographi.ca/en/bio/ morris_charles_1731_1802_5E.html (accessed 16/11/2018); Brian Cuthbertson, *The old attorney general: a biography of Richard John Uniacke* (Halifax, 1980), pp 1, 44, 75.   10 A naval veteran who had served with George Anson during his 1740–4 circumnavigation of the globe, Captain William McCleverty (1716–79) was most likely from Glynn, Co. Antrim, and took command, in 1763, of the *Hind*, a 24-gun vessel, 'stationed at Carrickfergus and Larne Lough for long periods of time'. His wife's family, the Johnsons of Glynn, owned a plantation on the island of St Croix, a Danish colony. Erica Fay, 'Captain William McCleverty, 1716–1779' in *Decies*, 68 (2012), 24–36 at 26–8, 30 (for quote), 33; Henige, *Colonial governors*, p. 10.   11 The Black family is known to have been involved in smuggling on the Isle of Man in the mid-eighteenth century. Black's uncle, Robert Black, was resident on the island for a spell, and his father visited the island with a consignment of rum in 1758. Three years later, planning a second visit, he proposed taking Black with him '[i]f the weather promises to be fair and settled.' John Black to Robert Black, 1 Sept. 1758 (PRONI, D719/51); George Black to John Black, 30 Oct. 1761 (PRONI, D4457/167); Cullen, *Anglo-Irish trade*, pp 148–9.   12 i.e., Black's wife, Bonne Clothilde.

Esther and Letty's little ones whom I hope to present some agreeable acquaintances to next summer.

Park[13] had been in Trinidad some weeks before I left it, he gave me a miserable account of the political and commercial state of our country and assured me I never would be able to live in it, however you will give me an impartial account.

I was in great anxiety when we heard of the Brest fleet[14] having got out, but we find they are gone to the Mediterranean where a good account will be given of them. We have also heard that the Union has been carried.[15] Amen!

Remember me affectionately to everybody. The pitching and heaving of the brig won't permit my being particular.

Your ever affectionate brother

John

13 A reference to either James or David Park of the Belfast Park family, and most likely the former. A member of the Park family appears to have engaged in the Isle of Man smuggling trade with Robert Black in the 1760s, and the family were also involved in the West Indian trade; James Park had been in business in Grenada between 1785 and 1796, and it was later said that, as a member of the St George's militia during the rebellion led by Julien Fédon, his 'bravery and eminent services ... saved the island.' Thereafter, James Park appears to have redirected his attentions to Trinidad. His brother, David Park, was also involved in trade in the island, and would later marry John Black's daughter Esther (see appendix, letter one, note 4). Black refers to 'Park' in letters two, four, five and six; and to 'Davy Parks' in letters ten, thirteen and fourteen. In letter sixteen he makes reference to both 'Park' *and* 'Davy Park'. Consequently, it is not always clear to which of the two brothers he is referring. In the current instance, however, the claim that 'Park ... gave me a miserable account of the political and commercial state of our country' is suggestive, for it is known that James Park had been present in Belfast in 1797 and 1798, and had had run-ins with United Irishmen, of whom he disapproved. James Park to marquis of Downshire, 18 Jan. 1798 (PRONI, D607/F/18); 'A certificate ... endorsing Park's application', 18 Jan. 1798 (PRONI, D607/F/19); 'Information of Major Park', 16 Feb. 1797 (PRONI, D607/F/20); 'Notarial copy ... of the Will of James Park', 29 Apr. 1815 (PRONI, D1905/7/19); 'Will and probate of David Park', 6 Dec. 1820 (PRONI, D1905/7/27); *BNL*, 31 Jan. 1815; Chambers, *Faces*, p. 89; Michael Craton, *Testing the chains: resistance to slavery in the British West Indies* (Ithaca, NY, 2009), pp 180–94; Gamble, 'Business community', pp 275, 288, 290–1; Pocock, *Shadows*, p. 217. 14 In April 1799, a fleet commanded by Admiral Bruix slipped out of the French Atlantic port of Brest, which had been under British blockade since 1795. Black's initial anxiety upon hearing this might well have been occasioned by the fact that ships that had escaped from Brest had earlier (in 1796 and 1798) ferried French troops to Ireland. Roger Morriss, *The foundations of British maritime ascendancy: resources, logistics and the state, 1755–1815* (Cambridge, 2011), pp 48–9. 15 A premature reference to the Act of Union – premature in that the act was not, in fact, 'carried' until the following year. It received royal assent on 1 August 1800 and came into force five months later on 1 January 1801. See J.C. Beckett, *The making of modern Ireland, 1603–1923* (London, 1966), pp 268–83 (esp. 279–80) and, for a fuller study, G.C. Bolton, *The passing of the Irish Act of Union: a study in parliamentary politics* (Oxford, 1966).

Letter Three

Written in April 1800, by which point his health had recovered and he had returned to Trinidad, Black's third letter ranks among his shortest. Addressed both to George Black Jr and his sisters, it reads as a follow up to an earlier letter, referred to in the opening line, but no longer extant, in which Black had informed his siblings of his 'return to the colonies'. As in his letter of July 1799, Black discusses the possibility of resettling his family in more salubrious climes, though the necessity of such a move is now attributed to the health complaints of the two youngest of his five daughters, all of whom are discussed here. Also discussed is the death of Black's uncle, Dr Joseph Black. 'Pray', Black inquired, financial considerations never far from his mind, 'to whom has he left his fortune?' Whether or not Black received a response to this somewhat mercenary query is unknown, but he was not, in any case, among the beneficiaries.

[c.19 April 1800][1]

My dear sisters and brother

   A few lines I wrote George by the *Highland Lassie* from St Vincent[2] would acquaint you of my return to the colonies and that my health was again perfectly restored. I got home on St Patrick's Day, found all well and many friends inebriated in celebration of the Irish patron's festival.[3] My health continues as it was used to do; I might hold it out some years longer but the situation of Mariquite and Julie will oblige me to pay another visit to the continent and as it is better to have only one house expense I intend carrying Mrs Black and all the family to the northward for 12 or 13 months. Where we will settle or indeed when we will go is uncertain. Nova Scotia I fear is too

---

1 While Black himself has not dated this letter, the original manuscript includes a second letter, penned by his wife, Bonne Clothilde Black, dated 19 April 1800. Annotations on the reverse of the manuscript indicate also that it was sent to Belfast 'care of Mr Archibald Ritchie, merchant in Port Glasgow', and that it crossed the Atlantic 'by the ship *Prince Edward* with a small *paquet*'. The *Prince Edward* arrived on the Clyde from Grenada in late June 1800. *Caledonian Mercury*, 28 June 1800.   2 St Vincent had been largely neglected by Europeans until the eighteenth century. The island was ceded to Britain, which had earlier claimed it, after the Seven Years War, but was captured by France between 1779 and 1783. Henige, *Colonial governors*, p. 169.   3 That St Patrick's Day should have been marked in Trinidad at this time is by no means remarkable, for by the end of the eighteenth century, as Anthony de Verteuil has noted, 'the Irish community formed a definite entity in Trinidad'. Precise numbers are unknown, but by 1802 the island's Irish population was sufficiently large to support an Irish Freemasons' lodge. De Verteuil, *Sylvester Devenish*, p. 5.

cold for Mrs Black, when I left it in February the mercury was at 12 below 0 and although a European born I felt it. I think Bermuda or some of the states to the southward in the Jerseys will better suit our purpose. I don't think we will get away this year, our crop falling an half short of what I expected from the dry weather and it is not altogether clear to me that any sugar at all will be made next year inasmuch the sources of vegetation are dried up. Never did I see (and I am a pretty old West Indian) such a season.

Julie is so replete, so plethoric and so fat, that the circulation in the capillary vessels is frequently interrupt[ed] and she is subject to a momentary convulsion, that has something [of] the appearance of epilepsy, but it lasts but about a minute or so. I am assured by the professional gentlemen it will cease on her becoming nubile, which I think the more probable from her enjoying in other respects the most perfect good health. Mariquite is on the other extreme, she is too tall much for her age and of course delicate and subject to feverish complaints and obstructions. Josefine, as fair, as sensible and as good a child as ever existed, I have great satisfaction in seeing universally beloved and admired. Adele and Esther [are] in rude health and promise to be all I could wish them.

I was and am much grieved to learn the afflicting situation of our dear aged parents from the letters I found here; the death of the doctor has also reached me this day by a gentleman who was at Edinburgh when it happened and who informs me he was in a state of childhood some time before his death.[4] He must have died very rich. Pray to whom has he left his fortune? Are any of you the better for it?[5]

---

4 A reference to Dr Joseph Black, who had died on 6 December 1799. The suggestion that he was 'in a state of childhood some time before his death' seems improbable. According to one friend, Black 'sometimes hinted his uneasyness at the thought of becoming silly, or slovenly, or squalid – and even of the last Struggle of life – and could not bear the thought of any undecencey of conduct or appearance', but had died peacefully; so peacefully, indeed, that 'for an hour there was not any change observable on his countenance'. Moreover, while his health failed towards the end of his life, his mind remained active: 'He was scheming a new Laboratory, to be built by subscription, of which he was to be the Contriver and the Architect – and never was without some gentle occupation.' *Partners*, ed. Robinson and McKie, pp 317–18; *CJB*, ii 1389; *ODNB* (Joseph Black).   5 As a result of his father's illness (see letter one, note 11) George Black Jr acted as 'sole trustee and executor' of his uncle's will, and was, indeed, 'the better for it'. Writing to James Watt in December 1799, John Robinson explained the provision that had been made for George Black, 'a very gentlemanly young Man', by his uncle: 'The doctor indeed always spoke of him in terms of particular regards,' he wrote, 'and has made him the greatest sharer of his Fortune. This, in Feb[ruar]y last amounted to £18,700, and must now considerably exceed £20,000. It is divided into 10,000 Shares, and is parcelled out among a great Number of Nephews and Nieces. Several annuities revert to Mr Geo Black, besides the largest share in the present partition.' Joseph Black's surviving testament suggests a slightly more complicated situation, with George Black receiving a portion of 1,800 shares. This, however, was to be inherited by George Black Jr, on the death of his father. Significantly, Joseph

I am anxious to hear from you and at same time dread the receipt of your letters. Something forebodes me afflicting news. God's will be done, we must all in our turn submit with resignation to the decrees of providence, but pray let me hear from you as soon as possible. I am at a loss yet what answer to make to what George has transmitted me; our revenues in these countries are so precarious that we never know what we are to have until we are absolutely in possession of it. Interest however I will not submit to, if I pay the principal it is much, for I am sure to a moral certainty that the concern is many thousands in my debt were I to state the accounts and I'll do it rather than pay any thing unreasonable; I can't afford to sport money having 5 daughters of whom two are as tall as myself.

Mrs Black sends Esther some jumby beans.[6] If there was a vessel going to Belfast I would send you and her some rum and sugar which would be more valuable, although less fashionable, and if it could be transhipped from Glasgow without any particular trouble or expense I could send it that way.

If I have parents (alas! it is very doubtful) and that they yet know my name, pray assure them of my inviolable affection and that my prayers are incessant for their recovery, but alas! at their age can it be hoped for?[7] I am ever my dear sisters and brother

Your affectionate brother

John

Black made clear that 'John Black the eldest son of my Brother George' was 'excluded from succeeding to any part of my estate or affects by being the heir of his father or otherways my will and desire being that My Nephew George Black aforesaid shall after his father's decease succeed in place of the said John to the enjoyment use and property of my estate above bequeathed to his said father'. *CJB*, ii, 1461–2; *Partners*, ed. Robinson and McKie, p. 325.   **6** Presumably jumbie beads, the poisonous but decorative red and black seeds of the *abrus precatorius* vine. Winer, *Dictionary*, pp 474–5.   **7** Although Black did not, at this point, know it, his father had died just over a month previously, on 6 March 1800. See letter one, note 11.

Letter Four

Notwithstanding his initial claim to be 'naturally averse to epistolary correspondence', Black's dispatch of 1 August 1802, the longest of his surviving letters, is detailed and wide-ranging. Matters discussed include Black's plans to send his wife and children to Ireland, the depression of sugar prices, the high rate of mortality among Europeans in Trinidad and the possibility of securing a position as commissioner for the sale of lands. Of particular interest is Black's description of his plantation – clearly a significant concern – and his reflections on the difficulties West Indian sojourners experienced in readjusting to life in Europe. Equally interesting, though, is the large 'cast' that populates the letter. As in earlier letters, Black makes reference to a number of relatives and related families, highlighting the importance he placed on familial connection. However, his references to Montgomerie, Crookshanks, Swiney, Leeson Blackwood and Park, Ulstermen who spent time in Trinidad, offer glimpses of the wider networks and webs of connection that linked his world.

[1 August 1802]¹

My dearest brother George

I am naturally averse to epistolary correspondence and more especially so when my head and hand are enfeebled by indisposition, as in the present instance, the consequence of a severe cold and fever under which I have been confined for upwards of a week, being a species of infirmity to which my pate, now perfectly bald, particularly exposes me. I cannot nevertheless allow our friend Park to leave us without bearing you testimony of my inviolable affection towards you all and to assure you in the sincerity of my heart, that peace being made and this colony annexed to the dominion of Great Britain,[2] my ambition has one great and desirable object, that of placing Mrs Black and my children under the guardianship of my relatives and of ending my days where I so happily began them. Indeed the preliminaries of peace were no sooner known than I renounced my former plan of passing some years in Nova Scotia and in consequence I immediately gave orders for the disposal of my property there.[3] My intention was to have sent Mrs Black and the children home this year and to have given her united with you full powers of attorney to arrange my affairs in

---

1 The date is given at the tail of the original, rather than the head. 2 A peace had been agreed between Britain and France in October 1801 and Trinidad was ceded to Britain in the Treaty of Amiens, signed the following March. War broke out again in 1803. Carmichael, *Trinidad and Tobago*, p. 52; Uglow, *In these times*, pp 283–4, 289, 339–40. 3 Black had spent time in Nova Scotia in 1799. See letters two, three, six and twenty.

such a manner as would soon have permitted my following her; many occur-
rences have since interfered to prevent that arrangement, but as it is probable
that the principal of those will be done away before next summer it is my serious intention that they shall embark on or before the 20 June next either direct
for Belfast or via Glasgow in which trade we have several excellent ships well-
appointed and equipped and it is even possible I may for a small additional
sum prevail on one of them to drop the family at Carrickfergus or the White
House road of all which you shall be duly advised.[4] The impeachments that
have presented themselves this year are *primo* the very discouraging state of the
sugar market and increased price of slaves, provisions, plantation utensils and
everything requisite for a plantation, all which we are paying for at present at
the highest prices of the war establishment in so much that so great is the dis-
proportion between the charges and revenues that it requires an uncommon
degree of economy to make the two ends meet and unless the price of sugars
increases, or that government come to the relief of the West India Planter by
a reduction of the duties, we must be inevitably ruined and this [is] a fact not
to be denied.[5] Our future prospects therefore depend on one or the other of
these taking place. Another business that at all events would have protracted
Mrs Black's departure is Josefines's pregnancy. She will lie in early in
December and being her first child, it would be an act of unkindness she does
not deserve at our hands to deprive her in that serious moment of her mother's
assistance. She is I confess one of the most amiable women you can imagine
and Lacoste makes her a very good husband.[6] She is respected and beloved by
all classes and colours of inhabitants.

4 Located some eight miles east of Belfast, on the northern shore of Belfast lough,
Carrickfergus was overtaken by Belfast, as a centre of trade, during the course of the seventeenth century, and is perhaps best known as the landing place of William III in 1690.
Also on the northern shore of Belfast Lough, though closer to Belfast, was 'the thriving
manufactory of Whitehouse ... a tolerably large village of good brick houses, with several
large buildings, for calico manufacture, bleaching, and printing.' Black uses the word 'road'
here in a maritime sense, i.e., 'a place in open water calm enough for ships to ride at
anchor'. 'Lydia', 'An excursion to Gracehill' in *Belfast Monthly Magazine*, 3 (1809), 106–
10 at 107; Gillespie, *Early Belfast*, pp 113–14, 117, 121. Miller, Schrier, Boling and Doyle
(eds), *Irish immigrants*, p. 96.   5 Black's complaints here are borne out by the work of
Seymour Drescher, who has demonstrated that the British sugar market experienced 'violent war-related fluctuations'. 'The price of sugar, exclusive of duties,' he notes, 'reached
its lowest quotation in decades between mid-1799 and the end of 1802, rose through 1805,
and then moved downward'. At the same time, 'sugar duties reinforced rather than soft-
ened the blows of war'. Drescher, *Econocide*, p. 126.   6 According to genealogical sources,
Josefine Black (1786–1853) married one Hugh Lacoste. That the two were married and
Josefine was pregnant by August 1802 is consistent with Pierre McCallum's account of his
experiences in Trinidad between February and April 1803, which makes reference to an
episode involving Black and his son-in-law – an episode which suggests that relations
between the two were not all sweetness and light: 'Some time since his daughter was married to a gentleman, whose name does not occur to my recollection, to whom he promised

Those were two powerful reasons and by the former one hangs a third which is that, on the cession of this island to G.B. being known, I had an offer of a loan of 8 to £10,000 by a house in London which I did not like to accept until after due consideration; but when I consented to the terms, they drew back on the grounds of the impossibility of turning sugars into money on any terms and that therefore they wished to suspend all negotiation until something in favour of the sugar markets be determined on, thus you see the price of sugars is the source of many inconveniences. I have received sales of 60 hogsheads remitted last year which after remaining three months in store neat [*sic*] me 12s/6d a cwt.[7]

I think it however impossible that this crisis can long exist, something must be done, and in that case I can obtain any money I want of which I will allow what may be wanted for Mrs Black and the children's support under your economy, until I myself can go home and conduct it which will be please God as soon as I can rid myself of my present very ungrateful situation, that of chief magistrate of the island[8] in the administration of justice under the Spanish laws which I must now continue to enforce until there is a change of the constitution and we are very uncertain as to when that will happen.[9] In the meantime, we have professional men in shoals like as many sharks waiting for the event.[10]

I have also laid out a large sum of money in slaves and lands within these two years, say nearly £8,000 sterling which however my ensuing crop will extinguish having 114 acres of remarkable canes, the bourbon quality, which

---

10,000l. as a marriage portion, and indeed gave bills of exchange to that amount to his son-in-law, drawn on a mercantile house in London ... the judge called one day on his son-in-law, just as he was about to forward them home for acceptance, and presented a pair of loaded pistols to his breast, then demanding the bills in a tone of voice intent upon bloody deeds, which so petrified the son-in-law with fear, that he returned them to his Honor without hesitation.' McCallum, *Travels*, p. 178; 'Josephine Black F, #405424', available at http://www.thepeerage.com/p40543.htm#i405424 (accessed 27/8/2018). 7 i.e., a 'hundred-weight'. John J. McCusker, *Essays in the economic history of the Atlantic world* (Abingdon, 2014), p. 53. 8 See note 28. 9 Trinidad's legal status was complex. 'At the time of the capture of Trinidad,' as A. Meredith John has written, 'the British had decided that the laws enacted by the Spanish should continue in force until the form of the island's government should be settled. Thirteen years later the future of the Trinidadian government was still in limbo: the colony had no legislative assembly, and Spanish law was still in force. Trinidad was administered by a royally appointed governor and by fiat from London.' Rendering this situation more complex still, Spanish legal expertise was scarce on the island and the question as to whether or not British law should be introduced was, as Kit Candlin has put it, 'hotly debated'. John, *Plantation slaves*, p. 20; Candlin, *Last Caribbean frontier*, pp 151, 202–3; Epstein, *Scandal*, pp 104, 275. 10 During the governorship of Picton (see note 29 below), '[s]ettlers ... crowd[ed] into the island'. These included lawyers, to whom Picton was antipathetic; he reputedly complained, in a comment which Black's words obliquely echo, that they 'were like carrion-crows, who flocked round carcasses and corruption'. McCallum, *Travels*, pp 144, 172–3; Epstein, *Scandal*, pp 104, 127.

to a certainty will yield me 500,000 pounds net sugar and about 20,000 gallons rum. And we are provided in force of every kind to take it off, i.e. 180 prime slaves, 60 mules, two complete sets [of] sugar boilers with a clarifier of 600 gallons, 2 3,000 gallon stills with 28 300 gallon vats for liquor and in fine a wind and mule mill on the most approved construction.

We have moreover our fuel houses perfectly stuffed and a great quantity prepared in the woods ready for emergency. Upon the whole I have no doubt of the quantity of sugar I mention being in the fields and I have also a certainty of making it <u>barring accidents</u> (for to those we are always exposed) to which end I shall commence crop on the first day of October and not cease until the whole be off.[11] All I look for with uncertainty is price and so far our London correspondents give us very poor encouragement.

Such are my hopes, my fears, my expectations and wishes and how far the whole or any of them shall be realised next year please God will determine.

I have received within these few days your very kind letter of 5 June by Mr Montgomerie who had a very favourable passage.[12] The detail you give me of our dear mother, sisters and your own very happy and comfortable situation, affords me the most pleasing and consolatory reflection. Would I could add one more to the number; it is an object I so devoutly wish the accomplishment of, that I fear it is too much happiness to be in reserve for me; I shall however do my best, and I am sure you will lend your assistance, although once more I must say, I depend for realizing it on the state of the sugar market to which I am totally dependent. I had also some time back a letter from my sister Younghusband[13] by a Mr Crookshanks[14] whom she particularly recommended to me and, finding him a young man of inoffensive manners, I took him into my own family (where he is at present) as well to save him the excessive expense of a tavern life as to preserve him if possible,

---

11 The harvesting of sugar cane and production of sugar were highly complex processes, requiring careful co-ordination. As cut sugar cane required immediate processing, its planting was phased to ensure it would ripen at different points. Harvesting was thus a protracted process with plentiful scope for 'accidents'. Dunn, *Sugar and slaves*, pp 189–201 (esp. 190–1).   12 Most likely a relative of the prominent Belfast merchant Hugh Montgomery, who was heavily involved in American and West Indian trade. Black makes several subsequent references in this letter to 'Montgomerie', and refers also to the 'the sailing of the *Industry*', this presumably being the ship on which he had had a 'favourable passage'. An American vessel, the *Industry* had been used by Hugh Montgomery and Co. as early as 1795, and was captained on this occasion by Thomas Hughes. It returned to Belfast by early December 1802 with a cargo including 20 hogsheads of 'damaged' sugars, which were advertised for sale 'by Auction for Account of the Underwriter at the Stores of HUGH MONTGOMERY & CO.'. *BNL*, 10 Dec. 1802; Benn, *Belfast from 1799 till 1810*, p. 122; Chambers, *Faces*, pp 84–7; Gamble, 'Business community', p. 263.   13 i.e., Letitia Younghusband née Black, Black's sister.   14 Possibly the A.E. Crookshanks whose name appeared on a list of signatories to an address presented to Colonel William Fullarton (see letter five, note 4) in July 1803. McCallum, *Travels*, pp 294–7.

by such means as experience has afforded me, from the effects of the yellow fever which has raged in an uncommon degree for six months past in this town, by which above 30 fair young men fresh arrived from England have already been carried off and it still continues its ravages so that I am in continual dread of his being attacked. I have had him bled and cooled by every proper means and I prescribe almost his seeing the sun after eight o'clock; this and his mode of life at my table, served in the French manner with a great proportion of vegetables, I conceive the best plan of preserving him; but still he risques much. Indeed I cannot conceive how any young man who could scrape acquaintance with a jailor would expose his life in this island under its present circumstances.[15] Not a man has escaped who has been attacked, the physicians confess their inability so that we must depend on domestic medicine in case of necessity and I am convinced it is the only means that offers a chance. You may assure his friends that every thing shall be done that can be done in case of necessity but I cannot answer for the event. Your friend Montgomerie does not *risqué* so much, he has been in Surinam and we observe the disease only attaches to people fresh from Europe who have never before been in a hot climate.[16]

Park will be able to give you a history of our situation in this respect which has really been melancholy. A fine young man from Larne of the name of Swiney was only a few days landed here when he was carried off almost without suspecting himself sick and many others have gone in the same manner.[17] Mrs Black and the children have been in good health for a length of time and indeed I never was better until this cold laid me up as Park will inform you. Mariquite is a strapping girl and considered very handsome. Julie the next in rotation is an immense overgrown child, very short and very plethoric. The consequence is she is diseased from excess of health or, to use the expression of the faculty, the container is not equal to the contained, hence she is subject to fits of a very singular nature very alarming in their appearance but very innocent in their effects for, although

---

15 An allusion to 'Conversations on Johnson, by Mrs Piozzi (Thrale) and Mr Boswell', a satirical verse by Peter Pindar (John Wolcot, 1738–1819), which contains the couplet: 'Quoth Johnson, "No man, sir, would be a sailor, / With sense to scrape acquaintance with a jailor."' Leigh Hunt, *Wit and humour, selected from the English poets; with an illustrative essay, and critical comments* (London, 1846), pp 35–7 (354 for quote); *ODNB* (John Wolcot). 16 Though confused, at times, with other sicknesses, yellow fever was a common illness in the West Indies, and was generally suffered, as Black notes, by 'people fresh from Europe'. Sufferers typically experienced 'a falling pulse accompanied by continued high temperature, the vomiting of partly digested blood and, in later stages, generalized haemorrhage'. David Geggus, 'Yellow fever in the 1790s: the British Army in occupied Saint Domingue' in *Medical History*, 23 (1979), 38–58 at 38–9. 17 Possibly a relative of the Belfast merchant Campbell Sweeny, who is known to have been involved in trade with Trinidad in the 1810s. McTear, 'Personal recollections', 211–12.

she has been afflicted with them for upwards of two years, her health has not been impaired, on the contrary, she is freer of ailment than any other of the family. I have had her with me through North America and Nova Scotia in hopes change of climate would procure her relief, but I found the succulent food of that country and wholesome air increased the disorder and of course I brought her home again. She is at present less subject to the fits and the general opinion is that the age of puberty which cannot be very distant will procure her relief. In the mean time we find taking now and then a little blood from her of use. Adele and Esther the two youngest, one of 8 the other of 5 years old, are two charming children, sensible to an astonishing degree and Esther in particular is a perfect *bijou*.[18] I hope some good schools are to be found with you for children of this description, for it will be impossible ever to separate them from their mother so as to prevent her seeing them daily. The attachment between a creole mother and her children is inviolable, which is accounted for by her nursing them and being their sole keeper and guardian from their birth I may say to their marriage, which often takes place at much too early an age.

I have as fresh in my memory, as if I had her yesterday, the mother of your amiable wife, with whom I have many a time danced at Dick Lee's school and afterwards well knew and admired when she became the wife of my respected friend Robert Stewart.[19] I don't recollect your Ellen but many a time I have nursed Mary who was a beautiful child, she is now I believe Mrs Clark.[20] The detailed account indeed you give me of the happiness of all around you and also of Mrs Bagenal, my old aunt Turnly and the Bordeaux

---

18 i.e., jewel.   19 George Black Jr had married Ellen/Ellinor Stewart (d. 1853), of the Ballydrain Stewarts, in February 1801. Her parents Robert Stewart (1742–1805) and Mary Isabella Stewart née Mitchell (1751–1785) had married in December 1769: Mary, 18 years old at the time of her marriage, was closer in age to John Black than to Stewart, who was born in 1742. She gave birth to five children in addition to Ellen – George, Jane, Mary, Annabella and Mattie/Helena – and died in 1785 'after a tedious illness'. Richard Lee was a dancing master present in Belfast in the 1760s; in April 1766 he advertised a new school, which he planned to open in the town of Lisburn. *BNL*, 25 Apr. 1766 and 20 Feb. 1801; Riddell, 'Great chemist', 64, 67, 69–71; Ward, 'Black family', 188. See also, for the Stewarts' connections with the Blacks, letter one, note 24.   20 Mary, the oldest of Robert and Mary Stewart's daughters (see note 19), was the wife of the Revd John Clarke, the curate of William Bristow, vicar of Belfast from 1772–1808. Clarke died in either 1799 or 1800, 'worn out by his excessive labours connected with the establishment of the Dispensary, and his unceasing and benevolent attentions to the poor'. Benn, *Belfast*, pp 385–6; Benn, *Belfast from 1799 till 1810*, pp 165–6; Riddell, 'Great chemist', 67.   21 'Mrs Bagenal' was Eliza Bagenal née Black (b. 1751), Black's cousin. The daughter of George Black's eldest brother (John Black IV), she was married to Walter Bagenal. 'Aunt Turnly' was Katherine Turnly née Black (1736–95), the youngest sister of George Black. She married Francis Turnly (d. 1801), a merchant from Newtownards, Co. Down, on 7 June 1768. The 'Bordeaux family' most likely refers to the family of Eliza Bagenal's father, who is said to have taken over the family's business in Bordeaux following the

family,[21] I have perused over and over with great satisfaction and the more I reflect on it the more I am impatient to consider with my own eyes the wonders of my native soil after 30 years absence.[22] I am equally rejoiced at the pleasing account you give me of Lord and Lady Macartney to whom I pray to you to render my humble and respectful compliments acceptable and assure them it would be the height of my ambition to pay them my devoirs in person at Lissanoure and also Mrs Black who is well known to her ladyship.[23] They are retired exactly in the style that must be highly pleasing to his lordship. *Otium cum dignitate*.[24] He has done his duty.

I consider by his having provided for you[25] he has in some measure cancelled any claim I might have had on him for protection, but he should recollect that if I should be an exile for so long a term of transportation, my exertions to serve his interest in my younger days laid the basis of my misfortune (this *entre nous*)[26] by exposing me to a line of expense that my means no ways entitled me to support, but depending on his promises to provide for me in such a manner as to recompense me.[27] This I doubt not he would have done had not the premature capture of Grenada prevented it, but a fair occasion now offers of serving me if he be so inclined, by the numerous employments and appointments government have to dispose of in this country, to many or any of which I am well entitled from my rank in the island of chief magistrate, president of the council and of the corporation and also master in chancery to take place under the new constitution being already in possession of the appointment.[28]

retirement of his father, John Black III. 'Black family tree' (PRONI, D4457/363); 'Births, marriages, deaths extracted from the Black family Bible' (PRONI, T1073/1); Benn, *Belfast from 1799 till 1810*, pp 166–8; Riddell, 'Great chemist', 64; Gamble, 'Business community', p. 255; *DIB*, ix, 528–9. **22** In the original manuscript a marginal annotation, in the form of a waved line, begins at the phrase '30 years absence'. **23** That Black refers to his wife, Bonne Clothilde (see letter one, note 4), being 'well known' to Lady Macartney, indicates that she had occupied a prominent social position in Grenada. **24** A classical phrase, associated with Cicero, *otium cum dignitate* may be translated as 'leisure with dignity', though it carried more precise political and social connotations in Cicero's writings. Arina Bragova, 'The concept cum dignitate otium in Cicero's writings' in *Studia Antiqua et Archaeologica*, 22 (2016), 45–9 at 48. **25** See letter one, note 18. **26** i.e., between ourselves. **27** See letter eleven, note 13. **28** Governor Picton (see note 29) established an advisory council in 1801. Over time, this body became an increasingly important part of the island's governing structure, but, as James Millette notes, 'it was an organ of autocratic control, not a platform for democratic debate'. Black was appointed to the council by Picton and also served as a member of the *Cabildo* – a 'municipal institution', which had been established under Spanish rule, and which is most likely what Black refers to here with the term 'corporation' – both as a *regidor*, or ordinary member, and as an *alcalde*, or judge. Millette explains the distinction as follows: 'there were two officials in whom the judicial functions of the *Cabildo* were almost exclusively vested. These were the *alcaldes ordinarios* who could not normally be chosen from among the *regidores* themselves. Barring the Governor the *alcaldes* were the

My ambition would point at being a commissioner for the sale of lands to which my general knowledge of the country (I have been through every corner of it in Indian hunting parties) particularly entitles me and also being perfect master of the three languages – English, French and Spanish. If a good occasion offers to hint this subject to his lordship, you might chance to serve me by bringing it forward. If not and that you dislike it, I would rather wave my pretension than you should be importunate.

It is to be observed however that I would not give up my appointment as master in chancery unless for something more beneficial and I conceive it will be worth from £1,200 to £1,500 sterling a year when the court is once fairly a going and it is an appointment I am specially calculated for on account of my experience in the affairs of the country and my knowledge of the languages. I hold it however only under Governor Picton's[29] commission which perhaps his lordship[30] might get me confirmed from the lord chancellor[31] in whose province it immediately lies.[32]

In the course of your intelligence of relations you have omitted the Purdysburn family and particularly Mrs Rowan of whom I would be glad to hear good news, but I fear the peace establishment will deprive some of her numerous family of situations which at least was a temporary provision.[33]

most senior officials of the *Cabildo* and they were judges. They were distinguished by the titles of *alcalde de primer voto*, or *alcalde* of the first election, and *alcalde de segundo voto*, or *alcalde* of the second election. The *alcalde* of the first election was senior to his colleague by reason of his having been elected one year before him … Though they were not *regidores* they took an active part in all the proceedings of the *Cabildo* and had a vote.' Black is known to have been a *regidor* under Spanish rule, in the 1790s, and was *alcalde* of the first election in 1803, hence his description of himself as 'chief magistrate'. He appears to have been appointed as *alcalde* of the first election as a replacement for John Nihell, an Antiguan of Irish ancestry who had offended Picton by questioning his abuse of power. McCallum, *Travels*, p. 177; Millette, *Society and politics*, pp 37–41, 151, 196–9, 267; Epstein, *Scandal*, pp 107, 133; Pocock, *Shadows*, pp 213–14; de Verteuil, *Sylvester Devenish*, p. 13.   **29** Thomas Picton (1758–1815) was a military officer appointed as governor of Trinidad following the Spanish capitulation in 1797. He held the position until 1803, during which time Luisa Calderón, a 13-year-old girl, was tortured during an investigation into a robbery. This led to a major metropolitan scandal, during which Picton was twice tried (see letter eleven, note 16). He went on to fight under the duke of Wellington on the Spanish Peninsula and was killed in 1815 during the Battle of Waterloo. *ODNB* (Thomas Picton). For two valuable recent studies, which shed light on Picton's governorship, see Epstein, *Scandal* and Candlin, *Last Caribbean frontier*.   **30** Macartney was made an Irish peer (Baron Macartney) in 1776. He became Earl Macartney in 1794, and was made a baron in the British peerage in 1796. Johnston, 'Grenada, 1775–79', p. 90; J.L. Cranmer-Byng, 'China, 1792–94' in Roebuck (ed.), *Macartney*, pp 216–43 at 218; W.R. Fryer, 'Verona, 1795–96' in Roebuck (ed.), *Macartney*, pp 244–65 at 265.   **31** John Scott, earl of Eldon (1751–1838). *ODNB* (John Scott, first earl of Eldon); Watson, *George III*, p. 581.   **32** A marginal annotation in the original manuscript (see note 22) ends here.   **33** The 'Purdysburn family' were relations of John Black's mother, Arminella Black. One of a

What also is come of Mrs Sharman, Hill and that scapegrace Jemmy?[34] We have lately had here a lad of something of the same stamp and at [the] same time one of the most agreeable companions I have met with, Leeson Blackwood Captain in the 7th West India Regiment in garrison at Antigua.[35]

He came over here on speculation, and notwithstanding his *etouderie*,[36] he made a hit that in the first instance produced him a profit from hand to hand of £1,100 sterling. Aided by that and some more money he drew for on Sir James, his brother,[37] he has purchased 600 acres of excellent land in a very eligible sea-side situation which will turn out very valuable if he can contrive to settle it, but this will require a large sum. Perhaps more than Sir James will be disposed to advance him from his being unacquainted with the unavoidable expense that is requisite to the establishment of a sugar property. Be that as it may, Leeson has made a beginning with about a dozen slaves who are cutting down the wood and making an opening for the buildings, provisions and pasturage and I expect him from Antigua immediately on the reduction of those

number of 'Gentlemens Seats' located in Belfast's southern hinterland, Purdysburn was home, in the mid-eighteenth century, to Arminella's uncle, Hill Wilson. 'Mrs Rowan' was Eliza Rowan (d. 1817), daughter of Hill Wilson and wife of Robert Rowan (1754–1832). Married in April 1777, she had ten children; eight were sons, of whom at least three, Frederick, Charles (*c.*1782–1852) and William (1789–1879), pursued careers in the military. *The antient and present state of the County of Down. Containing a chorographical description, with the natural and civil history of the same* (Dublin, 1757), p. 72; *GM*, 38 (1852), 91–2; Burke, *Landed gentry*, p. 609; Riddell, 'Great chemist', 64; 'Table talk', 214; *ODNB* (Charles Rowan), (William Rowan).   **34** 'Mrs Sharman' was Arminella Sharman née Wilson, another of Hill Wilson's daughters (see note 33) and the wife of William Sharman (*c.*1730–1803), a prominent member of the Irish Volunteers who was elected to the Irish parliament as MP for Lisburn in 1783. Hill and Jemmy were, most likely, siblings of Arminella, and the description of Jemmy as a 'scapegrace', combined with the fact of William Sharman's involvement in Volunteering politics, suggests that Jemmy was the James Wilson who was elected to the Irish parliament as MP for Co. Antrim in 1776 and who was said to have been 'disinherited by his father'. Peter Harbison, 'Gabriel Beranger (*c.*1729–1817) in County Down' in *UJA*, third series, 64 (2005), 154–9 at 154; McBride, *Scripture politics*, p. 121; *DML*, i, 2; G.O. Sayles, 'Contemporary sketches of the members of the Irish parliament in 1782' in *Proceedings of the Royal Irish Academy*, section c, 56 (1953/1954), 227–86 at 233; *DIB*, ii, 977–9 and viii, 847–8.   **35** Leeson Blackwood was one of 11 children of Sir John Blackwood (1722–99), landowner and member of the Irish parliament, and his wife Dorcas Blackwood née Stevenson (d. 1808). He died in 1804. Dorcas Blackwood was made Baroness Dufferin and Clandeboye in 1800, and the family estate was later inherited by Frederick Temple Hamilton Temple Blackwood, marquis of Dufferin and Ava (1826–1902), who served as viceroy of Canada from 1872 to 1878 and India from 1884 to 1888. *Burke's peerage and baronetage*, 105th ed. (London, 1976), pp 847–9; *DIB*, i, 572–3, 576–7. The Blackwood family were linked to the Black family through marriage, for which see note 40.   **36** i.e., carelessness.   **37** An older brother of Leeson Blackwood, Sir James Stevenson Blackwood (1755–1836) was a military officer and, from 1788 to 1800, member of the Irish parliament for Killyleagh, Co. Down. He helped supress the 1798 rebellion in Co. Down, voted in favour of the Act of Union and later held seats in

regiments which are to be confined to 6 battalions complete.[38] He talks of sell-
ing out and employing his money in planting but this I advised his deferring
until he should receive his brothers opinion on whom he is dependent, for his
uncle Leeson's legacy has gone long ago.[39] He is upon the whole however a
very pleasant fellow of uncommon good humour and very much esteemed by
every man of respect in this island.

He made this house his home and dined with us at all times when tired of
hard living with the military he wished to cool down *en famille*.

We talked over all our friends in the north very frequently and did not
forget our cousin Tom Banks in the number. Mr Montgomerie has informed
of the death of the old gentleman so that I suppose the family is reduced to
Tom alone.[40] You are also silent as to my Uncle Tom's family and how he has
disposed of his numerous offspring.[41] Esther wrote me some time ago that one
of his daughters who is a toast was about to be married to a Captain Galway
of the 64th[42] who has two brothers here, one a merchant,[43] my neighbour, the

Westminster. He became Baron Dufferin in 1808. *DIB*, i, 576.   38 The 7th West India
Regiment had been raised in 1795 and was disbanded in 1802. It was initially proposed that
the 7th, 8th, 9th, 10th, 11th and 12th regiments would be disbanded, but soldiers of the
9th, 10th and 12th regiments became part of a re-established 7th West Indian Regiment,
and soldiers from the 11th regiment became part of a re-established 8th West India
Regiment. Roger N. Buckley, 'The early history of the West India regiments, 1795–1815'
(PhD thesis, McGill University, 1975), pp 100, 209, 219–20.   39 Most likely Joseph
Leeson, earl of Milltown (1701–83), a maternal uncle of Leeson Blackwood's father. *DIB*,
i, 576–7 and v, 414–15.   40 The Black family was related to the Banks family through the
marriage in 1750 of Black's uncle, John Black IV (1717–82), to Jane Banks, whose father
was Thomas Banks of Belfast and whose uncle was Sir John Blackwood (see note 35).
Thomas Banks was most likely also the father of Stewart Banks (1725–1802), the 'old gentleman' referred to by Black. Sovereign of Belfast on several occasions in the second half of
the eighteenth century, Stewart Banks was described by John Black III, in a letter penned
in 1765, as 'our Worthy friend and family Allye', and died on 1 April 1802. The 'cousin
Tom' to who Black refers was in all likelihood the Thomas Banks whose name appeared on
an advertisement regarding the sale of a property, 'situated in Castle-street, late the residence of STEWART BANKS' in 1802. 'Black family tree' (PRONI, D4457/363); *BNL*, 6
Apr. and 21 May 1802; Ward, 'Black family', 179, 185, 187.   41 Thomas Black (1735–
1804) was the youngest son of John Black III and Margaret Black née Gordon. He is said
to have had a number of children with his wife Isabel Black née Towry, but the identity of
the daughter Black goes on to refer to here is unknown. 'Black family tree' (PRONI,
D4457/363); *CJB*, ii, 1437.   42 The 64th regiment had been despatched to the West
Indies in 1801 and Captain Galway was reported as having been injured 'slightly' in June
1803, during an attack on Morne Fortunée, a fortress on St Lucia, a British colony that had
been captured by France in 1802. *GM*, 73 (1803), 769; Joseph Wetherall, *An historical
account of his majesty's first, or the royal regiment of foot: General George, duke of Gordon,
G.C.B. colonel* (London, 1832), p. 73; Henige, *Colonial governors*, p. 168.   43 Most likely
the Richard Galway whose name appeared in 1805 on a 'petition of ... proprietors of lands,
planters and merchants' requesting the introduction of British law in Trinidad and who was
named, in 1807, as the island's postmaster. It is possible that Galway was related to a

other captain of the *Plover* sloop of war on this station. The regiment soon after came out and I was not without hopes of seeing my cousin with the regiment, perhaps in garrison here. I have however been disappointed in two ways, for the 64th is appointed to St Kitts[44] and Captain Galway is married to a Santa Cruz lady since the regiment came out. I mention this to you because Mr Montgomerie says he believes there was some sort of promise between Galway and my fair cousin whose name I don't know. Where is John Black of Bordeaux?[45] I would also wish to know how you have disposed of the old Ballintaggart concern. It was a place I was very partial to, but I have been so long exposed to a very active life and a sea port situation that a retreat of that kind, however seducing the lure of novelty might be for a little time, the charm would soon wear off and I should find it but a wearisome life. Indeed it's a general observation that when a man has passed upwards of 10 years in the West Indies he can never brook living anywhere else and I have invariably seen it turn out so, with all the old stagers I have seen attempt to stay at home. They all soon became disgusted with the European formalities and returned to our good West India hospitality in which all formality and ceremony had been long abolished.

This however shall not deter me of attempting it provided things turn out as I hope and expect and of which you shall [be] [–] and [–] advised.

Having thus wrote you for the benefit of the whole all I have to say, you will have the goodness to participitate my letter to all whom it may concern. It is a long incoherent scrawl but my head will not serve me in its present weak state to do more. By the sailing of the *Industry*,[46] which being a small vessel Mr Montgomerie will not I presume retain long, you shall hear farther from me and I'll endeavour to send you by her a sample of sugar of my own manufacture.

Should any other vessel (as is probable) offer for this place, I wish you would send us by her some butter for house use, say 3 or 4 firkins of superior quality (it is now 30 dollars a firken) and any other good things in salt that might be useful in a family. I would [be] glad also of 20 barrels of oatmeal for our negroes by every occasion and any other dry provision you could ship for the like purpose for all which you shall receive a consignment by the same

---

branch of the Cork Gallwey family that was established in the West Indies in the seventeenth century, but the precise nature of the connection is unclear. Henry Blackall, 'The Galweys of Munster (concluded)' in *Journal of the Cork Historical and Archaeological Society*, 74 (1969), 71–83 at 80–2; ['A gentleman of the Island'], *Political account*, pp 143–9; *The royal kalendar; or, Complete and correct annual register, for England, Scotland, Ireland and America, for the year 1807* (London, 1807), p. 250. **44** Occupied by both the French and the British in the seventeenth century, St Kitts had become a solely British possession in 1702. Henige, *Colonial governors*, p. 167. **45** Most likely a reference to Black's uncle, John Black IV (see note 21), or to his son, also John. *CJB*, ii, 1437; Ward, 'Black family', 186. **46** See note 12.

vessel to cover completely your advances. Oats also we are always in want of for our stocks.

With my tender love and affection to our dear mother, sisters, aunts, cousins, *cousines*, and friends of all descriptions, I remain with inviolable regard your loving brother and faithful friend.

Trinidad 1 August 1802

John Black

Park is just going off.

We have very unpleasant intelligence from St Domingo. The business is not at an end there yet.[47]

47 Most likely a referenct to events not in Santo Domingo, but to the French colony of St Domingue, where the enslaved, inspired by news of the French Revolution, rebelled in August 1791, in a rising that had repercussions throughout the Caribbean and that ulti-mately led to the emergence of Haiti as an independent nation. In February 1802 a force of 20,000 French troops, led by Victor-Emmanuel Leclerc, had arrived on the island. The rebel leader Toussaint Louverture was captured but the French faced stiff resistance and were defeated in 1803. Haiti declared independence the following year. Polasky, *Revolutions without borders*, pp 147–58, 259–63; Eakin, *Latin America*, pp 167–9. For Santo Domingo see letter eighteen, note 17.

Letter Five

Having written at length on 1 August 1802, Black's fifth letter, penned just a month and half later, is altogether more succinct. Its contents suggest that the letter of 1 August was accompanied by a third letter that has not survived: Black writes here of having previously 'mentioned to you the appointment of Colonel Fullarton to be first commissioner in the government of this island', but no reference is made to Fullarton in the earlier surviving letter. Whatever the case, Black's reference to Fullarton is of interest. While he was, in due course, to become highly critical of Fullarton, he appears, at this point, to have viewed him as a potentially useful contact. Fullarton aside, the letter also contains Black's first reference to Captain James Graves, who had requested permission to marry his daughter Mariquite, and highlights some of the more mundane, everyday considerations underpinning life in the West Indies; with food prices high, he requests that his brother help him source provisions for the use of his family and, reminding us that slavery was central to his world, 'food for negroes on reasonable terms'.

Trinidad 14 September 1802

My dear brother

Referring you to my letters by Park whose oral testimony would supply any deficiency, receive this assurance of my affection for you <u>all</u> by the *Industry*,[1] in which I have shipped for sample a barrel of coffee, and 4 cases containing each 12 bottles Martinique liqueurs assorted, but of those, two (although directed to your protection) are for the reverend Dean Graves, late of Elphin, now of Down, residing in Belfast or Carrickfergus, from his son Captain Graves of the 14th regiment in garrison here.[2] The coffee we have been obliged to put in the manifest but the cases you must manage as well as you can and I suppose Captain Hughes is a good hand at smuggling.[3] I would have added

---

1 See letter four, note 12. 2 Thomas Graves (1725–1848) was the Church of Ireland dean of Connor and rector of Carrickfergus from 1802 to 1811. His son, James William Graves (1774–1845), joined the 14th regiment in February 1791. He was made captain-lieutenant on 1 September 1795, shortly before departing for the West Indies, where he was to remain until 1803, serving in Puerto Rico, St Lucia, St Vincent and Trinidad. Samuel McSkimin, *The history and antiquities of the county of the town of Carrickfergus, from the earliest records, to the present time* (Belfast, 1811), p. 64; *RMC*, iv, 160–2; Burke, *Landed gentry*, p. 275; J.B. Leslie, *Clergy of Connor: from patrician times to the present day* (Belfast, 1993), pp 129, 355. 3 Thomas Hughes was captain of the *Industry* in 1802 (see letter four, note 12). Whether or not he was involved in smuggling is unknown. He would, however, have been far from unusual if he was, for smuggling appears to have been widespread in Belfast. In his

to those a sample of our rum and sugar, but all has been shipped long since. However, as this or some other vessel from Belfast will probably pay us a visit early next year, I'll send you a hogshead of each for family use, I mean for you, Letty and Esther. Indeed I wish a continual intercourse could be established, and I think a store well and continually supplied with good provisions would answer well. They have been uncommonly scarce this year in so much that butter in particular was at one time a dollar a pound. We now pay for it 22 dollars a firkin, beef 24, pork 30. Should any opportunity be coming his way, I would be very glad [if] you could send a supply of those articles for my own use, such as 8 or 10 half barrels of choice mess beef, 4 of Pork and 6 or 8 firkins of your very best butter. You have no idea of the consumption of those articles in a West India family who always prefer salted meat to fresh provided it be really good, such as I know you could procure it. In my former letters, I also mentioned negro provisions and I particularly recommended a few hogsheads of oatmeal. It now occurs to me also to recommend field pease, a few barrels for trial, oats in hogsheads for stock and if hearts and skirts could be shipped nearly as cheap as herrings they would be preferable food. In short you can perceive my aim which is to procure food for negroes on reasonable terms and whatever supply you ship shall be profusely remitted for by return of the vessel.

Mrs Black here reminds [me] of fine linen for shirting and table linen, objects which in the family cost me some hundreds annually.

In my last letters I mentioned to you the appointment of Colonel Fullarton to be first commissioner in the government of this island (a sort of phenomenon I don't yet well comprehend and requested your procuring me through Lord Macartney a recommendation to him, considering that they must be on terms of friendship from their having been on service in India together).[4] I

'Personal recollections', published in 1899, Thomas McTear noted that 'Belfast, during the last century and beginning of the present, was notorious as the headquarters for smuggling tobacco, silks, spirits, and other articles subjected to high duties on importation'. McTear, 'Personal recollections', 212. 4 A Scottish-born landowner, politician and colonial administrator, William Fullarton (1754–1808) was appointed, in 1802, as the leading member of a governing commission for Trinidad. His fellow commissioners were Commodore Samuel Hood (see letter six, note 18) and the incumbent governor of the colony, Thomas Picton, who was essentially supplanted. Conflict quickly developed and, as James Epstein has put it, 'Fullarton and Picton clashed violently over matters of colonial governance and the administration of justice'. Earlier in his career, Fullarton had fought in the army of East India Company, and he was, indeed, 'on terms of friendship' with Lord Macartney, who had served, following his governorship of Grenada, as governor of Madras. Writing to Macartney in March 1803, Black noted that 'Expressions of friendship and regard for your Lordship are often the Theme of Colonel Fullarton's Conversation and they appear to proceed from the feelings of his heart.' John Black to George Macartney, 20 Mar. 1803 (PRONI, MIC438/3); *ODNB* (William Fullarton); Epstein, *Scandal*, pp 17–18, 60, 130–1; T.G. Fraser, 'India, 1780–86' in Roebuck (ed.), *Macartney*, pp 154–215.

hope you have not neglected my request, for although I must be of his council, his master in chancery, and enabled from my experience and perhaps influence in the country to be of more service to him than he can be to me, still his lordship's recommendation must have its influence and I repeat my request that you will mention it to him. He owes me a good turn, and he ought to discharge the debt when he can.

My prospect of a very handsome crop increases as the year draws to a close. I am repairing our mills and fire places to commence making sugar as soon as possible, and if the price would but favour us you may expect the performance of my promise with respect to Mrs Black and the children as soon as the spring will permit. She is very anxious to get away and I assure you I am not less so, both for her sake and the younger children's, who are at the time of life necessary to commence their education.

I wish you to procure and transmit me information exact of what Dean Graves <u>is</u> and also his circumstances and family.[5] My reason for asking arise from an application by his son Captain Graves for Mariquite, which I have required time to consider of.[6] He is a fine young man, very correct, was on the continent with the regiment in the duke's campaigns and now commands the regiment here.[7]

This however *entre nous*.[8] If it takes place, you will have them soon with you for the regiment is ordered home and Captain Graves will immediately go to Belfast.

I have just received a letter from Captain Blackwood at Grenada where he has been ill; his regiment is reduced [to the] 7th West India and he is on his way here from Antigua to turn sugar planter.[9]

You will consider this letter as wrote to you and to all the family for I really have not time to address one to each, and therefore this must be a circular; but you have all my warmest wishes for your individual prosperity and happiness in which Mrs Black very cordially joins me and the youngsters. Josefine now unwieldy will lie in in November, I believe. She is the best of all God's creatures and universally beloved.

Mariquite is all fire and tow,[10] but a very fine woman. Esther however will be the finest woman of the family and <u>like her aunt</u> uncommonly sensible. In

5 That the living of Carrickfergus was valued at £250 a year in 1811 suggests that Dean Graves' circumstances were comfortable. McSkimin, *History and antiquities*, p. 64. 6 Captain Graves and Mariquite appear to have married before the end of the year. In his subsequent letter, dated 19 January 1803, Black remarked that 'in effect Mariquite was married to Captain Graves of the 14th on the 25 October (I think) and they make a very happy couple'. See letter 6. 7 A reference to the duke of York, under whose command Graves had served in Holland and France in the early 1790s. *RMC*, iv, 160; Uglow, *In these times*, pp 39–45. 8 i.e., between ourselves. 9 See letter four. 10 A variation on 'fire and flax', a saying that can be traced back to the fourteenth century. Apperson, Manser and Curtis, *Proverbs*, p. 200.

short, they are a very fine family for creoles as you will allow when you see them.

Assure my honoured mother of my inviolable duty and affection, and receive <u>all</u> my vows for your happiness and prosperity; I have not time to add more than that I am and ever will be your affectionate brother <u>John</u>.

Letter Six

Written with a 'confused head', following a night spent at a 'crowded ball', the sixth of Black's letters commences with his response to bad news – news concerning his mother's death, and news to the effect that his creditors were not disposed to come to terms. Fearing that his 'financial abilities' had been misrepresented, Black here adopts a somewhat self-justificatory tone, foregrounding his frugality and the difficulties he encountered in attempts to wring a profit from his estate. Financial matters aside, the letter contains a striking discussion of the high mortality rate among the enslaved in Trinidad, and an account of Colonel Fullarton's arrival on the island. It also contains family news, with Black informing his brother that his daughter Mariquite had, the previous October, married Captain James Graves.

Trinidad 19 January 1803

My dear brother

After passing the night with the family at a crowded ball given by Governor Picton[1] in celebration of the anniversary of the Queen's birth, I take the pen with a confused head to avail myself of a friend who sails for Greenock[2] this day to say what time permits me in reply to your kind letter of 24 November dated at Stranmillis at 12 o'clock at night. And in the first let me join in your natural affliction for the loss of our dear mother whom it pleased God to spare us to that advanced age when such an event might be expected.[3] To you and my dear sisters who have been always with her, the loss must have been sensible, but I unfortunate I, who have been estranged from everything consanguinely dear to me for nearly 30 years, the period I may say of a man's life, I feel it with probably less poignant sorrow, but perhaps more lasting impression and it appears to incite me still more to revisit my native soil before we are forever separated. The account you give me however of the disposition of the persons on whom that re-union principally depends is not consolatory. The more so as the reports which have reached them respecting my financial abilities are fallacious in the extreme and I am surprised very much indeed that Park, with whom I have always been on the most friendly terms, should attempt to mis-

---

1 By this point Picton was not, in fact, the governor of Trinidad, but one of three governing commissioners. See letter five, note 4. 2 Located to the west of Glasgow, Greenock was a port town on the Upper Clyde which had grown considerably over the course of the eighteenth century, and with which Belfast had well-established connections. Daniel Weir, *History of the town of Greenock* (London, 1829), pp 1–3; Gamble, 'Business community', pp 212–13. 3 The precise date on which Black's mother died is unknown, but his comments here suggest that the death occurred towards the end of November 1802.

97

lead them so much to my prejudice. I can assure you with the greatest sincerity that my income for several years preceding 1802 barely kept pace with my expenses and we live as frugally as the extent of my family and estate can possibly admit, but this year of 1802 in the fall has nearly brought this country to destruction by the mortality with which we have been afflicted in our slaves and stock and should it unfortunately be again the case in this fall Trinidad, which we are informed is considered so valuable a possession, will be completely done up.[4] I have an hospital at Barataria[5] well-ordered and attended; Park will tell you that no estate in this country offers a more healthful situation for slaves and notwithstanding those advantages, improved by the best medical attendance and a profusion of every thing, I have buried 36 slaves since 1 day of June last, many of them my very best and most valuable people, refiners, distillers and mill boatswains, and when I estimate the intrinsic value of those people (together with 27 mules and 5 draft oxen) without calculating the inconvenience that must necessarily arise by the want of my leading people at £4,000 sterling Park will tell you I do not exaggerate.

I have nevertheless been one for my numbers who has suffered the least, for I know properties where the mortality has exceeded 100 or 260 and there are many, many of 60 and 80. Park has also been a sufferer, but to what extent I am ignorant, for people generally keep those losses secret; the census now preparing for the information of the commissioners[6] will explain all and I am very apprehensive the general loss will be found to approach 4,000 slaves.

To an infant colony on which no great dependence (experience has taught us) can be placed with respect to its revenues, by reason of the uncertainty of its seasons, this is nearly a mortal blow. We had cherished hopes of a very plentiful crop to come to our relief and also an increased value of sugar on account of the total ruin of St Domingo[7] and the failure of the crop at Jamaica

4 Mortality rates among the enslaved in late eighteenth- and early-nineteenth-century Trinidad were notably high, and particularly so on sugar plantations. In part, this was a consequence of the undeveloped nature of much of Trinidad. Land had to be cleared in order to establish plantations and the onerous labour involved led to heavy losses: 'slaves', Bridget Brereton has written, 'were literally worked to death ... suffering from gross overwork, primitive conditions and exposure to tropical diseases.' However, even when plantations were established, mortality rates remained high. Writing of the life expectancy among the enslaved in the early nineteenth century, A. Meredith John has noted that 'fewer than half of newborns survived the first five years of life, and a newborn slave would live, on average, seventeen years'. Brereton, *Modern Trinidad*, pp 26–7; John, *Plantation slaves*, pp 162–3; Candlin, *Last Caribbean frontier*, p. xxiv.   5 Barataria was the name of Black's plantation. As detailed above, in the introduction, the name was also used in Irish political pamphlets as a synonym for Ireland, but it is not clear if Black himself named the plantation.   6 i.e., Picton, Hood and Fullerton. See letter five, note 4.   7 Most likely a reference to St Domingue, which had, by the 1780s, 'eclipsed all the colonies in the Caribbean to become the world's greatest sugar plantation center'. The rebellion that broke out in the colony in 1791 thus had a major impact on the European sugar market and increased demand for British-produced sugar. Eakin, *Latin America*, p. 166; Drescher, *Econocide*, pp 116–17.

by druth or drowth,[8] but the season has been hitherto worse than I have ever before known it, nothing but deluge of rain in all those Windward Islands (insomuch that a flood was down a few days ago in the River Ricagua near Barataria by which one of my best negroes was carried away and drowned) and our accounts of the prospect of sugar advancing are worse and worse. The quotations you mention indeed are very different and I shall be glad to know from you as soon as possible how far those prices may be depended on and what quantity you could engage to procure sale for. There are several of my friends disposed to try your market if you persist in encouraging it and I will undertake to procure you a consignment to the extent of the *vente*,[9] if you be sure of obtaining a price nearly equal to what you have quoted. From your situation in the customs you cannot I suppose be openly concerned in business, but our friend Jemmy Kennedy (whom assure of my inviolable regard) can step forward and it shall not be my fault if I be not of service to him. We learned a few days ago of the *Industry*'s arrival after a heavy passage. I hope Hughes's wants did not excite him to open the liqueurs for yourself and for Dean Graves and that you and my friends have found a glass of them comfortable by the fireside in your long, windy, rainy winter evenings. The fruit must all have been lost no doubt, as would a couple [of] turtle I had procured the morning Hughes broke ground, and who were too late to be embarked.

I mentioned to you the probability of a connection taking place with the dean's family and in effect Mariquite[10] was married to Captain Graves of the 14th on the 25 October (I think) and they make a very happy couple. He is a young man of much merit in his profession and well beloved in the regiment of which he has been for some time commanding officer here and just now promoted to a vacant company.[11]

He has been 15 years in the army and was with this famous regiment on the continent serving immediately under the eye of his royal highness,[12] who then marked him as a promising officer. He has lost much by the death of Sir Ralph Abercromby who was much attached to him.[13] The 14th and 57th have

8 'Druth' is an Ulster Scots term for dryness or drought. 'Drowth' is possibly a variant of 'drewth' or 'drouth', themselves variants of 'druth'. If so, then Black is here indicating that he is unsure as to how a colloquial word from his youth, the meaning of which he knew, should be spelt. Michael Montgomery, *From Ulster to America: the Scotch-Irish heritage of American English* (Belfast, 2006), pp 57–8.   9 i.e., sale.   10 In the original manuscript, Black renders Mariquite's name here as 'Marie Quite'.   11 Captain Graves was given command of the 14th regiment 'in consequence of the death or absence of senior officers'. *RMC*, iv, 161.   12 i.e., the duke of York. See letter five, note 7.   13 Sir Ralph Abercromby (1734–1801), a Scottish officer, commanded British forces in the West Indies between 1795 and 1797, during which period he encountered Graves. It is said that, having returned to Britain, he 'was … pleased to mention the services of Capt. Graves most favourably to the Commander-in-Chief.' Subsequently given command of forces in Ireland, Abercromby famously condemned the army, which had been violently suppressing the United Irish movement, as being 'in a state of licentiousness which much render it formidable to everyone but the enemy'. *RMC*, iv, 161; *ODNB* (Ralph Abercromby); A.T.Q.

been some time under orders for Europe and the transports had actually arrived for them when a counter-order arrived (after they had quitted their barracks to embark) in consequence of some suspicion at home of Bonaparte's sincerity which however appear to have been removed by Andreossi's arrival as ambassador.[14] We have heard therefore that the orders respecting those regiments are now to be observed and the 37th and 64th replace them so that I shall have probably the pleasure of seeing Mrs Rowan's sons.[15] The mother's situation I deplore and that of all the unfortunate family most sincerely.

I thank you for your hint respecting L.B.[16] The respect we were taught in our youth to show that family gives me reason to rejoice at having in my power to show him civility and give him advice. As I am neither merchant, banker or gambler, his vice can do me no hurt. I must say however his conduct here hitherto has been correct and I hope will continue so. He is very intimate with us and as you observe can make himself a very pleasant companion and I think him a safe one.

Colonel Fullarton and his *suitte*[17] arrived here 15 days ago in the *Ulysses* (Captain Hood[18] has remained at Barbados in the *Blenheim* but is now hourly expected), also his lady, her sister Miss Mackay and the family, all I believe from the mansion house at Fullarton.[19] It fell to my lot as senior member of the council to board the *Ulysses* long before she anchored, to be the mouth piece of General Picton's congratulations on his safe arrival and to take the proper arrangements with him for the style we had agreed on for his landing and reception. This took place the ensuing morning, with all the honours due his rank and the street completely lined by three regiments from the wharf to council chamber and here it again fell to my lot to receive him on the wharf

Stewart, *The summer soldiers: the 1798 rebellion in Antrim and Down* (Belfast, 1995), p. 52. **14** General Antoine-François Andréossy was appointed by Napoleon as ambassador to England several months after the signing of the Treaty of Amiens. He arrived in London early in November 1802, but returned to Paris the following May as peace broke down. P. Coquelle, *Napoleon and England, 1803–1813: a study from unprinted documents*, trans. *Gordon D. Knox* (London, 1904), pp 3–6, 70. **15** At least one of Mrs Rowan's sons (see letter four, note 33), Frederick Rowan, was a member of the 64th and is known to have served in the West Indies in 1803. Present during the capture of St Lucia, he narrowly escaped injury during the attack on the French fortress Morne Fortunée but later succumbed to 'the fever of the climate'. 'Table talk', 207, 213, 214.   **16** i.e., Leeson Blackwood. See letter four, note 35, and letter five.   **17** i.e., suite.   **18** An experienced naval officer, who had earlier served in the West Indies and the Mediterranean, Commodore Samuel Hood (1762–1814) was appointed in 1802 as a member of the Trinidad commission, alongside William Fullarton and Thomas Picton. He arrived in the island two months later than Fullarton and had left by the end of April 1803. Chiefly happy at sea, he was a somewhat diffident character and was said to be 'awkward and ungraceful'. *ODNB* (Samuel Hood); Epstein, *Scandal*, pp 130–1.   **19** William Fullarton travelled to Trinidad accompanied by his wife, Marianne Fullarton née Mackay; his sister-in-law, Georgina Mackay; and an 'entourage of subordinate officials'. His property in Ayrshire was named Fullarton, hence Black's reference to 'the mansion house at Fullarton'. *ODNB* (William Fullarton); Epstein, *Scandal*, p. 130.

and conduct him up. The commission was <u>there</u> immediately opened under a discharge of 21 guns and in presence of council and a great concourse of the first personages civil and military. It was read by the clerk and he and General Picton sworn as two of the three commissioners for executing the office of Governor of Trinidad. Since then little has been done but visiting and scraping, but we are summoned for council tomorrow to enter on business and then will see how the administration of Trinidad is to be managed. In the mean time the most perfect harmony subsists between the <u>consuls</u> to the great disappointment of many whom Park knows.[20] Tell him from me that he made on being sworn in the handsomest compliment to General Picton on the administration of his government, seemingly as if coming from his majesty and his ministers and this in an audible voice with an apparent intention that it should be well heard and understood by all present, many of whom put on long faces. General Picton is a brigadier by the commission of the forces in the Windward Islands and as such commands wholly the military here.[21] Communicate this to Park who will rejoice to know that his enemies have been baffled in all their attempts and are now fairly put down.

You may suppose that the colonel and I were not long together before he discovered me to be a nephew of our late uncle the doctor whom he speaks of in terms of admiration and of as having been one of his dearest friends.[22] This naturally brought Lord Macartney on the topic for whom he entertains the most inviolable attachment and speaks of his merits as a man and his talents as a statesman in the terms his reputation so deservedly merits. Those circumstances, my situation in the colony and the preference given me by General Picton to carry him his congratulations and receive his orders, have given me it would appear more than a common title to his favour for on all occasions public and private he has been particularly attentive to me and I hope I shall continue to deserve it. There will be no harm however in strengthening the connection by a recommendatory letter from his lordship (which however it should not appear I sought for) but I wave all <u>recommendation on his lordship's</u> part to places of

---

20 Over the course of 1802, opposition to Governor Picton's authoritarian rule had developed among recently arrived British settlers. Opponents of the governor inevitably invested their hopes in Fullarton and, as Epstein has noted, 'on his arrival the first commissioner was greeted by British opponents eager to indict the governor and prepared to go on record with details of his tyranny.' Black's reference to 'the great disappointment of many whom Park knows' might appear to suggest that Park (see letter two, note 13) sided with Picton's critics, but his subsequent comments indicate that this was not at all the case. Epstein, *Scandal*, p. 121. 21 Picton held the rank of lieutenant-colonel when appointed as governor of Trinidad in 1797. He was made brigadier-general in 1801 and, within the context of the governing commission established in 1802 (see letter five, note 4), retained authority for military affairs. *ODNB* (Thomas Picton); Epstein, *Scandal*, pp 17, 88–9. 22 Fullarton and Dr Joseph Black were both members of the Royal Society of Edinburgh, in Black's case a founding member. Likewise, both moved in Scottish Enlightenment circles. Riddell, 'Great chemist', 87–8; *ODNB* (Joseph Black); Epstein, *Scandal*, pp 49–50, 61–2.

pecuniary advantage; I will be well content to keep my place of master and examiner in chancery, for I see he has brought out such a tail or rather entail of needy people to provide for that I suppose we must endeavour to create places to allocate them, otherwise they will continue to be leeches on him which the salary £3,000 a year allowed him by government is no way adequate to support in this colony, extravagantly dear in what regards the necessaries of life.

Thus you see helter skelter I have endeavoured to give you an idea of my situation here <u>moral</u>, and as to the physical, we are all thank God in perfect health. Josefine brought a charming little girl[23] on the 2 December much about the time I suppose Esther[24] has lain in. She and her husband live very happily on Barataria and his conduct (whose worst feature was *etouderie*[25] a disease I was once terribly afflicted with) repairs much to my satisfaction his youthful *ecarto*, the offspring of inexperience.[26] Barataria was never in such high condition, it is the admiration of all travellers (for the high road goes through the midst of it) and will give a revenue of some relief to our losses, but it will require at least 3 years to bring them up. Nor do I think the colony generally speaking in less than 5 years can defray the losses and expenses of the late one. Hence you will see the perplexity of my situation; my desire leads me home and I see myself bound here faster than ever; could I even spare where[withal] to send Mrs Black and the children to you or elsewhere for their education I would sit down without repairing and drag it out, but under the present prospects I fear that even will not be feasible. I shall be anxiously expecting the result however of young Mr McIlveen's negotiations (if this is Jack I remember him perfectly well) and such other friends as you can employ.[27] I would do anything within the compass of my power, but I owe here from late purchases of land and losses of slaves an enormous sum and that I must pay off with dispatch, for in my peculiar situation I must not expose my conduct to censure who am professionally obliged to enforce payment from others.

I don't know how far Valentine Jones the 3[d] would be disposed to serve me; I well know his great abilities (he is allowed to be by all people the cleverest man

23 This is, most likely, the Eleonore that Black refers to in letter seven. Josefine and Hugh Lacoste are known to have had at least one other child, Esther Lacoste, who was born in 1805. 'Josephine Black F, #405424', available at http://www.thepeerage.com/p40543.htm# i405424 (accessed 27/8/2018).   24 i.e., Esther Pettigrew née Black, Black's sister.   25 i.e., thoughtlessness.   26 Black's precise meaning here is obscure. Ecarto is possibly a misspelling of *ecarté*, a card game which was later said to have 'long had the bad reputation of being merely a "rooking," or gambling game'. If so, then he may be suggesting that his son-in-law was given to careless and unnecessary risk taking. More literally, he may simply be alluding to an objectionable fondness for gambling. [G.F.P.], *Hoyle's games modernised* (London, 1863), p. 110. For a sidelight on Black's relations with his son-in-law see letter four, note 6.   27 The McIlveen family were prominently involved in the commercial life of eighteenth- and early nineteenth-century Belfast. The merchant Gilbert McIlveen had helped establish the Belfast Discount Office, a bank, in 1784, and 'young Mr McIlveen' is possibly a reference to his son, also Gilbert. Benn, *Belfast from 1799 till 1810*, pp 217–18.

that was at the head of the commissariat in these countries) and he is better experienced to give information on West India properties and West India concerns than any man in Ireland (and perhaps in England) certainly.[28] Park, I am sure, will also be aiding and abetting by your telling him of my dependence on his friendship, and Jemmy Kennedy's good offices I am sure will not be wanting. Thus prepared I think if the old gentlemen are reasonable some advantage must be gained. Ballintaggart was once I thought of all places the most beautifully romantic and as youthful impressions are lasting so I retain still the same high idea of it; I doubt however if the reality would now answer my expectations. I have been so long a stranger to still life and peaceful retirement that I much doubt whether I would not soon be wearied of the ewe hedges nicely cut into *sophas* and *fauteuils*,[29] the majestic grove of ash and elm that lead to the fishing alcoves on the borders of the fish pond where my dear Aunt Kitty[30] caught me with her fishing hook by the finger which I was obliged to ride to Richhill[31] behind Uncle Sam[32] to have cut out by Dr Cranston (does she remember this) and she all the time weeping and lamenting for the torture I must suffer; the park, the old state coach in the barn, the nice flower garden under the windows of the drawing room lined with Morocco leather and above all Dick Greenaway, the park and deer. All these were the delights of my soul at that time and I still reflect on them with inconceivable pleasure, but I return to say that I much doubt if my mind long accustomed to turbulence and disappointments would now find the same satisfaction in those rural pleasures. When I landed in Nova Scotia in August '99 they were in the midst of harvest, mowing and reaping.

28 Valentines Jones III was the grandson of the well-known Belfast merchant Valentine Jones I (1711–1805), and the son of Valentine Jones II (1729–1808), who 'spent a great portion of his life in Barbadoes'. He became commissary general of the West Indian commissariat, which sourced food for British forces in the West Indies, in the mid-1790s, but proved not, in the end, to be as clever as Black suggested: it was later discovered that he had been involved in extensive fraud by purchasing overpriced supplies from merchants and exploiting exchange rates, and he was sentenced to three years imprisonment in 1809. Benn, *Belfast from 1799 till 1810*, pp 183–7; *DIB*, iv, 1044–6; Janet MacDonald, *From boiled beef to chicken tikka: 500 years of feeding the British army* (Barnsley, 2014), pp 8, 33–6.   29 i.e., sofas and armchairs.   30 i.e., Katherine Turnly née Black.   31 Richhill was a market town located some four miles from Armagh, on the lands of William Richardson. Charles Coote judged it to be 'not extensive', but conceded that it possessed a 'very excellent markethouse' and that its 'appearance ... is considerably increased by the elegant demesne of Mr Richardson, whose residence is in full view from the street.' Charles Coote, *Statistical survey of the County of Armagh, with observations on the means of improvement; drawn up in the years 1802, and 1803, for the consideration, and under the direction of the Dublin Society* (Dublin, 1804), p. 345.   32 Samuel Black (1730–92) was a younger brother of Black's father, who went into business as a linen-bleacher in the vicinity of Belfast and was said, in 1758, to be 'well provided for on a bleach green reckoned one of the most compleat of its kind in Ireland situated on the river & new canal'. He served as sovereign of Belfast five times between 1779 and 1789. John Black III to Robert Black, 1 Sept. 1758 (PRONI, D719/51); 'List of children' (PRONI, D4457/329); *Town book*, ed. Young, p. 238; Ward, 'Black family', 188.

It is impossible to conceive or describe the pleasure I felt on seeing those delightful labours of which I had been so long deprived the contemplation of, and the smell of the new mown hay was new life to me (and I then had much occasion for it) but it soon wore off. It was the lure of novelty and winter no sooner began to show her dreary head by the fall of the leaf than my heart yearned again for West India luxuriant, eternal verdure and the attendant activity in our species of industry. To see one lonely man mowing a field of several acres of hay or to see 100 negroes holing a piece of cane land to a chosen song led by one of the number is wonderful odds to an active mind, and this last I have been so long inured to, that I can't conceive how a large farm can be cultivated with so few hands or how farmers contrive to live by it.

If my means however ever admit my offering for Ballintaggart I would purchase it more for the sake of keeping it in the family than for any enjoyment I would take there. If ever I settle at home, I must be near the sea and I must have a boat or something afloat were it but a wash tub in a tocher.[33] It is my hobby horse, every man has his own and this has always been mine.

I must conclude for I am tired and jaded by last night's debauch, a little of which goes far with me; but you shall hear from me again soon. In the mean time allow me to embrace your dear Ellen[34] and her little [one] for the love and respect I bore her amiable mother and excellent father;[35] Mrs Younghusband[36] and the family, Esther and Mr Pettigrew,[37] Miss Stewart[38] and her fire side and in short all those whom you well know I must bear the sincerest friendship for.

I remain my dearest brother

Your affectionate brother John

Don't send me any oatmeal or grain of any sort I have received a full supply from London. I would rather have linen such as shirting, sheeting and table linen.

Tell Park he has got the land at Point Cedro that was D'Aubreme's. He owes me at least that good turn which will be very valuable (McBurnie his neighbour is dead).[39]

---

33 Black is known to have owned at least two boats while resident in Trinidad. One was 'crushed to pieces' during a hurricane in August 1810, while the second was stolen from the harbour in Port of Spain in April 1814. Pocock, *Shadows*, p. 212.   34 i.e., Ellen Black née Stewart, George Black Jr's wife.   35 i.e., Robert Stewart and Mary Isabella Stewart née Mitchell.   36 i.e., Letitia Younghusband née Black, Black's sister.   37 i.e., Esther Pettigrew née Black and her husband James Pettigrew, Black's sister and brother-in-law. 38 Most likely a reference to Mattie/Helena Stewart, the unmarried sister of Ellen Black née Stewart, George Black Jr's wife. Riddell, 'Great chemist', 71.   39 A Mr M'Burnie is mentioned in the pamphlet literature concerning the governorship of Thomas Picton. *Letters of Decius* refers to Picton 'taking money out of Mr. M'Burnie's hands, as the *guardian* of *minors*! and employing on his estate fifteen slaves of this said minor, called *Savignon*; who, when he came from Granada [*sic*], being of age, to claim his money and slaves, was abused by this governor.' Whether or not this M'Burnie was Park's one time neighbour is unknown. *Letters of Decius*, p. 63.

Letter Seven

Internal evidence suggests that letter seven was written just days after Black received a response from his brother to letter five. In the earlier letter, dated 14 September 1802, Black had requested 'information exact' on the 'circumstances and family' of Dean Graves, father of Captain James Graves, and he notes here that '[t]he account you give me of the reverend dean and the family is very acceptable'. His chief aim in writing, however, was to prepare the way for the arrival in Ireland of his daughters Mariquite and Adele, who were due to travel with Graves (by now Mariquite's husband), whose regiment had been recalled to Europe. This, it is clear, was a source of much anxiety, both for Mariquite and her parents. As in previous letters, Black also makes reference to financial affairs, here discussing recent 'losses' and his 'embarrassed' circumstances.

Trinidad 3 March 1803

My dear brother

We approach with fear and trembling the moment so much wished for and now so much dreaded. A family so long united cannot contemplate the term of its separation without sentiments of affliction. The 14th have received orders from Europe and they and the 57th embark on the *Excellent* of 74 [guns], armed *en flute*[1] to sail the 20th *pre fin.*[2]

Mariquite's feelings since the order has been received are visible in her countenance and I dread the moment of separation both for her and her mother with apprehension; I myself feel enough, but conscious of her quitting the bosom of a tender parent, to enter into the arms of another, I endeavour to console myself. Adele my good little girl accompanies them and her I will consign to you and my sister's care for her education until her mother with Julie and Esther can join you. She is a child of the very best disposition, sensible much above what you would expect from her age and I wish her to be improved, by every species of qualification that education can procure her and that her talents may be susceptible of, for which expense I will provide you amply. The ship may be expected at Portsmouth about 1 May. The regiment will probably go to Hilsea Barracks[3] and Captain Graves' intention is to go up

---

1 A ship sailing *en flûte* was sailing as a transport, with guns removed. Philip Haythornthwaite, *Nelson's navy* (Botley, Oxford, 1993), pp 4–5. 2 i.e., before end. 3 Located close to Portsmouth, Hilsea barracks were first opened in 1756 and expanded in the mid-1790s. Raymond Riley, 'Military and naval land use as a determinant of urban development – the case of Portsmouth' in Michael Bateman and Raymond Riley (eds), *The geography of defence* (London, 1987), pp 52–81 at 59.

to London and obtain 6 or 12 months leave of absence and then immediately join the family at Carrickfergus, where I hope Mariquite will be made welcome. The account you give me of the reverend dean and the family is very acceptable and the connection becomes therefore the more agreeable; Captain Graves is a young man of great worth, and will I doubt not make an excellent husband to Mariquite whom he doats on; you will find her a child of nature, bred in the woods of this country, but whom civilized life and polished society will make an amiable woman of.

She is I fear pregnant, and in the pains necessarily to follow, far removed from her mother's care, we must commit her to your brotherly tenderness.

You will find Graves a distant character at first and the appearance of a stiffness, inherent to his profession, but that will wear off as you get better acquainted and you will find him at bottom possessed of a warm friendly disposition, and high feelings of honour. He served with the regiment on the continent throughout the campaign and also in this country under Sir Ralph Abercromby with whom he was a favourite, and the reputation of the regiment you may know has ever stood unblemished. As Mariquite carries a negress with her who has been for many years her servant, I fear Adele will be an encumbrance (as will Fanny)[4] in the long journey they have to make by land; I wish it was possible therefore that you could contrive to have Adele and also Fanny, if Mariquite would consent to it, conveyed to you directly from Portsmouth to Belfast without going to London, Mariquite is not aware of the encumbrance of a negro servant in such a route, nor have we been able to dissuade her from carrying her; on this as for everything else that may tend to their ease or satisfaction I commit them to you and to providence.

I have received only two days ago your letter of 21 December with its enclosures and am sensibly obliged to Lord Macartney for the kindness he has shown me in his letter to myself and Colonel Fullarton with whom I had already become familiarly acquainted,[5] as you would learn by my letter by Mr David King to Greenock.[6] I shall answer his lordship's letters by Captain

---

4 As discussed above, in the introduction, Fanny was most likely an enslaved person, rather than a servant. Black's anxiety concerning Mariquite's plan to travel with her likely reflected a fear that doing so would have legal repercussions.   5 While the letter dated 21 December is missing, a subsequent letter from Black to Macartney, dated 20 March 1803, indicates that Macartney had provided Black with a 'recommendation' to give to Fullarton. This, Black predicted, would 'no doubt have its due influence', though he was here being unduly optimistic. As Fullarton himself explained, in a letter to Macartney dated 3 April 1803, the souring of his relations with Picton had complicated matters. 'Unfortunately', he wrote, 'in the present state of Trinidad Discussions have gone so far between Br General Picton and me, that those who are Connected with him by Habits and Cooperation as Mr Black has been, cannot fail to feel a proportional alienation from me.' John Black to George Macartney, 20 Mar. 1803, and William Fullarton to George Macartney, 3 Apr. 1803 (PRONI, MIC438/3).   6 Possibly the same David King who was later a member of the Glasgow partnership of Francis Garden and Co., which is known to have been involved in

Graves and take that opportunity of introducing him which I request you will in the meantime prepare his lordship for and to Graves a gracious reception.

I observe the *Industry* had got home which I had almost despaired of, and when I considered the weather she experienced and their wants, I only wonder you received any of the liqueurs full; the dean says nothing of it to his son, so I suppose he was well satisfied with the partition.

My said recited letter by King will explain to you how well I am able to pay £3,560 sterling after the losses I have lately sustained, they might as well ask me for the Sans Souci diamond.[7] I am I assure very little able to pay £2,000 sterling without receiving value for it, but notwithstanding having by many years hard industry contrived to pay off the debts of the partnership in which J.B. and Co.[8] were a half concerned (and which they shall bear their share of in case of litigation) I will also engage to pay that sum also to be done with them, but I must have a reasonable time for it and if they will agree to this I will send you my oblig[atio]ns, perhaps bring them myself payable in as short a term as I can possibly (my other encumbrances considered) hope to accomplish it, with interest from the dates respectively and if they leave the term to myself that confidence will operate on my mind generously, for I am that sort of character to do that from benevolence which coercion or litigation would make me revolt at.

That fact is that my late losses have embarrassed me so much that I have very painful moments, for should I be called away, before I can liquidate and extricate myself by a couple [of] years' frugality and good crops and good prices, my children would be the sufferers. I have reason to believe however I can obtain a loan on favourable terms and if I succeed it will assist me. My present crop will be important, if the season permits our reaping it, but that seldom happens. It now offers very fair and we may be for once agreeably disappointed.

If Hugh Montgomerie sends out a vessel you may send me some articles for family use by her, but no meal or oats or grain of which I have received a supply from London. I'll remit you by her in rum and sugar of my own manufacture and you will see then what such produce would yield *communibus annis*[9] with you. Lord Macartney I see had got Lord Hobart's promise[10] to my

the West Indian Trade. Devine, 'Business élite', 65.   7 An oblique reference to a complicated financial affair the French philosopher Voltaire was involved in while resident at Sans Souci, the palace of Frederick II, king of Prussia. Accounts of the episode vary, the salient points being that Voltaire had accepted some diamonds as a security for a cheque while illicitly speculating in Saxon bonds and that there was a controversy over the return of these diamonds. Roger Pearson, *Voltaire almighty: a life in pursuit of freedom* (London, 2005), pp 216–18, 221–2; David Fraser, *Frederick the Great: king of Prussia* (London, 2000), p. 256.   8 Possibly John Black and Co., though Black is not known to have been involved in a partnership of this name.   9 i.e., 'on the annual average'. *Black's*, p. 296.   10 Robert Hobart, fourth earl of Buckinghamshire (1760–1816), became secretary of state for war in March 1801. His role was expanded to secretary of state for war and the colonies the fol-

confirmation in the place of master and examiner in chancery, but I wish his lordship not to let the secretary forget it, for between ourselves Governor Fullarton has here the whole of Renfrew and Caithness shires well recommended to him and we old standers will all be kicked out to make way for them.[11] They are all ready to devour us. I never saw such a set of wolves.

I am obliged to make Mariquite a promise to send her mother and sisters as soon after her as my finances will permit and that promise I will certainly keep, but as I have totally forgot what might the annual expense of Mrs Black and the 3 children amount to, including their education and living frugally in your own style, I wish you as soon as may be inform me fully on that subject or what would be better what sum you will hold me harmless for, annually payable by semester. The latest day I should wish to embark them from this country is the 20 July and if I could contrive to save as much as would amount to the first semester only, crop would come round again before the second would fall due, which would be very convenient and we could go on *toties quoties*,[12] until the savings here would enable me to increase the allowance as far as my means can permit and I am very sure the expense at home would not amount to ¼ of what it is here because what it is here would astonish you although I live almost misanthropically, for I am tired of the follies of life and also of making new acquaintances. My ambition is to renew those of my juvenile days and to see how a country can be changed in its appearance, customs and manners in 30 years. This really is worthy of philosophical speculation.

Thus far I can go and no further, for the sloop of war the commodore sends down to Tortola to catch the packet has just fired her signal for sailing, so *adieu* my dear brother, with assurances of my warm affection to Letty,[13] Esther[14] (who I hope is safe out of the straw) and all yours and theirs.

I remain ever your affectionate brother

John

Josefine[15] [is] in high health making sugar at Barataria and raising her charming child, my god daughter Eleonore.

---

lowing July, and he held the position until 1804. Earlier in his career he sat as a member of the Irish parliament, and he had also served as governor of Madras. *ODNB* (Robert Hobart, fourth earl of Buckinghamshire); Watson, *George III*, p. 581.   11 While plans were discussed, early in 1803, to settle Scottish highlanders in Trinidad, it is by no means clear that Black was aware of this and his comments here appear to reflect a more general anxiety that Fullarton, a Scottish landowner, albeit one whose property was located in Ayrshire rather than in Renfrewshire or Caithness-shire, would favour Scottish settlers and exercise patronage on their behalf. *ODNB* (William Fullarton); Epstein, *Scandal*, pp 196–9.   12 i.e., 'as often as'. *Black's*, p. 1528.   13 i.e., Letitia Younghusband née Black, Black's sister.   14 i.e., Esther Pettigrew née Black, Black's sister. Black's subsequent comments suggest she was pregnant, or had recently been so.   15 i.e., Josefine Lacoste née Black, Black's daughter.

Letter Eight

Following on from letter seven, Black penned letter eight on 20 March 1803 – the day on which his daughters Adele and Mariquite boarded the Excellent *for their journey to Britain. The distress caused by this separation is, again, readily apparent, with Black noting that his wife 'is in the most poignant affliction'. Much of the letter is concerned with practical matters, including travel itineraries, letters of introduction, the money being carried by Mariquite and Adele and Black's wishes concerning Adele's education. However, Black also makes reference to his future plans, noting his 'inviolable determination' to send his wife to Ireland, and touches upon the political trouble brewing in Trinidad. Observing 'that we are all at loggerheads', he here condemns Colonel Fullarton as 'a most dangerous man'.*

Trinidad 20 March 1803

My dear brother and sisters

The day of parting with our dear children is arrived and with resignation I commit them to the protection of providence and yours. They have ever experienced from us the most tender affections and I trust sympathy in the breast of you my brother will prevent their perceiving the want of us. Our feelings at this trying moment can be better conceived than described; their poor mother is in the most poignant affliction, she knows not where or to whom they are going, and I who do am not insensible to their situation. I well know that once with you they are in good hands and much better off than they are here, but the apprehension of sickness on the voyage, especially in a ship that carries 1,000 men, among which it is possible some epidemical disease may break out, gives me much uneasiness. Let God's will be done and let us with confidence in it hope for the best.

I wrote you my dear brother about 3 weeks[1] ago by the packet to announce to you their departure and that by prudent calculation the *Excellent* may be expected to arrive at Portsmouth by the 20 May and I think it probable I am right. It strikes me that your regard for me and impatience to see anything proceeding from a brother from whom you have been so long estranged might tempt you, if your concerns permit it, to cross the water to receive them, and I confess having cherished the hope so warmly as to assure Mariquite she will find you there which would be to me most satisfactory.

I have given her letters for Lord Macartney[2] and our uncles Alexander and James;[3] she has also letters for Mrs Lacoste[4] at the duke [of] York's seat at

1 See letter seven. 2 It is possible that Black is referring here to his letter to Macartney dated 20 March 1803, which was, in fact, given to Mariquite's husband, James Graves, on

Oatlands in Surrey[5] and several others which will procure them friends every-where, but to you and my dear sister, I look up as parents to replace us from whom they are to be so far removed.

You will find Captain Graves a valuable character but entirely the soldier and full of the spirit of his profession, he is doatingly fond of Mariquite and will I am sure make her always an affectionate husband.

From the account you give of the dean's family I have reason to think she will be kindly received and deservedly cherished. You must make my respects acceptable to the dean to whom I intend writing at a leisure moment. Graves carries with him in bills about £350 sterling, besides some loose money for travelling expenses. Mariquite has also some money of her own, perhaps 50 or 60 and Mrs Black has given Adele 10 or £12 in dollars with which poor thing she thinks herself immensely rich. They have both superfluity of clothing, but I don't know how far it may be adapted to the mode with you or the climate.

Adele is a child of the most endearing disposition and very sensible; she will I am sure soon gain all your affections. Nature has done much for her, art and your precept and example will do the rest and I am sure she will make an amiable and even learned woman. The mark on her eye was occasioned by my lancing a very large bile there when she had the small pox; a steady hand to touch it now and then with caustic would remove it and I wish it to be done as far as practicable with safety. With respect to her education, I leave it per-fectly to you; all I can say is that, besides literary talents, I wish her to be taught everything she shows a taste for, particularly music and dancing, both being her hobby horse. As to her religion, provided she has one well instilled I am almost indifferent whether it be Protestant or Romish. The want of an established church here has always occasioned the children to follow their mother to mass and me too till lately;[6] but Adele will now go with you to our own mode of worship and adopt it in future as her faith; so will Mariquite no doubt under the reverend dean's auspices.[7]

---

whose behalf Black requested that Macartney exercise his patronage. John Black to George Macartney, 20 Mar. 1803 (PRONI, MIC438/3).   3 Alexander and James Black, born in 1729 and 1733 respectively, were younger brothers of Black's father. Having 'been a long time in Business in the mercantile way the one in France and the other in Spain', the pair had set-tled in London and established a partnership in the early 1760s, before attempting, ultimately without success, to establish themselves as farmers. 'Black family tree' (PRONI, D4457/363); *CJB*, i, 348–9, 360–1.   4 Most likely a relative of Hugh Lacoste, husband of Black's daugh-ter Josefine.   5 Oatlands Park in Surrey was acquired by Frederick, duke of York (1763–1827), the favoured son of George III, in 1791, but was principally occupied by his wife Frederica Charlotte, from whom he had separated shortly after their marriage. The Regency personality Beau Brummell was a regular visitor. *ODNB* (Prince Frederick, duke of York); Ian Kelly, *Beau Brummell: the ultimate man of style* (New York, 2006), pp 143–4.   6 Formerly a Spanish colony, Trinidad was predominantly Catholic and the Church of England was not instituted as the established church in the island until 1844. An Anglican minister was, however, present from 1797. Carmichael, *Trinidad and Tobago*, pp 127, 130, 292.   7 i.e.,

As my inviolable determination is to send you Mrs Black next year, you must acquaint me as nearly as possible what she could live decently for *en famille* annually as you live, that I may calculate accordingly. I forgot to say that I will make good to you at all and every time when you call for it Adele's expenses; I allow Mariquite also £250 annual which with Graves' appointments may entitle them to live comfortably, until his promotion and my affairs admit my doing better for them. Exclusive of what he carries I have given him a credit on my correspondent in London for £200 so that there goes about £600 in the family.

It will be requisite to take great care of Adele as your winter sets in. Colds are the only sickness these young creoles are exposed to and they are particularly so from their natural inclination to be lightly clothed. We have had several examples of young persons from this country being lost in England from inattention to this object.

Flannel on the skin from November forwards is a good precaution; in America I used fleecy hosiery but this again I think too warm for youth.

I have not yet been able to conclude my money matters, but the negotiation is far advanced and I think I will succeed of which I shall inform you.

Graves carries with him honourable testimonies of his services in this country, from the commander of the forces and from Brigadier General Picton, and having been 12 years in the army with unsullied reputation I think Lord Macartney's influence would not fail to serve him. I have recommended him to his lordship in such terms as best suited the purpose and you must back me. Graves will inform you verbally the situation of this government; we are all at loggerheads and all I can say is that administration could not possibly have chosen a man more unfit for the purposes he was sent out than Colonel Fullarton, he is perfectly what Lord Shelburne termed him, a low intriguing, insidious *commis de bureau*,[8] and when such a character is attempted to be blended with the high ingenuous and honourable proceedings of two such men as Brigadier General Picton and Commodore Hood you may suppose a little what discord such a composition must produce but nothing equal to the reality. The commodore detests his public character and they have both told him in so plain terms at council board their opinion of him that he has almost retired from public affairs.[9]

the Revd Thomas Graves, Mariquite's father-in-law.   8 i.e., an office clerk. Early in 1780, with the American War of Independence raging, Fullarton was involved in a scheme to enlist highland troops and, though a gentleman-landowner, rather than a soldier, was given a military rank. Speaking in the House of Lords, William Petty, earl of Shelburne (1737–1805), attacked such appointments and described Fullarton as a 'clerk'. Fullarton, who was MP for Plympton Erle, responded in a speech to the House of Commons, sharply accusing Shelburne of 'ungentlemanly behaviour'. The spat resulted in a duel, during which Shelburne was shot in the groin. Epstein, *Scandal*, pp 51–2; *ODNB* (William Petty, second earl of Shelburne), (William Fullarton).   9 Relations between Picton, Hood and Fullarton deteriorated rapidly and Black's comments here correspond with Epstein's observation that,

I hope in God he will be immediately removed for, as a man of property myself, I think him a most dangerous man in the government of an island whose population is composed of the vagabonds of the revolution of all opinions to a very great number of which, above 5,000, are mulattoes that would not fail to cut our throats and enrage the slaves if occasion offered and this man from philanthropic principles has shown himself publicly their friend and protector.[10] In short he seems to choose and prefer the lowest company; neither General Picton nor any of his friends have ever been invited to his house.[11] All this I say to you reservedly, but should Lord Macartney enquire anything about it you may inform him of my sentiments which are almost general.

With prayers for a happy meeting for my dear children with you all I remain my dear brother and sisters[12] your affectionate brother, John.

I say nothing for Mrs Black,[13] she has wrote you in the fullness of her heart.

just three months after his arrival, 'Fullarton was speaking to neither Picton nor Hood'. Epstein, *Scandal*, p. 130.   **10** Trinidad is known to have had a large 'mixed race' or 'free coloured' population. Many of this group had moved to Trinidad from French colonies and, with events in France and St Domingue fresh in the mind, they were viewed with intense suspicion by the planter elite. Fullarton, however, interacted with the 'free coloured' openly, and sought to uphold their rights in the face of planter hostility. Indeed, he had complained, at the start of March 1803, that the island's planters 'conceive themselves to have an absolute Right to beat, maltreat or Imprison any Black or Colored Person without assigning Reason'. In addition, by early 1803, Trinidad was home to a group of British radicals, including the journalist Pierre McCallum who later helped publicize Picton's authoritarian rule and who, it is possible, was sponsored by Fullarton. Brereton, *Modern Trinidad*, p. 25; Candlin, *Last Caribbean frontier*, pp xv, 10, 55, 63, 100; Epstein, *Scandal*, pp 136–9 (esp. 138), 156–83 (esp. 161–2); Millette, *Society and politics*, pp 33–4.   **11** If not invited, Picton did, on one infamous occasion, visit Fullarton's residence; the two had a blazing row which was later much discussed, with Picton being said to have used 'language not only unbecoming of a Gentleman, but highly blameworthy as a public character.' Epstein, *Scandal*, pp 138, 151–2.   **12** i.e., Esther Pettigrew née Black and Letitia Younghusband née Black, Black's sisters.   **13** i.e., Bonne Clothilde Black née Fournillier, Black's wife.

Letter Nine

Written following 'a night of affliction', on the morning of 21 March 1803, letter nine reads as a coda to letter eight. The shortest of Black's letters, it offers further, vivid evidence of the anguish caused by his daughters' departure from Trinidad.

Trinidad 21 March 1803. Sunday morning 6 o'clock[1]

My dear brother

After passing a night of affliction I rise to avail myself of the *Benson* of Glasgow to say that our dear children embarked last night at eight o'clock and the *Excellent* is now under way gradually removing from us what is most dear, soon to be seen no more. It is impossible to describe our sufferings, the whole family and neighbourhood, with floods of tears, keep their eyes on the ship so long as a sail can be perceived above the horizon. Mrs Black is in despair and Mariquite's acute feelings, if losing sight of the land don't assuage them, give me everything to apprehend for her life in her critical situation. To that providence which has hitherto preserved her I must commit her and I trust it will afford her strength of body to support the anguish of her mind.

The ship I consider will arrive at Portsmouth about 1 May. If I could hope you would be there to receive them it would be consoling indeed. Graves' first intention was to go up to London, to show Mariquite the capital, but on further reflection considering the expense of travelling with 4 persons and a great deal of baggage I recommended his renouncing that idea and to go from Hilsea barracks as soon as he can obtain leave of absence directly for Ireland by the way of Liverpool, whence he will pass to Dublin and so to the north.

Not having adopted this plan (which however he may think of altering) until an hour before we parted, I had not time to give him an introduction to the family in Dublin to whom I beg you will mention him.[2]

The *Benson* is a fast sailer but it is very improbable that she will arrive before the *Excellent*. At all events, this letter will serve to acquaint you and the dean's family of their departure hence and enable you to take your measures in consequence.

I have provided them amply with everything I could possibly foresee a want of, but whatever you think necessary either for Adele or Mariquite and be pleased to advance I will gratefully restore.

The last request my dear girl made me on the wharf was to send her her

1 The date is given on the original as 20 March, but it is clear that this is a mistake, letter eight having been written on 20 March and this letter being written the following morning. 2 Thomas Black, youngest brother of Black's father, was a merchant in Dublin. *CJB*, ii, 1437, 1460.

mother as soon as possible, which I promised I would do so and I will religiously keep it. She will lie in in August I think. If I could contrive to send her by that time what a happiness! If not, to your care and my sisters I confide and oh! my dear brother let her not want for the best assistance.

The first child birth is hazardous; she is strong and well made; all I fear is that her bodily strength will be so reduced by her present sufferings, as to make her unable to get through. Since the orders came for the regiments holding themselves in readiness to sail this day (and that is nearly 2 months ago) she has never sat an ordinary repast and her alteration as to flesh and appearance is alarming.

May the almighty preserve them and conduct them safe to port, my reliance is in his goodness. With prayers for your happy meeting of which I am sure you will give me the speediest notice by packet and kind and affectionate remembrances to my sisters[3] and your dear Ellen,[4] I remain my dear brother your afflicted but affectionate brother

John

---

3 i.e., Esther Pettigrew née Black and Letitia Younghusband née Black.   4 i.e., Ellen Black née Stewart, George Black Jr's wife.

Letter Ten

A period of nearly four years elapsed between the writing of letter nine and letter ten. That Black had not written at all during this period seems highly unlikely, but no letters survive for the period 1804–6 and it appears that George Black Jr's letters to Trinidad had been infrequent: 'you suffer twelvemonths to pass', Black notes here ruefully, 'without giving us a sign of life'. Communication with Mariquite and her in-laws had, however, been more regular, and Black here passes on news of Graves' promotion. In addition, he discusses the possibility of establishing trading connections between Belfast and Trinidad, and broaches the subject of his daughter Adele's return to Trinidad. Of interest, too, is Black's suggestion that he might meet Adele at New York, 'whither we intend to return', suggesting, as it does, that he had spent part of the period following her departure for Ireland in America.

Trinidad 5 February 1807

My dear brother

Whence does it proceed that such a length of time has passed since you have given me the satisfaction of hearing from you? Are you living? Is my sister living? Is my child living? And you suffer twelvemonths to pass without giving us a sign of life and were it not of our sometimes hearing of you through Mariquite and the dean's family, we should suppose you or we had passed to the land of oblivion. But we know you are not only all alive but all well and the problem to be solved is why you would not take the trouble of telling us so. I believe we Blacks are all of the same humour; we are none of us afflicted with the *cacoethes scribendi*[1] but when we set too we can write as much and as well as our neighbours; for my own part I accuse myself in point of correspondence to be a genuine branch of the family and you are I believe well entitled to be my younger brother.

The second November mail has brought us the very comfortable intelligence of Graves being appointed to the lieutenant colonelcy of the 5th Garrison Battalion and the regiment is permanently fixed on Dublin duty.[2] This relieves us from a load of apprehension for, as the brigade to which the 14th belonged had been reviewed and reported fit for service, I dreaded the

1 i.e., the habit of writing. 2 Upon returning to Britain from the West Indies in 1803, Black's son-in-law, James Graves, was raised to the rank of major. Late in 1805 he participated in an expedition to Hanover and the following November he was promoted to lieutenant-colonel of the 5th Garrison Battalion, 'which corps he joined, formed, and disciplined for a few month in Dublin'. In March 1807, however, he moved to the 18th Royal Irish Regiment, which was despatched to the West Indies the following month. *RMC*, iv, 161.

thoughts of Mariquite being again separated from her husband and obliged to return to Ireland across the channel in the midst of winter without friend or protector. Thank God they are now comfortably settled in a very respectable establishment and Graves must be a very bad economist indeed if in the command of a regiment with the perquisites attached to his place he cannot contrive to live handsomely without running in debts.

He has the advantage of being amidst or near his family and I suppose when he can be absent from duty you will sometimes have a visit from them.

I have never received a line from you ever on the subject of the sugars consigned [to] Neilson and Hunter,[3] nor do I know what they have sold for, or if that has been remitted you. Pray inform me fully on this subject.

Davy Park informed me some time ago that he had reason to think some of his friends at Belfast would put a vessel on this trade. I wish they would, I will give it every encouragement in my power and now that the importation of salted beef, pork and butter is positively prohibited from America, surely it becomes an object to supply us with those articles from your market. Your linens printed and plain are an article in great demand for the Spaniards to whom many thousand pieces of the north of Ireland seal is [*sic*] annually sold here by the Glasgow merchants.[4] I want much myself to try your market with our sugars and rums and many of my friends would join me, but no opportunity has offered since the *Isabella*[5] called here at an improper season and addressed to persons whose interest it is to discourage the Belfast trade and prevent any Belfast man from coming to the market.[6]

I would very willingly at present ship you 50 to 100 hogsheads, by way of experiment, for it is in vain to send our sugars to England or Scotland. They would in the present state of the stagnated exportation barely suffice to pay the charges which exceed all reasonable bounds.

I write this by a running brig to Greenock now heaving up and I hope as you find we are all to the fore you will make an uncommon effort and write us a letter to tell us how you are, and how Adele is and how Adele progresses

---

3 Neilson and Hunter was a Glasgow partnership, which appears to have had links with the Eccles family of Glasgow (see letter fifteen, note 12) and to have traded with Trinidad. The partnership was dissolved in 1820. ['A gentleman of the Island'], *Political account*, p. 146; *London Gazette*, 11 Nov. 1820, p. 2118.   4 Linen was, by far, Belfast's most important export in the early nineteenth century. In 1809, the town exported 13,827,522 yards of linen, to a value of £1,910,909. Benn, *Belfast from 1799 till 1810*, pp 120–1.   5 Possibly a reference to the 'fast sailing new brig, ISABELLA', advertisements for which appeared in the *Belfast News-Letter* in 1805. This ship was, however, destined for New York, and prospective passengers were requested to 'apply to Newry'. *BNL*, 17 May 1805.   6 If Belfast's merchants were not trading with Trinidad, as Black appears here to suggest, they were certainly trading with the West Indies. 'In 1809, and many years previously,' George Benn noted, in his *Belfast from 1799 till 1810*, 'there was much direct trade with the West Indies.' As letter eleven indicates, Black himself was well aware of this. Benn, *Belfast from 1799 till 1810*, p. 122.

and if George still continues to be a good little boy according to Adele's account of him.[7]

The time is coming round when Adele must think of returning to papa, who is growing old and wishes to have her and her piano to amuse him at home when he will be no longer able to go abroad. Mamma is getting old too, though she don't think so. Grey hairs are no proof of age, people here are grey at five and twenty sometimes. I hope however that we shall first meet again at New York, whither we intend to return as soon as our finances, increased by the value of sugar, will bear it, but of that at present the prospect is very distant.

I have no news to tell Adele. Papa, mamma, Josefine, Eleonore and little Esther are well, as are all her little friends and acquaintances, but Mademoiselle Matthieu is dead a few days ago of a sore throat and left Adele her blessing, which is all she had to give. On the other [hand] her cat is well and has a numerous offspring of cats and kittens to the 5th or 6th generation and I hope will live to see Adele come home again.

Bonaparte has performed miracles and he has declared he never will make peace until he obliges England to deliver up all her conquests to their respective nations.[8] I wonder if he intends to comprehend Trinidad in the number. I should not admire to become a Spaniard again.

Mrs B writes my sister which I much doubt if she can read, however I suppose you have some French interpreter's among you. Adele will translate.

Tell her I expect she will now write to me and tell me what she thinks of going to meet us at New York, [and] that in the mean time I love her tenderly and hope when I do see her to find her what I expect worthy of all my affection. I hope she will soon see Mariquite either in the north or by paying her a visit in Dublin when convenient.

My sister[9] must think me a strange incoherent fellow; I confess it, but I am not the less attached to her and truly grateful for all her goodness to my Adele. Assure her so and that if ever we have the happiness to meet she will find me so, but that I despair of it.

To you I will always be an affectionate brother, but write to me and above all things tell me how much I owe you for Adele.

John Black

---

7 The George referred to here was George Macartney Black (1802–57), son of George Black Jr. He became a clergyman, married Sarah Anne Auld (d. 1869) in 1830 and fathered at least three children: Emily Marguerite/Margaret Black (later Richardson), George Robert Stewart Black and John Joseph Black. 'Black family tree' (PRONI, D4457/363); Ward, 'Black family', 188; Riddell, 'Great chemist', 66.   8 Long running peace negotiations between Britain and France had broken down in September 1806. Coquelle, *Napoleon and England*, pp 79–142.   9 i.e., Ellen Black née Stewart, Black's sister-in-law.

Letter Eleven

Central to Black's concerns in letter eleven is patronage – in particular a scheme in which he hoped a cousin, Frank Turnly, would assist him in securing the 'deputation' and half of the remuneration of the port collectorship of Trinidad. The letter also includes an account of the fire which destroyed much of Port of Spain in March 1808, news of the movements of Black's daughter Mariquite and her husband, who had returned to the West Indies, and reflections on the nature of Belfast's connections with Trinidad, with Black noting that Trinidad had 'no direct intercourse with Belfast' and that Belfast's merchants were 'devoted to Jamaica'. Lines appended to the end of the letter indicate that Esther, Black's youngest daughter, was in New York. Black had earlier intended to send her to Belfast, but this plan had evidently changed and subsequent letters reveal that she had been entrusted to the care of Madame de Malleveault, a Martiniquean royalist who was resident in New York.

Trinidad 1 August 1808

My dearest brother

We were put in possession yesterday of Adele's and my dear sister's[1] letters dated from Stranmillis in May, by which we learned with much concern for the first time that she had been in a bad state of health after her late accouchement and that you had had the affliction of losing the child, on which we who know well what a parent's feelings are on those occasions most sincerely condole with you. Experience has taught us how poignant it is to sensible minds to have those afflictions retraced in our memories and therefore having once said that we join in your grief very sincerely, we will be mute on the subject, hoping and trusting in providence that our dear sister having been supported through so trying a conflict and recovered her health will continue to enjoy it uninterruptedly and long be spared to be a comfort to you and her dear little ones. We are as we should be penetrated with gratitude for her parental tenderness of our dear Adele and doubt not but that, when it please God to reunite us, we shall find her endowed with principles imbibed from her precept and example which will constitute her happiness in this world and procure her favour in that to come. We are pleased to find in her style the same naïveté of expression for which she has from her earliest infancy been remarkable, and although not formed strictly according to grammatical rules, it displays the first fruits of a fertile genius, with the innocence of natural expression which we far prefer to the flights of a school mistress conducting

---

1 i.e., Ellen Black née Stewart, Black's sister-in-law.

the hand of her scholar. We are pleased to find that the trifles sent via Glasgow have got safe to hand and have proved acceptable; it would be very agreeable to us to send something more substantial to our dear Ellen, but having no direct intercourse with Belfast, we are obliged to have recourse to detours, by Glasgow, or Dublin and formerly through New York which we have found the uncertainty of. I have often recommended you to prevail on some of your merchants to try this country with their butter, their salted provisions and their linens, but all to no purpose; they are devoted to Jamaica, and have lately lost the *George* Captain McKibben bound there with a valuable cargo which has been taken and carried to Cayenne.[2]

You would learn by letters[3] I addressed you soon after the conflagration[4] of the arrival of Graves and the family[5] who stayed with us a fortnight and on the 31 May proceeded in the *Unique* brig of war for Curaçao.[6] I have no account of them direct or indirect of them [*sic*] since. Curaçao is directly to Leeward of us about 250 leagues and we have no sort of intercourse with it, they might as well be in Russia almost with respect to us. We have now however a prospect of communication through the Spanish Main and our friends at Caracas, which having declared for Fernando Septimo and the alliance of England we are again in habits of friendly intercourse with them and by that means we may contrive to forward and receive intelligence from Curaçao.[7]

2 The ship in question was, in fact, the *Georgetown*, which was owned or commissioned by the merchants M'Clure, Bailie and Whitla of Donegal Quay, Belfast. It appears to have been captured early in May 1808 by the *Serpent*, a French ship. *BNL*, 8 Mar. 1808; 'The marine list' in *The Tradesman: or, Commercial Magazine*, 1 (1808), 360–8 at 363; J.R.R. Adams, *Merchants in plenty: Joseph Smyth's Belfast directories of 1807 and 1808* (Belfast, 1991), pp 29, 66. 3 Missing. 4 Fire broke out in Port of Spain on the evening of 24 March 1808. Much of the town was destroyed and around 4,500 were left homeless, but not Black: as he goes on to relate, his property had a 'wonderful escape' and survived unscathed. Carmichael, *Trinidad and Tobago*, pp 93–5. 5 James Graves had returned to the West Indies with the 18th Royal Irish Regiment in 1807. See letter ten, note 2. 6 A Dutch island, Curaçao was held by the British for two spells during the Napoleonic wars: between 1800 and 1803, and between 1807 and 1816. The 2nd battalion of the 18th Royal Irish Regiment – Graves' battalion – was garrisoned in the island in 1807. *RMC*, v, 161; Gert Oostindie, 'Slave resistance, colour lines, and the impact of the French and Haitian revolutions in Curaçao' in Wim Klooster and Gert Oostindie (eds), *Curaçao in the age of revolutions, 1795-1800* (Leiden, 2011), pp 1–22 at 13. 7 In March 1808, during the French invasion of Spain, Fernando VII became king when his father, Carlos IV, abdicated. Early in May 1808, however, Fernando himself was forced to abdicate by Napoleon and, within Spain, royalist juntas were established. These events had a significant impact in Spain's colonies: as Eakin notes, 'colonists had political and economic autonomy dropped in their laps by the Napoleonic invasion, and the power of the British navy to keep the French from crossing the Atlantic.' In 1811, Venezuelan independence was declared, but in 1808 colonial authorities retained control. Curaçao had extensive trading connections with the Spanish Main, and it was as a consequence of this, combined with the political developments, that Black looked on Caracas, the capital and administrative centre of Venezuela, as

Indeed I would not be surprised or at all displeased to find that the 18th Royal Irish (and of course in the Spanish idea a regiment of Catholics) should be removed to Caracas as auxiliaries and that some other corps from Jamaica relieved them at Curaçao.[8] If auxiliaries are sent there they would be the properest regiment certainly from their reputation as Catholic to which the Spanish attach much importance.

You would learn by those letters also of the wonderful escape I had in preserving my house from the late dreadful destruction by fire. My neighbours to the north and south of me were sufferers, that to the north a printing office 3 story high of timber entirely only separated from me by the street of 32 feet wide. The heat alone of such a body of fire ignited my buildings but the fury of the flames did not leave us long in suspense. In 22 minutes the printers house was consumed and fell in and from that moment we were out of danger. It was a miraculous escape; however, it was not owing to good fortune but good guiding and I take that merit to myself.

I come now to the subject of which I crave all your attention if you think the matter at all feasible, if not you are to bury it in oblivion and keep the secret to yourself.

You were so kind once as to use your influence with Lord Macartney to obtain for me from government a confirmation of the place of master in chancery in this island which Governor Picton had conferred upon me by commission.

Lord Macartney readily undertook the office and I received a very handsome letter from him acquainting me of his having applied to Lord Hobart, then secretary of state for this department,[9] who promised I should have the appointment under his majesty's commission whenever a change of the laws here should take place, which was the earliest period at which I could use it.

The death of our friend[10] and the removal of Lord Hobart[11] from the office makes me consider all that arrangement as null as if it had never taken place and that consequently, when the change of laws does take place, my office

a possible avenue for communication with Graves and his family. Eakin, *Latin America*, pp 173–4, 179; Oostindie, 'Slave resistance', pp 3, 5; Candlin, *Last Caribbean frontier*, p. 53; Burkholder and Johnson, *Colonial Latin America*, pp 315, 323.   8 In actual fact, Graves would move to Jamaica and take command of the 1st battalion of the 18th Royal Irish Regiment in 1809. *RMC*, v, 161; letter sixteen.   9 i.e., secretary of state for war and the colonies. See letter seven, note 10.   10 i.e., George Macartney, who had died on 31 March 1806. *ODNB* (George Macartney, Earl Macartney).   11 In May 1804 Hobart was replaced as secretary of state for war and the colonies by John Pratt, earl of Camden (1759–1840). Pratt held the position until the summer of 1805, and was succeeded by the one-time reformer, Robert Stewart, Viscount Castlereagh (1769–1822) – a figure well-known, and not universally admired, in Ireland. Castlereagh lost the position when the Ministry of the Talents was established in 1806, but returned to it in 1807. Watson, *George III*, pp 581–2. *ODNB*, (Robert Hobart, fourth earl of Buckinghamshire), (John Pratt, first Marquess Camden), (Robert Stewart, Viscount Castlereagh).

(intended at least for me) will be filled by some more fortunate but I'll venture to say less meritorious aspirant or supplicant, for I can plead having served the king in his civil government in these colonies 31 years without fee or reward or ever having enjoyed or held any office or appointment by which I put a *maravedis*[12] in my pocket, and that I believe you yourself can vouch for, having been appointed a member of his majesty's council[13] for Grenada by mandamus dated on September 15 1777, then under Lord Macartney's government, and re-appointed when the island was restored by the French in 1783 under General Matthews.[14]

When this island was ceded to Great Britain by the Treaty of Amiens,[15] I was called to his majesty's council by General Picton and I claim the merit of having been one of his best friends and firmest supporters (which I considered was defending his majesty's authority and government) throughout all of the trying circumstances in which the intrigues of a designing man and his faction had involved him and out of which he has extricated himself with honour to us and to his friends.[16] The numerous documents which have been laid before

---

12 i.e., a Spanish coin.   13 As distinct from its legislature, which was elected, Grenada's council comprised twelve members – typically 'prominent residents' – appointed by nomination. Writing on 25 May 1777, Macartney had recommended 'John Black, esquire, as a person properly qualified to be of the Council' in a letter to Lord George Germain, secretary of state for the American colonies. *Journal of the Commissioners for Trade and Plantations from January 1776 to May 1782: preserved in the Public Record Office* (London, 1938), p. 106; Johnson, 'Grenada, 1775–79', pp 104–5.   14 Grenada was taken by the French in 1779, during the governorship of George Macartney, and held until 1783. Upon its return to Britain, General Edward Mathew, a veteran of the American War of Independence, was appointed as governor. Mathew's father, William Mathew, had earlier been Lt-Governor of St Kitts and the Leeward Isles, and his daughter, Anne, married Jane Austen's brother, the Revd James Austen. Johnson, 'Grenada, 1775–79', pp 123–4; Deirdre Le Faye, *Jane Austen: a family record*, 2nd ed. (Cambridge, 2004), pp 71–2; 'General Edward Mathew: profile and legacies summary', available at https://www.ucl.ac.uk/lbs/person/view/2146645387 (accessed 27/7/2018); Henige, *Colonial governors*, pp 122, 131, 167.   15 See letter one, note 19.   16 By July 1803, Hood, Picton and Fullarton had left Trinidad, and in the years that followed the conflict between the latter two was played out in the metropolitan centre. Fullarton (Black's 'designing man') laid charges against Picton before the privy council – charges relating to executions that were carried out in Trinidad under Picton's rule (in all thirty-five had taken place and it was alleged that twenty-nine were unlawful); and charges relating to the torture of Luisa Calderon, who had been accused of theft in 1801. Arrested in December 1803, Picton was released on a bail of £40,000 and a complex sequence of legal proceedings ensued. In January 1807, after a lengthy investigation, the privy council dropped the charges relating to the executions, but Picton was tried twice for the torture of Calderon and in 1808 received what Epstein has rightly described as 'a perplexing special verdict, finding torture to be legal in Trinidad at the cession of the island to Britain and Picton not to have been influenced by malice against Calderon, "independent of the illegality of the act" as based on British law.' This led to the further argument and the case was eventually dropped in 1812. Epstein, *Scandal*, pp 15–26 (esp. 18–19, 26), 130–1; *ODNB* (Thomas Picton).

his ministers at different periods respecting the locality of this colony and its population, soil, productions and laws, in all which reports I have been a principal actor, must make my name known to the present secretary of state Lord Castlereagh,[17] and with my name my labours in the service of the public. In the late Chinese emigration,[18] one of the strangest speculations that ever entered into the mind of man and that man was Fullarton, the whole direction of those unfortunate settlers 200 in number was confided to my direction and the expenditure attending the experiment amounting one way or other in this country to nearly £10,000 sterling has all gone through my hands, but without a penny of it I assure you sticking to my fingers, as would have been probably the case had it been trusted to others, and finally, since the fire, I have had the charge of the colonial treasury in consequence of the treasurer's inability to attend to the duties of his office by sickness and the quarterly accounts to the secretary of state's office go signed by me in that capacity but this also is gratuitous service.

I say in virtue of all this my name and my service cannot be unknown to Lord Castlereagh and as to his patronage our cousin Turnly owed his fortune at Canton, so our cousin if he is grateful to his patron would be disposed to serve him in his turn.[19] And here is how he may serve him and me too very essentially.

17 See note 11.   18 In 1806, in an attempt to establish 'a race of free cultivators, kept distinct from the Negroes and by their interest attached to the White Planters', a group of 200 Chinese were transported to Trinidad. 192 survived the journey (191 men and one woman), but the majority left within a few years: writing in 1814, the then governor of Trinidad, Sir Ralph Woodford (see appendix, letter two, note 2), observed that only 'about thirty' remained. Black was, as he goes on to claim, given 'direction' of the experiment, but it was not, as he suggests, Fullarton's idea; the possibility of introducing Chinese labour had, in fact, first been raised by a naval officer, Captain William Layman, in 1802. Carmichael, *Trinidad and Tobago*, pp 66–8; Epstein, *Scandal*, pp 205–19 (esp. 205–6, 216).   19 Turnly was Francis Turnly (*c*.1766–1845), one of several children of Black's aunt, Katherine Turnly née Black and Francis Turnly. He joined the East India Company in the mid-1780s and spent fifteen years in China, returning to Ireland a wealthy man in 1801. He subsequently purchased property in Co. Down and Co. Antrim and, prior to his death in 1845, devoted himself to an idiosyncratic scheme to bring about the integration of human society. That Turnly had returned to Ireland in 1801, prior to the appointment of Castlereagh as secretary of state for war and the colonies (see note 11), raises questions as to whether or not the latter had exercised patronage on his behalf. However, the Stewart family's connections with the East India Company appear to have been long-standing. Turnly's father was a tenant of Castlereagh's grandfather, Alexander Stewart (1697–1781), who was, through his marriage to Mary Cowan, half-sister of Sir Robert Cowan, governor of Bombay from 1728 to 1734, 'an important source of patronage in the East India Company'. Alexander Stewart's death in 1781 would preclude him from having exercised patronage on Turnly's behalf, but it is possible that Castlereagh's father did so. Moreover, Castlereagh himself *is* known to have exercised patronage on behalf of Henry Pottinger (1789–1856), another Co. Down man who served in the East India Company. Benn, *Belfast from 1799 till 1810*, p. 171; David Kennedy, 'Francis Turnly, 1766–1845: a prophet of the United

The collector of this port Charles Grant Esquire, brother of the master of the rolls and one of the best men living, is lately gone home in a reduced state of health and he told me in confidence he did not intend to return provided he could obtain a comfortable situation at home and this he will not fail to do as well from his own merits (for he possesses in an eminent degree the confidence of the board), as from his brother's influence; hence it will arise that the office of collector of this port will be vacated and there will be Scotch pretenders enough to obtain it.[20] I have not vanity to propose to our cousin Frank to solicit an office which is worth £5,000 currency a year for myself, but it might suit Lord Castlereagh to confer the appointment on some of his noble relatives who might condescend to give me the deputation, finding proper security for the discharge of the trust and allowing him a half of the revenues. Such things are frequently done and I don't see why his lordship may not be disposed to avail himself of so favourable an opportunity to serve some of his friends or his family as his predecessors in office have done before him. If Mr Turnly could manage a negotiation of this nature and succeed he would serve one of his own family who has not the pleasure of knowing him, but even to this day and forever will bear in remembrance his dear mother and cherish her virtues as long as he lives.

But if this cannot be obtained, or if it is of a nature out of his influence with his lordship to undertake, I must then request his assistance to obtain the confirmation of the office which Lord Macartney obtained a promise of for me from Lord Hobart, or the gift of any other good office in the colony to which his lordship may think my services entitle me when it suits his lordship's convenience.

When you consider the numerous family of children and grandchildren I have to support and reflect on the depressed state of the sugar market and the increased price of the necessaries of life and of the supplies requisite to maintain a sugar estate, these nearly absorbing the whole of the revenues, you will see how much I stand in need of some assistance from government, and I will make bold to say how much I am a creditor to that assistance by my long and gratuitous services. If however my friend Turnly should undertake to serve me and not succeed, I must be content to work my way through as well as I can, but I shall not be the less grateful for his endeavours.

When I say the office of collector is worth £5,000 currency, I mean it has been hitherto esteemed at that value, but if a peace takes place the trade will increase very considerably and the emoluments of the office with it.

Nations' in *Irish Ecclesiastical Record*, fifth series, 110 (1968), 40–51 (esp. 40–2); Henige, *Colonial governors*, p. 97; *DIB*, viii, 245–6 and ix, 75–80, 528–9. **20** Grant's brother was William Grant (1752–1832), a prominent juror and parliamentarian. That the brothers were Scottish explains Black's reference to 'Scotch pretenders', though this was not the only occasion (see also letter seven) on which he commented on Scots seeking position in Trinidad. *ODNB* (William Grant).

Thus my dear brother I have laid open my mind to you; if you can serve me, you want no stimulus to do so; if you cannot there is no help to it; I am inured to disappointments and can bear them.

You will find my second of exchange for £200 on Ottley and Brown of Dublin enclosed.[21] The first went in June by the packet.

I embrace my dear sister[22] and her children, Adele, my sisters Younghusband and Pettigrew[23] and their descendants and will ever remain my dearest George your affectionate brother John.

Mrs Black, Josefine, Esther Lacoste, Julie, Jenny and all the family are well and join me in love to you all.[24]

Esther is very well at New York and if we can credit the reports of her we receive from our friends promises to be a very accomplished woman. Adele must exert herself or Esther will carry the day. Take care Adele,[25] you know how much I love you and how much I should be disappointed if our Irish girl was not superior to a Yankee.

21 Ottley and Brown was a partnership of John Brown (1779–1808) and Brook Taylor Ottley. Brown, who was killed in Antigua a month after this letter was written (see letter thirteen), was the son of another John Brown (c.1740–1805), a well-known figure in the commercial life of Belfast in the late eighteenth century, and Isabella Brown née Callwell. Ottley, a former officer of the Lancashire Fencibles, married Brown's sister Isabella (1778–1845) in 1799, and the two men established a partnership in Dublin with interests in the West Indies. *DML*, ii, 477 and iii, 712; Chambers, *Faces*, pp 61–4. 22 i.e., Ellen Black née Stewart, Black's sister-in-law. 23 i.e., Esther Pettigrew née Black and Letitia Younghusband née Black, Black's sisters. 24 In addition to his wife, Bonne Clothilde Black née Fournillier ('Mrs Black'), Black is referring here to two of his five daughters ('Josefine and Julie') and his granddaughter ('Esther Lacoste', daughter of Josefine Lacoste née Black and Hugh Lacoste). The precise identity of Jenny is, however, unknown. 25 i.e., Adele Black, another of Black's daughters.

Letter Twelve

Written just two weeks after letter eleven, letter twelve is, in many ways, a follow-up to the longer missive that preceded it. The letter is chiefly concerned with patronage, with Black returning to the scheme, outlined in letter eleven, concerning Trinidad's port collectorship. However, he also comments on events in Spanish America, where Spanish colonists had risen in support of Fernando VII and French envoys had been captured.

Trinidad 15 August 1808

My dear brother

My last was by the packet covering my second of exchange for £200 on Ottley and Brown of Dublin;[1] here is the third and I'll keep the fourth until I hear of the fate of the foregoing.

I communicated to you a project, which if I could succeed in it through the interest of our cousin Frank Turnly with Lord Castlereagh would make me very comfortable for the rest of my days. It was founded on the probability of the collection of this island being vacated by the retreat of the present collector Mr Grant who is gone home in a bad state of health and never intends to return if he can obtain a suitable situation at home which there is no doubt he will, through the interest of his brother who is master of the rolls. I did not aim so high as the collection altogether for myself you may suppose; I proposed that our cousin Turnly should endeavour to prevail on his lordship to confer the appointment on some of his own noble relations and give me the deputation on equitable terms, which was to allow him a half the revenues and they may be considered £5,000 a year. My pretensions to such a place under the crown are better founded than perhaps any other man's who has not parliamentary interest. I have been serving the king in civil employments since 12 September 1777 when I was by his majesty's mandamus appointed to the council of that Island[2] and am now senior member of council here; I also served 3 years as chief judge here without fee or reward, and I have been for 3 months past, and now am, acting treasurer, the titled treasurer being from disease and age incapable of doing his duty, but this also is a gratuitous service and I can conscientiously say that in my life I have never reaped a shilling benefit from any services in which I have been employed by government and they have been numerous and important.[3] If I had been as importunate as others, I might have succeeded as well, but I never asked any-

---

1 See letter eleven. 2 i.e., Grenada. See letter eleven, note 13. 3 See letter four, note 28.

thing for myself while I could do without it, but now the depressed state of the sugar market and the ruinous prospect before us all who depend on colonial produce obliges me to prepare for the worst and endeavour to obtain something from government towards supporting my family in that class of life to which they have been hitherto accustomed. Lord Castlereagh must be well acquainted with my name for he sees it to [*sic*] many classes of public accounts and to all reports of council relating to this island and for farther particulars I would refer his lordship to General Picton, with whom I am in habits of intimacy, or to Captain Holmes,[4] formerly Governor Hislop's secretary [and] now member of parliament for Grampound, and with this last Gentleman his lordship is very intimate.[5] It is, I'll admit, a bold push to ask for so good an appointment all at once, but when you reflect that I have been 35 years in the West Indies, and of that 31 serving the king gratuitously, I hope it will not be deemed exceeding my merits.

If however better interest should carry it, I would then put in for the treasurer-ship (in which I am now acting by order of Governor Hislop) and as the present treasurer is very old and infirm, and probably never will be able to do his duty again, I would allow him a handsome annuity out of the revenues for his life provided the appointment devolves to me on his demise by the king's commission. The salary is fixed at £1,500 currency a year without any other allowance so you see it's no great matter, for £1,500 a year in this county is not worth £300 with you. Mr Collin the treasurer is an American, who was in former times civil secretary to General O'Hara[6] when he was governor of Senegal and in consequence of a letter of recommendation from O'Hara to Sir Ralph Abercomby he obtained the appointment of treasurer when the island was taken and has no other merits to entitle him to the employment.[7]

---

4 William Holmes (1779–1851) was the son of a Co. Sligo brewer. After a spell in the army, during which, as Black indicates, he was stationed in the West Indies and employed as secretary to Thomas Hislop (see note 5), he embarked on a political career in 1808. Known as 'Black Billy', he was a long-serving Tory party whip and was associated with the 'ultra' faction within the party. *ODNB* (William Holmes).   5 A military officer who had served in the 11th and 8th West India regiments, Sir Thomas Hislop (1764–1843) was lieutenant-governor of Grenada between 1803 and 1804, and governor of Trinidad from 1804 to 1811. He subsequently served as commander-in-chief at Madras and controversially ordered the killing, despite their surrender, of the governor and 300 strong garrison of the fort of Talnar during the Third Anglo-Maratha War (1817–18). *ODNB* (Thomas Hislop); Henige, *Colonial governors*, pp 122, 182.   6 Charles O'Hara (*c.*1740–1802), an officer in the Coldstream Guards, served as governor of Senegambia, which comprised most of what had formerly been French Senegal along with territory on the Gambia River, from 1765 to 1775. He went on to fight in the American War of Independence, and was governor of Gibraltar from 1795 to 1802. *ODNB* (Charles O'Hara); Henige, *Colonial governors*, pp 118, 170.   7 Sir Ralph Abercromby led the force that initially captured Trinidad from Spain in 1797. As Millette notes, in addition to appointing Josiah Collin as treasurer, Abercromby

Had Lord Macartney lived, I could have had his interest with government to support my pretensions, but as he is no more I am obliged to have recourse to my cousin Frank[8] (who I remember [as] a child and his sister Peggy who died young) who I am informed is much protected by Lord Castlereagh our colonial secretary.

We have great accounts from the neighbouring continent. The Spaniards are <u>all up</u> (as you call it) to defend the rights of Ferdinand the 7th who has been proclaimed king in the provinces of Guayana, Cumana, Caracas and Santa Feé.[9] No doubt the same spirit will be found to prevail in Puerto Rico, Havana,[10] Mexico and Peru.[11] The French had sent out officers to take charge of the governments of all those places, but we were before hand with them. Several of these emissaries have fallen into the hands of our cruizers and those who arrived have been seized and imprisoned by the Spaniards.[12]

also gave him 'the many-faceted position of superintendent of imports and exports, receiver of duties and regulator of the ports of the Colony.' Abercromby was also responsible for the appointment of Picton as governor. James Millette, *Society and politics*, p. 57; Epstein, *Scandal*, pp 94–5.   8 i.e., Francis Turnly.   9 See, for events on the Spanish Main, letter eleven, note 7.   10 The Spanish West Indian islands of Puerto Rico and Cuba (of which Havana was the capital) were not untouched by events in Spain, but were, as Burkholder and Johnson have noted of Cuba, 'spared the turmoil common in the mainland colonies', and did not declare independence. Burkholder and Johnson, *Colonial Latin America*, p. 340; Eakin, *Latin America*, pp 197–8.   11 In Mexico, news of events in Spain 'raised the level of political debate and drove a wedge between creole and peninsular members of the elite' – that is between those born in Mexico and the so-called *peninsulares*, born in Spain, who had travelled out to the colonies and who alienated the creoles with what were perceived as their 'condescending cultural and social attitudes'. In the short-term, the *peninsulares* gained the upper hand and succeeded, in 1808, in deposing the Spanish viceroy, José de Iturrigaray, who they suspected of siding with the creoles. This led, in 1810, to a rebellion, headed initially by the creole priest Miguel Hidalgo y Costilla (1753–1811), and in 1821 Mexican independence was declared. In 1808 Peru remained loyal to Fernando VII, thanks in no small part to its viceroy, José Fernando de Abascal, who 'countered every move towards constitutionalism and reform'. Peruvian independence was, however, secured late in 1824. Burkholder and Johnson, *Colonial Latin America*, pp 325–6, 330–9; Eakin, *Latin America*, pp 163–4, 187–93.   12 Early in October 1808 the *Belfast News-Letter* published what it described as an 'Extract of a letter from Trinidad to a gentleman in this town', which contained similar reflections on events on the Spanish Main. The author explained that 'Bonaparte has been publicly burnt in effigy' and that 'the cargo of *dors* viz. Gubernadors, Corregidors, Comadors, Auditors, &c. &c. sent by Boney to Saguira from Bayonne, has been safely lodged in the castle at Puerto Cavallo, with the exception of one unfortunate, who, for his insolence to the Captain of the British frigate Acaste, was immediately sent to the infernal region by a Spanish officer.' That the date of this letter was given as 1 August 1808, the same date which Black's previous letter (letter eleven) bears, is suggestive. However, as French is described, in the extracts published in the *News-Letter*, as a 'cursed infectious language', it seems unlikely that Black, whose wife appears to have been a French creole (see letter one, note 4), and whose family had long-standing French connections, was the author. *BNL*, 4 Oct. 1808.

I have no accounts yet from Graves at Curaçao but the brig which carried him down is at Cumana on her way up and expected here daily.

I send this by way of Barbados whence armed ships very frequently sail for Liverpool and Glasgow.

With my love to your better half, to Adele, to Esther,[13] to the Ballydrain family[14] and all who belong to you. I am my dear brother, yours affectionately

John

---

13 i.e., Esther Pettigrew née Black, Black's sister.   14 i.e., the family of Letitia Younghusband née Black, Black's sister. See appendix, letter three, note 15.

Letter Thirteen

Dated 5 October 1808, letter thirteen is chiefly striking for Black's frank acknowledgment of his financial troubles, and his reflections – inevitably disapproving – on the abolition of the trade in enslaved people. Touching, in passing, on the port collectorship, he concedes 'really and truly' that he is 'in want of something of that nature to help me out', and in the ensuing discussion outlines the difficulties slave-owners faced in turning a profit and bewails 'the ill-founded calculations of his majesty's ministers and the ridiculous philanthropy of Mr Wilberforce'. The letter also makes reference to the unfortunate fate of John Brown, a Belfast-born merchant killed in Marie-Galante; gives news of Black's daughters Mariquite and Josefine; and mentions Adele, from whom Black had received a letter that gave him 'great pleasure'.

[Trinidad 5 October 1808][1]

My dear brother

Although I have not much to say in addition to my late letters, I cannot let Davy Park go home without his being the bearer of a letter from me. His departure is sudden and unexpected, and is occasioned by the death of Mr Brown who, happening to be at Marie-Galante on commercial affairs when the French landed there on a depredatory expedition from Guadeloupe, was made a prisoner by the enemy and unfortunately killed while in their hands by the fire of our own soldiers.[2] He is very much regretted by all who had the pleasure of his acquaintance and by myself especially.[3] He was a very fine young man of great promise, his cruel fate must have been a dreadful shock to his poor mother[4] and the family.

---

1 The date appears at the tail of the original manuscript, rather than the head.   2 John Brown (see letter eleven, note 21) was killed in September 1808. Having been captured by the French while sailing 'from Antigua to another island', he was taken to Marie-Galante, one of the French Antilles, which was, in due course, attacked by the British. When the French decided to surrender Brown was freed 'for the purpose of communicating with the British', but his 'joy at his deliverance made him neglect the precaution of taking with him a flag of truce and on approaching the posts of the British, he received a ball in the heart'. *The Athenaeum*, 5 (1809), 280; Henige, *Colonial governors*, pp 24, 36.   3 Brown had earlier studied at Trinity College Dublin, and those who had had 'the pleasure of his acquaintance' included the poet Thomas Moore. Moore described Brown, in a note in his *Irish Melodies*, as 'one of my earliest college companions and friends, whose death was as singularly melancholy and unfortunate as his life had been amiable, honourable, and exemplary', and copied an account of his death into his journal in January 1843. *The journal of Thomas Moore*, ed. Wilfred S. Dowden (6 vols, Newark, 1983–91), vi, 2315, 2366.   4 See letter eleven, note 21.

If the subject of my late letters is within the competency of my cousin Turnly, I hope and trust you will prevail on him, aided by the influence of my good aunt[5] who I have never forgotten, to exert himself in the pursuit of either of the objects pointed out.[6] I confess to you really and truly, that I am in want of something of that nature to help me out; sugar believe me does not defray the expense of making it, without making any allowance for the interest of capital. Consequently, we are retrograding every year and those who owe money must be ruined at last. Our means are decreasing; the prohibition of the slave trade[7] renders it impossible to replace the mortality which in inevitable; our expenses and interest increasing and very little prospect of obtaining any permanent relief from government so that the colonies and colonists must gradually decline and end in total ruin, not only to the proprietors but to all those who depend on such properties for their support. To sell is equally ruinous; for no man in his sense would purchase that by which he is in a manner sure to sink his capital by, and indeed the fact is that there are no purchasers at any price. Many properties in this country are for sale under execution for debts but nobody offers, not even the creditors, so you see what a blessed situation the ill-founded calculations of his majesty's ministers and the ridiculous philanthropy of Mr Wilberforce[8] has placed us in – a philanthropy that will terminate by consigning thousands of whites to beggary, for the sake of a country of savages who are 10 thousand times happier with us as slaves than at home free, if a man can be called free whose life and property (if he has any) is always at the disposal of his king.

I need not press upon you this subject more explicitly, if I did not want aid I would not seek it, I have been 34 years in the West Indies permanently, most of that time doing one service or other to government without ever having profited a shilling by it and surely now I cannot be considered as importunate. I have no friend however through whom I could convey my humble petition, except through our cousin from his intimacy (as I conceive) with Lord Castlereagh, the arbiter from his office of all that is to be given in this colony. I have lately heard that a gentleman of the name of Kingston, who when an officer of the 60th Regiment at Belfast married Miss Goddard (since dead) grand daughter of John Rainey[9] and who has been for some years in this country [–]

---

5 i.e., Katherine Turnly née Black.   6 See letters eleven and twelve.   7 The British parliament having voted to abolish the trade in enslaved people early in 1807, the 47 Geo. III, c. 36 – under which the trade in enslaved Africans was 'utterly abolished, prohibited and declared to be unlawful' – came into force on 1 May of that year. Morgan, *Slavery and the British empire*, pp 170–2.   8 William Wilberforce (1759–1833), a parliamentarian, social reformer and evangelical, was the 'leading spokesman', within parliament, of the abolitionists, and one of the best-known politicians of his day. *ODNB* (William Wilberforce); Morgan, *Slavery and the British empire*, p. 161.   9 'Miss Goddard' was Eliza 'Bess' Goddard, daughter of John Goddard (d. 1807) and Eliza Goddard née Rainey (c.1743–1836). An acknowledged beauty, Goddard was involved, between 1791 and 1794, in what James Quinn has described as a 'stop-start affair' with the United Irishman Thomas Russell (1767–1803), but married Kingston, a captain, 'said to have had a fortune of 6,000', in 1795. She

his time, has lately gone home to endeavour to obtain the <u>survivorship</u> of the present treasurer under favour of Mr Canning[10] to whom he is known. You must probably know this Mr Kingston, who is from Cork, his father married in second marriage Miss Donaldson of Belfast.[11] He has always passed in this country for an extraordinary character and but ill succeeded in his pursuits. So may he in this if to my prejudice. I still continue to do the duties of the office but without reward.

Davy Park will give you an account of the state of this country better than epistolary expression can convey it. He must do it (to do it well) however as a planter not as a merchant, for the harder the times are for us, the more their harvest is copious.

I enclose you two letters from Mrs B, who is not at this moment thoroughly well, occasioned by cold contracted by getting a wetting and not immediately changing her clothes which in this climate is always followed by suppression and fever. I trust it will be of no consequence.

Adele's letter gave me great pleasure. It is I can perceive all her own production, innocence and vivacity form the outline of it. Her hand also is much improved and promises to be a good one; I am glad you have got so good a preceptress for her, especially too a descendent of a relative. Graves did not say a word unfavourable of her, far from it. I have at length letters from them at Curaçao. They are quite in transports with their situation there and so they may well be. The country is like a garden, uncommonly healthful and beautifully bespangled with neat country seats with grounds laid out in the Dutch style.

They occupy an elegant house or rather a corner of it (for it's big enough for 4 families like theirs) a *l'otra banda* or opposite side of the lake which forms the inner harbour of the town.[12] The distance by land to town is con-

most likely died late in December 1800. The Raineys, her mother's family, were a well-connected Belfast family with links to the Ballydrain Stewarts (for whom see letter one, note 24). *DML*, iii, 79, 715, 721; James Quinn, *Soul on fire: a life of Thomas Russell* (Dublin, 2002), pp 37, 145, 148–51; *DIB*, viii, 662–4. **10** George Canning (1770–1827), a prominent Tory politician, served as foreign secretary between March 1807 and September 1809. He and Lord Castlereagh fought a duel on 21 September 1809. Castlereagh, having discovered Canning had attempted to unseat him as secretary of state for war and the colonies, was the challenger, and Canning was wounded in the exchange of fire. *ODNB* (George Canning); Watson, *George III*, pp 477–8, 483, 582. **11** The second wife of Kingston senior was Ann Donaldson, who had earlier been married to Christopher Conron of Cork. Her father was Hugh Donaldson (d. 1762) of Belfast, a merchant who traded with the West Indies and 'had a hand in all aspects of Irish-American trade'. *DML*, i, 12, 17; ii, 125; and iii, 654–5, 715; *Letterbook of Greg & Cunningham*, ed. Truxes, p. 117. **12** The town in question being Willemstad, which was located on the shores of St Anna Bay. Over the course of the eighteenth century, part of Willemstad became known as Otrobanda, this name deriving from *oversijde* which, Linda M. Rupert notes, Dutch residents employed 'throughout the eighteenth century to refer to the neighbourhood across St Anna Bay, often employing variations of the phrase, *de overzijde van de haven* ("the other side of the harbour").' Cornelis C. Goslinga, *A short history of the Netherlands Antilles and Surinam* (The Hague, 1979), p. 60;

siderable because you are obliged to make the circuit of the lake, but by water it's not more than 20 minutes row and as commanding officer (with the appointments of a brigadier) Graves has a boat manned always at his orders.

Mariquite says she and the children never enjoyed better health and Tom Graves had got the appointment of brigade major, which besides giving him a cover at the governor's table, makes a very handsome increase of his appointments.

Josefine and her two little ones[13] are in high health; I had yesterday letters from Esther[14] and from the lady in whose care she is.[15] This and other reports make brilliant representations of her improvement which with every allowance for exaggeration must be remarkable. I am only afraid she will outstrip Adele, if Adele be not very attentive.

I reserve till another occasion by our packet to answer more particularly your letter on other matters to which it relates; all I can for the present [say] is that blood can not be drawn from a stone.

With assurance of my constant regard for you all who are yet present to my memory as if I had seen you yesterday, and my love to my good and dear Adele.

I am ever your affectionate brother
John

You see how intimate we are become with the Spaniards who show they are still possessed of the true Castilian valour when fairly tried.[16] Bonaparte will be overthrown from the elevated situation he had got to by the determinate resistance of these people, which will encourage all the countries labouring under his despotism to do the same.

Linda M. Rupert, *Creolization and contraband: Curaçao in the early modern Atlantic world* (Athens, GA, 2012), p. 132.   **13** i.e., Esther Lacoste, daughter of Josefine Lacoste née Black, and a sibling. As noted above (see letter six, note 23), Josefine Lacoste's first child was most likely named Eleonore. However, the fact that Eleonore is named only in letter seven, and is not mentioned in letter eleven, where Black *does* refer to Josefine and Esther Lacoste, suggests that she died in infancy and that the other child referred to here was a third child.   **14** i.e., Esther Black, Black's daughter.   **15** Black's subsequent letters reveal the lady in question to be Madame de Malleveault, a French Martiniquean who had 'quitted Martinique from her antipathy to the code Napoleon' (see letters seventeen and eighteen). De Malleveault was the widow of a royalist naval officer, Louis Charles François de Malleveault de la Varenne. Eliza, her daughter, accompanied her to the United States and there met and 'captivated' Thomas Butler – son of Pierce Butler, a prominent Irish-born plantation owner and signatory of the United States constitution – who she married in Martinique in February 1812. Malcolm Bell, *Major Butler's legacy: five generations of a slave-holding family* (Athens, GA, 1987), pp 1–2, 210–11; Janice E. McKenney, *Women of the constitution: wives of the signers* (Lanham, MD, 2013), pp 33–5.   **16** France had invaded Spain in March 1808. By June, widespread resistance had emerged and Britain, gripped by what Boyd Hilton has termed 'Spanish fever', provided assistance – initially in the form of money and materiel, though by the end of the year, with the French driven from Portugal (see letter fourteen, note 11), British troops had moved into Spain. Hilton, *A mad, bad and dangerous people?*, pp 213–14; Esdaile, *The Peninsular War*, pp 49–53, 58, 88–9, 104, 141–3.

Letter Fourteen

Picking up on themes touched upon in letters twelve and thirteen, letter fourteen, written on 13 November 1808, discusses developments in (and Trinidad's connections with) South America, and events on the Iberian Peninsula, where Spanish opposition to the 'treachery' of Napoleon served, in Black's judgement, to 'prove what a people can do when they are unanimous and determined to maintain their independence'. Equally interesting is the fact that Black shows himself here to have been in continued contact with Trinidad's former governor, Thomas Picton. Noting that Picton had informed him that he had encountered Letitia Younghusband née Black at Harrogate, Black proceeds, in a revealing passage, to reflect on Picton's character and defend his conduct, arguing that 'any acts committed by him during his government in this country were the acts of necessity to prevent greater evils'. What George Black Jr made of this defence, and whether or not he had been influenced by the 'injurious reports' of Picton's opponents, is, regrettably, unknown, though it is perhaps telling that Black felt that he needed to justify Picton in this way.

Trinidad 13 November 1808

My dear brother

An armed brig, which will sail this day for Glasgow, affords me a good opportunity of writing and I avail myself of it to say that we are all well to windward and leeward. I mean here and at Curaçao whence we have now frequent intelligence through the medium of our Spanish friends on the continent, with whom we live in habits of intimacy. They bring us a variety of their productions and take away our manufactures in quantities. Fine Irish linens, long lawns which we call estopillas, prints etc. are in great demand.

Their imports are composed of a great variety of articles, some for consumption in our own market, others for the European.

For us they bring oaken, cows, horses, mules, sheep, goats, hogs, tortoise, turtle, turkeys, fowl, corn, plantains, water and musk melons, salted beef or rather hung beef called tasajo, d[ried] fish of various kinds and tobacco. For exportation, cotton, indigo, hides, balsams, tinctures, gums, dye woods, medicinal productions, oils, spices, sassafras, larsaparilla, vanilla, cascarilla and specie.[1]

1 'Larsarparilla' is, most likely, a reference to sarsaparilla. It, sassafras and cascarilla (chinona) were South American medicinal plants in which there was an extensive trade. John Redman Coxe, *The American dispensary, containing the natural, chemical, pharmaceutical, and medical history of the different substances employed in medicine*, 9th ed. (Philadelphia, 1831),

The former are bought by small vessels from the coast of Cumana and Barcelona and the Island of Margaritta, but the latter, which are objects of great value, come from the River Orinoco, which is navigable 300 leagues from its mouth running through a country the most fertile and yielding naturally the richest productions in the world.[2]

A free and protected commerce with such countries, you may suppose, adds greatly to the activity of business with us; it does so effectually and our dry good importers are now milking the cow. Are there no people in Belfast who have the spirit of adventure? The ports of Buenos Ayres and Montevideo are also open to British commerce; the inhabitants of that country had tasted the sweets of a free intercourse with us during the short period we were among them and no sooner were the events which have taken place in Spain known there than the ports were opened to us.[3] A number of speculators that had gone to Rio Janeiro with rich investments had proceeded to Montevideo, the business having been overdone at the Brazils, even at St Salvador.[4] We

---

pp 205–6; Stefanie Gänger, 'World trade in medicinal plants from Spanish America, 1717–1815' in *Medical History*, 59 (2015), 44–62.   **2** Cumana and Barcelona were ports on the Spanish Main, located at the mouths of the rivers Neveri (Barcelona) and Manzanares (Cumana). Margarita (Marguerite) was an island located close to Cumana, which, although 'extremely barren', was considered 'as a commercial or military station … extremely desirable'. Further east lay the Gulf of Paria, into which the river Orinoco flowed and in which Trinidad lay. Trading connections between Trinidad and these territories were, by 1808, well-established. In his *Travels in parts of South America* (1806), F. Depons explained that 'Trinidad, which was ceded to the English at the peace of Amiens, situated at the eastern extremity of Terra-Firma, from which it is only four leagues distant, is extremely convenient for the contraband trade with Cumana, Barcelona, Marguerite and Guiana. The gulph of Paria, which washes the eastern [*sic*] part of Trinidad, receives the waters of the river Guarapiche, which enters the province of Cumana, and by which animals are transported from Terra Firma to Trinidad. The articles received in return, arrive by the same channel, or are landed at different points in their course, without the smallest danger. It is there that the cargoes enter that are destined for Barcelona, from which place they are separated, and sent to Caraccas and other cities.' F. Depons, *Travels in parts of South America, during the years 1801, 1802, 1803, & 1804; containing a description of the Captain-Generalship of Carraccas, with an account of the laws, commerce and natural productions of that country; as also a view of the customs and manners of the Spaniards and native Indians* (London, 1806), pp 26–7, 28–9, 73, 86.   **3** Buenos Ayres (Buenos Aires) and Montevideo were ports located in the estuary of the La Plata River – Buenos Aires in what is today Argentina, and Montevideo in what is today Uruguay. Buenos Aires was invaded by the British in 1806 and 1807, and in 1808 Santiago Liniers, a French military officer who had led the opposition to the British and acquired power, introduced free trade. Eakin, *Latin America*, pp 182–3; Jay Kinsbruner, *Independence in Spanish America: civil wars, revolutions and underdevelopment* (Albuquerque, 1994), pp xxi, 57–8.   **4** Rio de Janeiro and St Salvador were, respectively, the capital and former capital of Portuguese Brazil. Rio de Janeiro was made the capital in 1763, by which point it had become 'the most important commercial centre in Brazil … the gateway for Portuguese colonists, African slaves, and supplies to the gold and diamond fields in Minas Gerais, and the main legal exit for gold production.' St

have this intelligence by the *Stork* sloop of war, Captain Le Geyt,[5] in 5 weeks from Rio Janeiro, she went out with the pope's nuncio[6] and is on her way to join the admiral now off Martinique with the fleet in blockade, preparatory to its being besieged, which we have reason to think it will before X'mas.[7]

Spain continues to add laurel to laurel, and to prove what a people can do when they are unanimous and determined to maintain their independence.[8] Divide and *impera*[9] has been always Bonaparte's maxim. By this stratagem it is that he has subdued all those who have hitherto yielded to his oppression. In Spain he tries to play the same game, but his treachery has been discovered, his projects frustrated and the resistance they have shown, and triumphs they have gained, may incite others to follow so glorious an example, and the union of Europe may yet lay prostrate the tyrant, and the world be restored to peace and its former equilibrium. He is preparing a great army to reduce them, but if that people undisciplined and unarmed could resist and defeat the armies he had so insidiously introduced among them, what may not now be expected from them, when formed into regular armies, which have acquired confidence by victory and are supported by the strong arm of Great Britain.

Salvador, however, numbered 'among the most populous cities of the New World' and was itself 'a hub of transatlantic commerce'. Eakin, *Latin America*, pp 90–1, 154; Stuart B. Schwartz, *Sugar plantations in the formation of Brazilian society: Bahia, 1550–1835* (Cambridge, 1985), pp 75–6; Henige, *Colonial governors*, p. 260.   **5** George Le Geyt (1777–1861) was an experienced naval officer who had been given command of the *Stork* in 1803 and who, by 1812, 'had been upwards of 20 years in constant active employment (one-half of that time in the West Indies, and upwards of six years on the American station).' John Marshall, *Royal naval biography; or, memoirs of the services of all the flag officers, superannuated rear-admirals, retired-captains, post-captains and commanders, whose names appeared on the admiralty list of sea-officers at the commencement of the year 1823, or who have since been promoted ... with copious addenda, supplement – part iii* (London, 1829), pp 99–102; *London Review and Weekly Journal of Politics, Literature, Art and Society* 3:77 (21 Dec. 1861, supplement), 796.   **6** i.e., Lourenço Caleppi. In November 1807 the Portuguese royal family fled Portugal, which had been invaded by the French, for Brazil. Caleppi was instructed to join the exiled court and did so in September 1808, having first visited London. Evidently pleased with Le Geyt (see note 5), he gifted him a snuff box. *London Review and Weekly Journal of Politics, Literature, Art and Society* 3 (21 Dec. 1861, supplement), 796; Eakin, *Latin America*, p. 173; Samuel J. Miller, *Portugal and Rome, c.1748-1830: an aspect of the Catholic Enlightenment* (Roma, 1978), p. 381; Hans-Jürgen Pien, *Christianity in Latin America*, revised and expanded edition (Leiden, 2013), p. 310.   **7** Placed under blockade in November 1808, the French colony of Martinique was invaded late in January 1809 and was held by the British until 1814. The admiral referred to here is Sir Alexander Inglis Cochrane (1758–1832), rear-admiral of the red, who jointly led the attack on Martinque with Lieutenant-General George Beckwith (1752/3–1823), former governor of Bermuda and St Vincent. Edward Pelham Brenton, *The naval history of Great Britain from the year 1783–1836* (2 vols, London, 1837), ii, 253; Henige, *Colonial governors*, pp 43–4, 95, 169; *ODNB* (George Beckwith), (Alexander Inglis Cochrane).   **8** Here, Black is possibly alluding to the Spanish defeat of French forces at Bailén, the previous July. Esdaile, *The Peninsular War*, pp 77–83. See also letter thirteen, note 16.   **9** i.e., rule.

Portugal now relieved from French fraternity will also contribute with her treasures and armies.[10] It is the same cause; in defending Spain, they defend themselves. I shall make no observation on the late convention there. It makes the same impression here as at home and our only hope is that [it] has been smashed and our navy ordered to stop the transports and carry the whole to England. Time will clean up the mystery.[11]

Davy Park left this 10 October in a ship for Liverpool. The unfortunate death of Mr Brown[12] called him suddenly home and he was the bearer of a letter from me. I hope he has arrived safely. I have a letter from General Picton at Harrogate.[13] He says he has become acquainted with my sister Younghusband[14] whom he recognised by a strong family resemblance. He expresses himself much pleased with her and the girls; I hope they were equally so with him and that his agreeable manners and interesting conversation will have removed any prejudices with which their minds might have been impressed by the injurious reports his enemies had disseminated. General Picton is an honourable man, humane in his prejudices and sincere in his friendships; any acts committed by him during his government in this country were the acts of necessity to prevent greater evils and without which we should have experienced catastrophes similar to those which happened in the neighbouring islands during the frenzy of the French revolutionary doc-

---

10 Late in 1807, prior to invading Spain, France had invaded Portugal, and in July 1808 a British army, led by Sir Arthur Wellesley (1769–1852), had landed in the country. Defeated at Roliça on 17 August and Vimeiro on 21 August, the French came to terms and withdrew from Portugal the following month. Hilton, *A mad, bad and dangerous people?*, pp 213–14; Esdaile, *The Peninsular War*, pp 87–102; *ODNB* (Wellesley). 11 Black is referring here to the so-called Convention of Cintra, under the terms of which the defeated French army was permitted to return, by sea, to France, with the assistance of the Royal Navy. These terms were met with outrage in Britain, where disappointment at a squandered opportunity to press a military advantage mingled with fears about establishment corruption and a public inquiry was held, albeit one which, in Boyd Hilton's description, 'turned out to be a lengthy exercise in obfuscation'. Hilton, *A mad, bad and dangerous people?*, p. 214; Esdaile, *The Peninsular War*, pp 101–2; Uglow, *In these times*, pp 476–7. 12 See letter thirteen. 13 Picton is known to have been writing from Harrogate to Trinidad at this time, and to have been sharing news of events in Spain. In May 1838, the *United Services Journal* published an article entitled 'Anecdotes and original letters of Sir Thomas Picton', which included transcripts of letters that had been provided by a 'gentleman ... long resident in Trinidad'. In one extract, dated 'Harrowgate, 1 Sept. 1808', Picton reported that 'The Spanish people have showed great energy; far more than the government was capable of, even if it had been inclined to resist. Bonaparte committed himself most assuredly, and must make great exertions to retrieve his character as a statesman, which is now at stake. I was on the point of embarking with 6,000 men, and incurred considerable expense in fitting myself out, when I was disappointed by some rascally machinations at the Colonial office.' 'Anecdotes and original letters of Sir Thomas Picton' in *United Services Journal and Naval and Military Magazine* 27 (1838), 77–88 at 77, 80. 14 i.e., Letitia Younghusband née Black.

trine.[15] I shall not have time to write to Adele, because I want to give her a summary of events for times past, present and those which may happen in time to come and that requires time and reflection. You may assure her however of my never forgetting her a moment and that I look forward with infinite pleasure to the period when I shall receive her back from her Irish parents, the same Adele in candour and innocence that I parted with, but improved in knowledge, and possessed of those accomplishments which are acquired by education and immured by precept and example. Esther continues to deserve well of all our acquaintances at New York and of her mistress. She is under the inspection of a lady who is not inferior to Madame de Genlis in talents natural or acquired, but her principles are in the reverse of that celebrated authoress.[16]

The enclosed letter for Mr H.J. Tomb you will peruse, seal and deliver.[17] The tableau it presents of my feelings and circumstances is drawn after nature and as you are thus fully in possession of my sentiments I hope you will mind what I have requested you in several letters to propose to my cousin Frank Turnly and let me know the issue or the hopes of issue.

With assurance of my affectionate regard for your good Ellen, Esther, Letty[18] and all the little ones, I am always, whither in the cellar or the garret,[19]

Your brother who

Loves you John

---

15 See, for some of Picton's 'acts', letter eleven, note 16.   **16** Stéphanie-Félicité de Genlis (1746–1830), an aristocratic French governess, authored numerous books, including treatises on education, and was initially supportive of the French Revolution. Her views on education have been judged 'discriminatory with regard to sex and social class, but … truly modern in their practical orientation, the simultaneous attention to mind and body, the emphasis on foreign languages and mathematics, and their civic awareness in offering education to all citizens without exception.' Marie Naudin, 'Stéphanie-Félicité, Comtesse de Genlis (1746–1830)' in Eva Martin Sartori and Dorothy Wynne Zimmerman (eds), *French women writers* (Lincoln, NA, 1994), pp 178–87 (182 for quote).   **17** Most likely Henry Joy Tomb, a Belfast merchant. Tomb's father, David Tomb, had been a member of the Jones, Tomb, Joy and Co. partnership, which is known to have traded with the West Indies in the late eighteenth century. Black later (in April 1809) remarked that 'Park has brought out powers from Mr Tomb to settle the old business on generous terms', and it is possible that it was with Jones, Tomb, Joy and Co. that he had run into financial difficulties in Grenada in the early 1780s. Benn, *Belfast from 1799 till 1810*, p. 174; Gamble, 'Business community', pp 32–3, 46–7, 344–5.   **18** i.e., Ellen Black née Stewart, Black's sister-in-law, and his sisters Esther Pettigrew née Black and Letitia Younghusband née Black.   **19** Possibly an allusion to *The Author* by Samuel Foote (*c.*1721–77), in which a character is described in the following terms: 'The offspring of a dunghill! born in a cellar – hold, hold – and living in a garret! a fungus, a mushroom!' Samuel Foote, *The Author* (London, 1778), p. 9; J.C. Grocott, *An index to familiar quotations selected principally from British authors with parallel passages from various writers ancient and modern*, 4th ed. (Liverpool, 1871), p. 39; *ODNB* (Samuel Foote).

Letter Fifteen

The last of a sequence of five letters Black wrote in 1808, letter fifteen is a short letter, but one that is varied in content. Opening with a reprimand, Black points out that his brother is 'several letters in ... debt', before turning to share news of the death in Trinidad of John McDonnald, an Ulsterman, educated in Belfast, whose sisters stood to inherit a sum of £3,000, and who had, Black claims here, 'been my intimate friend and that of the family for the last 10 years uninterruptedly'. Notwithstanding this 'intimacy', McDonnald makes no prior appearances in Black's correspondence, a fact that serves to illustrates the point that Black's surviving letters, detailed as they are, present an incomplete picture of his world. McDonnald aside, Black also offers an update on James and Mariquite Graves' situation, touches again on Trinidad's connections with Spanish America and makes reference to the American embargo on foreign trade, which was clearly being flouted, an American vessel having recently arrived in Trinidad.

Trinidad 1 December 1808

My dear brother

It's long since I heard from you. You are several letters in my debt and I claim my eight. Our second October mail has reached Barbados we know 10 days ago, but we are yet ignorant of its intelligence or its contents. Perhaps it may be the bearer of news from you.

We are all well as yet thank God, although we have had and still continue to have a season more than usually mortal for cadues,[1] of whom a number have been removed. Yesterday I performed the last duties to a very old friend and acquaintance whom I sincerely regret, John McDonnald,[2] who was educated in his youth at Manson's school[3] in Belfast and has been my intimate friend and that of the family for the last 10 years uninterruptedly. He died of a bilious fever which degenerated on the 5th day into the putrid yellow fever and baffled all our endeavours to save him, though he had the best of constitutions, not having been ailing before for 9 years, though exposed to all the

---

1 The precise meaning of this word is unclear, though the context would suggest it refers to Europeans resident in the West Indies. 2 Possibly James McDonnald who had been involved, as master of the *Matty*, in the Belfast–Jamaica trade in the early 1790s. *BNL*, 26 Nov. 1790. 3 David Manson (1726–92), 'the best-known educationalist in eighteenth-century Ulster', settled in Belfast in 1752 and opened a school three years later, in 1755. Central to his educational philosophy was the rejection of corporal punishment and the employment of games and exercise. Adams, *Printed word*, pp 17–19 (17 for quote); Barnard, 'Educating', pp 121–2; *DIB*, vi, 352–3.

fatigue and misery of a West India planter settling a new estate out of the forest. The enclosed letter for his sisters Elizabeth and Mary Ann McDonnald, wives of Mr Pusham and of Mr Fawcet, communicates to them the disposition of his will and as he could not point out precisely the place of their residence, but said it was in the neighbourhood of Bangor or of Newtown Ards,[4] I address it under cover to you that you may have it safely delivered, and I wish you to inform me what sort of people those are and of what class in life. £3,000 sterling is a pretty wind fall to most people, but to those who have been dragging through the world with hardship and difficulty it will be a great blessing. It may be in time much more, if West India property ever rises again, but I confess I despair of it.

I have a very late letter from Graves via Caracas; they were then all well and Mariquite nearly ready to lie in. She has had an attack of fever with serious symptoms, but a general eruption in the skin carried it off, without its returning. The island is uncommonly healthful. The regiment has only buried 3 men in 12 months and no officers. The children were as well as possible; how fortunate for them since they were condemned to exile to have come to so good a climate.[5]

The American embargo deprives us of news from Esther.[6] Congress are now sitting and debating about taking it off. In the meantime the New England states have lost patience and are proceeding to sea with their exports in spite of custom house officers, gun boats and all the president's array of Mars.[7] We have a schooner this morning from New Bedford[8] laded with fish,

4 Towns in Co. Down. Located north-east of Belfast, on the southern shore of Belfast Lough, Bangor was 'antiently famous for its abbey' and later developed as a resort town. The market-town of 'Newtown Ards' (Newtownards) lay some 4 or 5 miles south-west of Bangor (and 8 miles east of Belfast). It, too, was 'celebrated from a very early period for the number of religious foundations in its immediate neighbourhood' and, by the mid-nineteenth century, comprised 'one spacious square with several wide streets and others of inferior character, and … about 1300 houses, many of which are handsomely built'. Philip Luckombe, *A tour through Ireland; wherein the present state of that kingdom is considered* (London, 1780), pp 346–7; Samuel Lewis, *A topographical dictionary of Ireland*, 2nd ed. (2 vols, London, 1840), ii, 434–5; Jonathan Bardon, *A history of Ulster* (Dundonald, 1992), p. 398.   5 Genealogical sources suggest that Mariquite and her husband had six sons (Thomas Cockburn, James William, John Crosbie, William Henry, Robert Stannus and Alexander Hope) and seven daughters (Clotilda Bona, Anna Victoria, Emily Georgiana, Francis Charlotte, Mary Arabella, Annabella and Josephine Lacoste). Precise dates of birth are unknown. 'Marie Victoire Black F, #284502', available at http://www.thepeerage. com/p28451.htm#i284502 (accessed 7/8/2018); Burke, *Landed gentry*, p. 275.   6 With American shipping subject to hostile attention from Britain and France, the American government prohibited foreign trade in 1807 in a bid to safeguard the neutrality of the United States. The embargo lasted until 1809, but was widely resented and flouted. Davis and Mintz, *Boisterous sea*, pp 209–302.   7 i.e., war. The military and navy were employed in order to uphold the embargo. Davis and Mintz, *Boisterous sea*, p. 302.   8 A town in Massachusetts. On 23 August 1808 a town meeting in New Bedford voted to petition the

flour, rice, tobacco and other notions as they call it, which came to a good market, if he can obtain entry, but this cannot be for some of his articles.

You may suppose I am impatient to know if my cousin F.T.[9] is inclined to assist me in the way I pointed out; if not *patientia!*[10]

Our trade with the provinces within the captain generalship of Caracas goes on briskly, they take off great quantities of goods by contraband, which the heavy duties they levy, on what they call a free trade, encourages. These amount to 15 ½ inwards and 12 ½ outwards *ad valorem*[11] but these valuations are so moderate that the duties do not really exceed 25 per cent in all.

The British and German goods are there in great demand and articles of every species of our manufacture find a ready sale at a great advance. A merchant of my acquaintance at Caracas has sent me a very comprehensive list which I'll endeavour to translate and send you a copy of, for the information of your commercial friends.

This goes by a brig for Glasgow (Mr Eccles')[12] and if I can find leisure I'll add to it a few lines for Adele, if not I will by a ship for London to sail the 5th, in the mean time I embrace her. With my love to my dear sisters and all the little ones round the ingle (for when this gets to you it will be fiercely cold) and wishing a merry Xmas and many happy New Years I am ever your brother who loves you

JB

president 'requesting that the existing embargo be repealed or suspended, in whole or in part', and that same year the town's collector was removed as a result of his laxity in upholding the embargo. Walter H.B. Remington, 'New Bedford in the beginning' in *Old Dartmouth Historical Sketch*, 49 (1920), available at https://www.whalingmuseum.org/explore/library/publications/old-dartmouth-historical-sketches/odhs-no-49 (accessed 8/8/2018); Walter Wilson Jennings, *The American embargo 1807–1809: with particular reference to its effect on industry* (Iowa, 1921), p. 117.   **9** i.e., Frank Turnly, Black's cousin.   **10** i.e., patience.   **11** i.e., 'according to the value'. *Black's*, p. 57.   **12** Most likely a reference to Robert Eccles of Glasgow, or to one of his brothers. The family is known to have had extensive links with the West Indies, and with Trinidad in particular. Robert Eccles, and his brothers James and Thomas, were shareholders in 'Robert Eccles and Co., West India merchants', and following the abolition of slavery a William Eccles was awarded compensation in relation to the freeing of the enslaved on six Trinidadian properties. In letter sixteen, Black refers to Robert Eccles and Co. as 'very old friends of ours'. Letter sixteen; 'William Eccles, profiles and legacies summary', available at https://www.ucl.ac.uk/lbs/person/view/7555 (accessed 8/8/2018); Devine, 'Business élite', p. 59; Stephen Mullen, 'John Lamont of Benmore: a highland planter who died "in harness" in Trinidad' in *Northern Scotland*, 9 (2018), 44–66 at 48, 49.

Letter Sixteen

In letter sixteen, dated 26 April 1809, Black is chiefly concerned with making plans for his daughter Adele's return to Trinidad from Belfast. Having first mentioned this in letter ten, where he noted that '[t]he time is coming round when Adele must think of returning to papa', he here discusses the practicalities of her return and expresses his preference that she travel by the Louisa, *a ship owned by the Glasgow partnership of Robert Eccles and Co., 'who are very old friends of ours'. Letter sixteen also reveals that Black's attempts to secure an interest in Trinidad's port collectorship had failed, hints that his complicated dealings with Belfast creditors might be concluded 'on generous terms' and contains a lengthy complaint about the wetness of the season in Trinidad and a gloomy prediction that 'our crop will be a wretched one'. A reference to Mariquite and James Graves indicates that the latter had been promoted and was now in Jamaica.*

Wednesday 26 April 1809

My dear brother

Park brought me yours of 10 January with its enclosure. What cannot be cured must be endured.[1] If the Turnlys can't serve me, I must be content to struggle through as well as I can, the journey is almost over and the worst part of the road past, at least I hope so.

I have Adele's return home much in mind, Esther I expect in the course of the year from New York, and I wish to see us all together once more. Mrs B's health is not of the best, she is at that time of life when her constitution must undergo a change for the better or worse. If she weathers that period, she may long survive it, but I am not without apprehensions.

Mr Cachard's stay will I fear be protracted here much longer than I had some weeks ago reason to expect.[2] Law is a bottomless pit and those who engage in it never know how or when it will end so that I fear we must relinquish the hopes we had entertained of getting Adele out with that family.

---

1 A saying dating, in English, from at least the late fourteenth century, when it appeared in William Langland's *Piers Plowman*. Apperson, Manser and Curtis, *Dictionary of proverbs*, p. 124.   2 Possibly Francis Cachard, who had married Caroline Devenish in Liverpool in 1806. Devenish's father appears to have been James Devenish, an Irish planter who had moved to Trinidad from Grenada *c.*1784, and whose estate, 'Peru', was one among the island's earliest sugar plantations. In all likelihood, the 'Mr Cachard' referred to here is the same as the 'gentleman of the [name] of Cacharde' that Black's daughter Adele refers to in appendix, letter two. 'Caroline Cachard: profile & legacies summary', available at https://www.ucl. ac.uk/lbs/person/view/29845 (accessed, 10/09/2018); de Verteuil, *Sylvester Devenish*, pp 10–11.

I have two other modes of conveyance which would accommodate well could she be conveniently transported to London or to Glasgow. At the former Mr Joseph Marryat[3] would receive and forward her by one of his own ships, under the care of some family coming out of which there are frequently examples, at the latter the house of Robert Eccles and Co. who are very old friends or ours and to whom she was known in her infancy, particularly to Miss Eccles. These gentleman have two and will henceforward have 3 ships on this trade which are continually going and coming and generally make each 3 voyages in the 12 months. The *Louisa*, [Captain] Reid of 300 tons, as fine a ship as ever was built and as well commanded, arrived here yesterday from Greenock having been only 92 days absent. The *Fame* sails this day for Greenock (and carries this letter)[4] and they have a new ship ready for launching at home which will be here in 6 weeks or two months, so that you see opportunities from thence are never wanted for this island. For besides these, there are a dozen more of the same description on the trade which are as expeditious as Mr Eccles'. Of all those however I would prefer the *Louisa* both on account of the ship and on account of the man with whom I would have no objection to her coming out even without a family, provided a good discreet woman servant could be procured to attend her. If she likes the climate she can remain. If not I'll send her home again by the same road, scot-free.

In London she would be well received by Mr Marryat (who is the son of an odd sort of a doctor[5] who was in Belfast in my time very intimate in our uncle Legg's[6] family) and she is or was a great favourite of General Picton who is Marryat's friend and is always at his house. The general would protect and take care of her as well as anybody.

3 An absentee slave-owner with extensive business interests, Joseph Marryat (1757–1824) was, from 1805, Trinidad's Westminster agent. He upheld the interests of planters such as Black and served as MP for Horsham from 1808 to 1812 and for Sandwich from 1812 to 1824. His children included the writer Frederick 'Captain' Marryat (1792–1848). *ODNB* (Joseph Marryat), (Frederick Marryat).   4 A note on the rear of the letter indicates that it was, in fact, sent 'by the *Louisa* to Greenock'.   5 Joseph Marryat's father was Thomas Marryat (1730–92), a one-time Presbyterian minister who abandoned the ministry and devoted himself to medicine in 1760. A Londoner by birth, he spent the period *c*.1766–74 in Ulster, where, the *Oxford dictionary of national biography* records, 'he set aside two hours every day to non-paying patients, allowing him to test his medicines on them'. That 'he tended to administer enormous doses of drastic medicine regardless of the patients constitution' might perhaps account for Black's description of him as 'an odd sort of a doctor'. *ODNB* (Thomas Marryat).   6 The Leggs/Legges were a long established Belfast family. The uncle referred to by Black was possibly the Belfast merchant Benjamin Legg (d. 1760), Legg's wife was a 'Miss Wilson of Purdy's Burn', and Black's mother, Arminella Black was related to the Purdysburn Wilsons (see letter four, note 33). There were, however, other links between the Blacks and the Leggs. A sister of Jane Black née Eccles, wife of John Black II (1647–1726), Black's great-grandfather, was married to a Legg, and the paternal grandmother of Ellen Black née Stewart, wife of George Black Jr, was a Legg. Benn, *Belfast*, pp 266–8, 334; Benn, *Belfast from 1799 till 1810*, pp 164–6, 198–201; Ward, 'Black family', 186–8; Riddell, 'Great chemist', 64–70.

The *Louisa* will leave this again in about a month at farthest and you would find her at home about 1 July. If you could manage matters so as to have her in Glasgow about that time it would be an excellent opportunity and a fine time of year to come out. If it were possible I would wish Adele to see the old seat at Ballintaggart ere' she comes out, that she may give me a pastoral account of it; I would like also that she had a peep at Dublin etc. but I fear you are so sedentary a man that there are little hopes of her travelling.

Park has brought out powers from Mr Tomb[7] to settle the old business on generous terms I think all things considered and you may depend in my using every exertion to accomplish them. I don't want inclination. My yearning to revisit my native soil is perpetual and unabated, but this country has always difficulties to combat with that seem peculiar to itself.

Produce has looked up and, since Ireland has been comprehended in the distilling bill, looks still higher.[8] But our crop will be a wretched one. We have not an half off and the hyronage or rainy season has set in with violence since the 3^d instant; a period early beyond example. Our seasons here are divided here [*sic*] into wet and dry. Not into hot and cold, for our winter is our hottest weather. Our dry season begins at Christmas and should end in May. But this year we have not had 8 days dry weather successively since Christmas. On the principle of long foul long fair,[9] we expected a protraction of the usual period of the rain setting in; but to our great grief and astonishment, they set in on the 3 April with a thunder storm and until yesterday continued with increased violence in so much that our rivers have been flooded, our roads rendered impassable and the low lands in many place inundated. I have little better than one third of our canes cut, for I had been going on *poco a poco*,[10] to keep our stock in heart, always in hopes of the weather getting into its usual temperature, but disappointments are and ever will be I fear the order of the day in this ill-fated country. Wet day or dry day however, we must put our shoulders to the wheels and work through for there is no leaving 150 [–] sugar in the field when the prices are so encouraging. Therefore we must make hay although the sun does not shine.

I received letters yesterday from Caracas by which I find that Graves is at Jamaica whither he has been removed as I expected in consequence of the

7 See letter fourteen. 8 The previous June, following lobbying from the London Society of West India Planters and Merchants and parliamentary investigation and debate, the 48 Geo. III, c. 118, 'An Act to prohibit the Distillation of Spirits from Corn or Grain, for a limited Time', had been passed. It was hoped that this act, which was renewed in 1809, would stimulate the use of sugar in distillation and, in so doing, create a market for surplus sugar supplies. Ryden, 'Sugar, spirits, and fodder', pp 42, 52, 54–5, 62; Lowell Joseph Ragatz, *The fall of the planter class in the British Caribbean, 1763–1833: a study in social and economic history* (New York, 1928), p. 319. 9 A proverb, possibly of Scottish origin, also current in North America. James Kelly, *A complete collection of Scottish proverbs explained and made intelligible to the English reader* (London, 1818), p. 43; Whiting, *Early American proverbs*, p. 143. 10 i.e., little by little.

death of Lieutenant Colonel Honeyman.[11] He left Curaçao in February since which I have no letters from him. It's a good move for him because his appointments and situation at Jamaica will be much superior to what he had at Curaçao, to say nothing of the [–] which is in high vogue at Jamaica and Graves is a knowing one.

You neglected to inform me what class or description of people Mrs Pusham and Mrs Fawcet are, for whom I sent you letters which they received and have answered. They appear by their correspondence to be of the middling sort, they are not the less heiresses to a handsome property which I expect will be out of debt in a year or two more and then they may sell it very advantageously which should be their object.

West India properties thrive only under the eye of the master; I never knew one that did not suffer by his absence and many a one ruined by it.

Adele must be very alert in learning anything she requires to know before she leaves Ireland. Except with respect to music and dancing, she will have few opportunities of improvement here. I could have wished much she had met with an occasion to attend one or two sets of lectures on natural and experimental philosophy. Those serve to open the mind and inspire it with an idea of the omnipotence of the creator more than all the studies of books that contemplation can afford.

I would wish her also to be well supplied in linen, that is a profusion of shifts. It is a very costly article of apparel with us. All the rest we can obtain here almost as cheap as at home.

It will be a trying moment both for you and for her to separate, but you must not despair of meeting again. It shall be if I can by any means accomplish it.

I hope my good and dear sister[12] is by this time safely delivered of her burthen and that she and the stranger and George and all the family are as well as we wish them.[13] Give my love to the Ballydrain family and to Esther and all her [–].

I am always my dear George

Your loving brother

John

Pray who is my sister's sister Davy Park saw at your house? Is it my dear little Mary that I used to carry about [on] my shoulder at Ballydrain?[14]

11 Lieutenant-Colonel Robert Honyman, who had commanded the 1st battalion of the 18th Royal Irish Regiment, had died in Jamaica from 'the fever of the country' in November 1808. James Graves joined the 1st battalion in March 1809. *GM*, 79 (1809), 182; *RMC*, v, 161.   12 i.e., Ellen Black née Stewart, Black's sister-in-law.   13 George Black Jr and Ellen Black née Stewart had two sons, George Macartney Black (1802–57) and John Black (1811–68), and at least three daughters, whose dates of birth are unknown: Mary Isabella, Ellen and Letitia Adelaide. *BNL*, 18 Feb. and 7 Aug. 1825, 18 Apr. 1838; Ward, 'Black family', 188.   14 Possibly Mary Clarke née Stewart (see letter four, note 20), sister of Ellen Black née Stewart.

Letter Seventeen

As in letter sixteen, which was written just a month previously, Black's chief concern in letter seventeen is his daughter Adele's return to Trinidad. He here raises the possibility that she might travel, in convoy, with Mr de Gourville, a family friend who had spent time with Black in North America and whose daughter Fanny was, at the time of writing, living with Black and his wife in Trinidad, though he reiterates his preference that she travel by the Louisa *in the event that this should prove impossible. In addition, Black makes reference to the anticipated return from America of his daughter Esther. Thus letter seventeen raises the possibility of a family reunion of sorts and it is clear that Black is keen that, with the exception of Mariquite Graves, 'we shall be united once more'. The letter's content is not, however, universally positive: returning to the subject of the weather, Black notes that the sugar crop has been 'lost' and makes a self-pitying reference to the 'miseries of we poor sugar makers'.*

Trinidad 25 May 1809

My dear brother

I write by the *Louisa* Captain Reid belonging to Messrs Eccles and Co. of Glasgow, the ship by which I would prefer Adele taking her passage, and the friends to whose care I would have her consigned, if she is to come by that route. The only objection I feel to her coming by this ship is that she is armed and runs it,[1] and although she has in common with all our running ships for years run safe without encounter, still the possibility of capture would induce me to prefer her coming in convoy. *Tant va la cruche a l'eau qu 'a la fin Elle y reste*[2] and so it might be with the *Louisa*. We have in London a very intimate friend who intends coming out in convoy with his daughter in September and he knows Adele well and would take care of her as of his own child, who is Adele's contemporary.

His name is Mr de Gourville, his eldest daughter Fanny is now in the house with us. He lived with us in America and, Mrs Black and Mad[ame] De

---

1 Armed merchant vessels that did not sail in convoy were known as 'running ships'. While capable of crossing the Atlantic more swiftly than ships that sailed in convoy, they were more costly, requiring additional manpower and expenditure on weaponry. T.M. Devine, *The tobacco lords: a study of the tobacco merchants of Glasgow and their trading activities*, c.*1740–90* (Edinburgh, 1975), pp 145–6. 2 A variation on the French proverb *'tant va la cruche a l'eau, qu'à la fin elle se brise'*, i.e., 'the pitcher goes so often to the water that it is broken at last'. Wolfgang Mieder, *Proverbs: a handbook* (Westport, CT, 2004), p. 170; Whiting, *Early American proverbs*, p. 340.

Gourville (now dead) having been brought up together, the greatest intimacy has always subsisted between the families, hence we should consider Adele under Mr de Gourville's care in company with his daughter Julie as safe and protected as if with ourselves.[3] I should suppose that opportunities of some of your friends to be depended on frequently happen to London by whom Adele could be sent to Mr Marryat where she would find Mr de Gourville and General Picton. I would have her addressed direct to Mr de Gourville if I knew his number and street; but Mr Marryat who is a member of parliament will easily be found and he will either keep Adele under his own care or hand her over to Mr de Gourville if he be yet in London, for there is a possibility that he may have already embarked before this letter reaches you and then we must have recourse to the *Louisa* and take our chance.

If however she comes this last way a careful woman of 40 must be sent out with her as a servant. Captain Reid is as good a man of his kind and as confidential a one as any existing but still she will have occasion for the service of a female servant on board, for such things as it would be indelicate for a cabin boy or ship's steward to assist her in.

I think however we shall be in time for Mr de Gourville to whom I write by this occasion and also to Mr Marryat who will advise you of de Gourville's motions for your government and by them you will regulate yours accordingly.

I expect Esther from New York every minute. The lady with whom we left her there had quitted Martinique from her antipathy to the code Napoleon but, the island now being ours, she is on her way out and brings Esther with her.[4] So we shall be united once more. Mariquite excepted, who is now removed to Jamaica, the metropolis of the West Indies.

We are literally submerged. It has rained since the 3 April incessantly. Our crop is lost. Our roads impassable. Our rivers flooded and the sugar market at home from the capture of Martinique and the Swedish revolution reduced to its former ebb.[5] When and where will the miseries of we poor sugar makers end?

3 'Mr de Gourville' was, in fact, the Chevalier Dupont du Vivier de Gourville, who had travelled from Trinidad to London on Governor Picton's behalf several years earlier. His daughter Julie was married to 'Count S. du Bourblanc' shortly after this letter was written. *GM*, 79 (1809), 676; Joseph, *Trinidad*, i, 141; Naipaul, *El Dorado*, pp 155–6, 185, 259. 4 Having held the French island of Martinique between 1794 and 1802, the British recaptured it again in 1809 and held it until 1814. The lady in question, Madame de Malleveault (see letter thirteen, note 15, and letter eighteen), was by no means alone in her dislike of Napoleonic rule. As Flavio Eichmann has demonstrated, the *grand blancs* of Martinique – that is, its planter elite – 'saw Napoleon as a usurper on the French throne' and frustrated attempts to implement his innovations and reforms. Henige, *Colonial governors*, p. 43; Flavio Eichmann, 'Local cooperation in a subversive colony: Martinique, 1802–1809' in Tanja Bührer, Flavio Eichmann, Stig Förster and Benedikt Stuchtey (eds), *Cooperation and empire: local realities of global processes* (New York, 2017), pp 115–43 at 117, 124–5, 127–8. 5 Among planters and their allies, the capture of Martinique raised fears that Britain's

If Adele comes out via London I shall order Mr Marryat to supply her wants and furnish her with a piano forte which I suppose will be acceptable. In other respects, particularly in linen, coming from the fountain head[6] I hope she is well provided.

With my love to Ellen, the children, the fireside, Adele, Ballydrain and all Esther's interest, I remain my dear brother
Yours most affectionately
John

already over-supplied market would be further swamped with sugar. Legislation was passed to prevent this, though the Trinidad agent Joseph Marryat (see letter sixteen, note 3) opposed it, as David Beck Ryden has explained, on the grounds that 'it did not matter whether or not British sugar could be sold in British markets, given that it would be added to the same limited *external* market which was available to British planters'. That external market contracted still further as a consequence of events in Sweden. In 1809, the Swedish king, Gustav IV Adolf, a British ally, was deposed in favour of Charles XIII, and a new constitution was adopted. In due course, Sweden entered the continental system with which France denied Britain access to European ports. Ryden, 'Sugar, spirits and fodder', 53–4; Robert Gildea, *Barricades and borders: Europe, 1800–1914*, 2nd ed. (Oxford, 1996), pp 42–3, 51; Pasi Ihalainen and Anders Sundin, 'Continuity and change in the language of politics at the Swedish diet, 1769–18' in Pasi Ihalainen, Michael Bregnsbo, Karin Sennefelt and Patrik Winton (eds), *Scandinavia in the age of revolution: Nordic political cultures, 1740–1820* (Abingdon, 2016), pp 169–92 at 182. 6 i.e., coming from the north-east of Ireland, where the production of linen was a major industry. See letter ten, note 4.

Letter Eighteen

Announcing Adele Black's return to Trinidad, letter eighteen, dated 6 January 1810, marks something of an end point in Black's correspondence, for although two further letters survive, these date to 1836 and letter eighteen is the last of the main body of letters. It conveys Black's pleasure in Adele's 'talent, accomplishment ... [and] amiability of disposition'; clearly, her sojourn in Belfast had been a success, and Black's sense of gratitude towards George Black Jr, who had welcomed her into his family, is evident. Requesting a statement of Adele's 'expenses', in order that he might reimburse them, Black urges that this be sent promptly, informing his brother that 'it's enough to be under the weight of such signal services as you have rendered me in the raising and improving my child without adding to it pecuniary ones.' The letter also contains details of the movements of Black's youngest daughter Esther, who had not yet returned to Trinidad, but had travelled to Martinique and was expected in a matter of days, and reference to gifts – 'walking sticks, of our beautiful leopard wood', 'birds and other curiosities' and two 'monkey throttles' for Mary Clark, who suffered from asthma – that were being sent back to Belfast. There is reference, too, to public affairs, with Black discussing the anticipated British assault on Guadeloupe, and a telling passage in which Black appears to acknowledge that his longed for return to Belfast would not take place and that Trinidad had, in fact, become 'home'.

---

6 January 1810, Saturday

My dear brother

I write by the *Louisa* and compute that before now you have received our letters advising Adele's arrival with us and how happy we were made by that event. No incident has yet happened thank God to give us uneasiness. Her *embonpoint*[1] at first made me very apprehensive but by bleeding, physicking and boiling in tepid baths, we soon lowered her to the temperature of the climate and she has enjoyed uninterrupted good health. We had indeed the creole stuff to work upon; Mary[2] has been treated in the same manner and has not as yet had her acclimating fever, but I am under no fear for her when it comes, we have taken so many and so proper precautions.

Esther arrived at Martinique with Madame de Malleveault on the 20 November, so you see I had managed well to bring them home nearly at the same time.[3] Want of a proper opportunity has detained her longer than I expected, but this instant I have received a letter to announce her departure

---

1 i.e., plumpness.   2 Most likely a servant that had accompanied Adele on her journey from Ireland, Black having earlier requested that 'a careful woman of 40 must be sent out with her as a servant'. See letter seventeen.   3 See letter thirteen, note 15.

from Martinique this day and I hope to receive her on Monday in time for a ball in the style of a lord mayor's feast, to be given on that evening by our chief judge,[4] at which there will be upwards of 400 persons of all classes at least, so many are invited. Adele is very much admired and beloved by all our friends and acquaintances and there does not a day pass without our discovering some new talent, accomplishment or amiability of disposition to render her if possible more and more dear to us.

It was but yesterday we found out that she is an excellent pastry cook, and tomorrow being Sunday, she is to give us a dinner of her own ordering. French cooks are terrible bad hands at making puddings of any description, especially plumb puddings; our old cook has conducted our kitchen this 5 and 20 years, and most of that time he has been drunk or nearly so, but Adele has undertaken to reform him and she says she will make him a good pastry and pudding cook yet. In short there is nothing in the domestic way that she is not ready to undertake and she acquits herself very well. Aunt Black taught her to do everything that appertains to housewivery and Uncle Black to ride Puff and she is an excellent horsewoman, a qualification she is not very likely to forget, for not a day passes that she is not either riding or driving the chaise, but the former seems to be her forte.

She has sent a box by the *Louisa* containing some very nice stuffed birds for the darling George,[5] for so she always calls him, and I have sent a small case containing two walking sticks, of our beautiful leopard wood,[6] called by the Spaniards *gatiado* or catted wood, from the shades which resemble the skin of a tabby cat. One is for my good brother in law John Younghusband, marked on the gold head J.Y., the other for yourself marked G.B. in cyphers. The heads or pommels are very elegant, done by a goldsmith here, the ferrules are silver. Both cases go under Captain Reid's particular care and will be forwarded by the first good occasion after his arrival either by him or the Eccles.

---

4 George Smith, who had earlier served as chief justice in Grenada, was appointed as chief justice of Trinidad in 1808. He arrived on the island in May 1809 and left under a cloud in 1811, having fallen out with both the governor, Thomas Hislop, and the island's so-called 'English Party', which sought the introduction of English laws – as Epstein notes, Smith believed that 'the British constitution was incompatible with the institution of slavery'. Although English, Smith had Irish connections. He knew the Belfast reformer William Drennan (1754–1820) and, prior to his appointment as chief justice of Grenada in 1805, his wife had abandoned him for the former United Irishman Roger O'Connor (1763–1834), brother of the better-known United Irish leader Arthur O'Connor (1763–1852), and father of the Chartist Fergus O'Connor (*c.*1796–1855). *DIB*, iii, 461–3, and vii, 226–9, 275–7, 245–8; *DML*, iii, 720, 722; Carmichael, *Trinidad and Tobago*, pp 86–93; Epstein, *Scandal*, p. 273. 5 i.e., George Macartney Black, son of George Black Jr. 6 In his nineteenth-century history of Trinidad, E.L. Joseph described the leopard wood as a 'hard but small tree', of which only the central core – 'about one third as thick as the whole trunk' – was of value. 'This heart', he noted, 'when polished, is a dark red or chocolate colour, spotted most beautifully with black, like a leopard.' Joseph, *Trinidad*, p. 80.

In the box with the birds and other curiosities will be found two monkey throttles which are considered in this country as a certain cure for the asthma with which Adele says Mary Clark is afflicted.[7] The manner of using them is simple enough. The patient must always drink water out of it, and to keep it fresh and clean those who use them generally keep them floating in the water pot. I have certainly seen the good effects of this remedy in several instances here, particularly in the family of Mr Begorrat[8] an intimate friend of ours, whose daughter Rosie was very subject to attacks of the asthma on any sudden changes of the weather or being exposed to cold, but since she has used the monkey throttle by drinking water out of it, she has never had a return of the complaint. It is proper I should describe what this monkey throttle is however. We have here a very large species of the monkey tribe which is the colour of dirty red hair with which he is covered.[9] In the throat immediately beneath the under jaw he is provided with this excrescence which communicates with the wind pipe and gives him the appearance of a native of Chamouni with his *goitres*.[10] I know of no use he makes of it except to make a very loud and hollow noise, which at some distance would be mistaken by a stranger for the bellowing of an enraged bull, and this noise our forests echo with every morning at day light (especially in cold raw mornings) from thousands of those animals, always collected on the summit of the highest trees. You can have no

7 Possibly Mary Clarke née Stewart (see letter four, note 20), sister of Ellen Black née Stewart, or one of her children.   8 Begorrat was St Hillaire Begorrat, in James Millette's words 'one of the pillars of Trinidad society'. Born in Martinique, he settled in Trinidad in 1784 and possibly introduced Tahiti sugar cane to the island. Like Black, Begorrat had been close to governor Picton. Indeed, Epstein suggests that he and Picton 'formed a fast and lasting friendship based on ties of mutual dependency'. Millette, *Society and politics*, p. 45; Brereton, *Modern Trinidad*, p. 17; Epstein, *Scandal*, pp 104–6. See also, for Begorrat's relationship with Picton, Candlin, *Last Caribbean frontier*, pp 75–95.   9 Black is here describing the red howler monkey, one of the distinguishing features of which is a large hyoid bone. The use of this bone in the treatment of asthma appears to have derived from indigenous South American practice. Thus, in an article on South American medical science, published in the *Philadelphia Journal of Homoeopathy* in 1855, C.W. Brink noted that 'there are some tribes who believe that water drank from the hyoid bone of the howling monkey cures asthma'. Winer, *Dictionary*, p. 755; C.W. Brink, 'A paper on the state of medical science in South America' in the *Philadelphia Journal of Homoeopathy*, 4 (1855), 358–75 at 361.   10 Chamouni, an Alpine valley, overlooked by Mont Blanc and much praised in the early nineteenth century, had become known as a result of the travels, during the 1740s, of Richard Pococke (1704–65), future bishop of Ossory, and William Windham (1717–61). Alongside 'cretinism', *goître* – 'a swelling in the front of the neck (of the thyroid gland, or the parts adjoining)' – was a condition associated particularly with the Alpine valleys. Thomas Raffles, *Letters, during a tour through some parts of France, Savoy, Switzerland, Germany, and the Netherlands, in the summer of 1817* (Liverpool, 1818), pp 226–7; Mariana Starke, *Information and directions for travellers on the continent*, 6th ed. (London, 1828), p. 37; *A handbook for travellers in Switzerland and the Alps of Savoy and Piedmont* (London, 1858), lxi–lxii; *ODNB* (Richard Pococke), (William Windham).

idea of the peal of roaring they set up. The roar of a lion enraged by the pursuit of his hunters cannot exceed it.[11]

I state this to show that the cup, though not very elegant, is cleanly and that no repugnance may be shown by Mary to use it. The monkey is graniverous and lives entirely on fruits, which the forest furnishes him.

I hope my brother Younghusband will be gratified by this mark of my reconnaissance for all the kindness and attention he showed Adele, both him, my sister and the Harrisons. Indeed the goodness of all my friends to her is her continual theme. She speaks of you all with a sensibility that I am sure proceeds from her heart, a heart warm with affection and refined by the purest sentiments of her inviolable regard for you all. It would be to me the perfection of happiness, to conduct her back to you, never more to be separated; but alas!, where the goat is tied, there he must browse,[12] thanks to Mr Wilberforce and his proselytes, he has consigned all the poor West Indians to live at home. We are on the eve of another addition to our sugar colonies to increase our supplies and help us poor dogs over the style. The navy and army are assembled at Prince Rupert's Bay Dominica to attach Guadalupe and a brig of war has come for our Governor Hislop who is to command a division as major general.[13] They will leave Dominica the 15th at night, land the 16th in the morning and I fancy the business will soon be settled. We shall have 8,000 men besides the navy lads who in expeditions where dispatch is necessary are superior to soldiers and equal to bear more fatigue. There will be some hot work there however. Ernouf is a desperate fellow.[14] He has abandoned all his sea side ports and fortresses and taken fort in the high lands of the Cabes Terre whence it will cost labour to expel him.[15] But it will be done, in the end. General Carmichael has come up from Jamaica to have a share of the glory.[16] I have not

11 In his *History of Trinidad*, Joseph echoes Black's description of the howler monkeys' 'bellowing', explaining that this monkey 'has two pouches under his chin; these he compresses when he wishes to bawl, and I believe this aids his lugubrious and discordant howl. When a number of these animals set up their cries, which they generally do before rain falls in the woods, the sense of hearing becomes a misfortune to those who are within half a mile of them.' Joseph, *Trinidad*, p. 37. 12 A French proverb, dating to at least the early seventeenth century. Richard Chenevix Trench, *Proverbs and their lessons: being the substance of lectures delivered to young men's societies at Portsmouth and elsewhere*, 5th ed. (London, 1861), p. 84; Apperson, Manser and Curtis, *Proverbs*, p. 233. 13 The French colony of Guadeloupe was captured by Britain in February 1810, and held until 1814; George Beckwith (see letter fourteen, note 7) led the British forces, with Hislop (see letter twelve, note 5) given command of the first division. *ODNB* (George Beckwith), (Thomas Hislop). 14 'Ernouf' was Manuel Louis Jean Augustin Ernouf, governor of Guadeloupe from 1803 to 1810. Henige, *Colonial governors*, p. 36. 15 Cabes Terre appears to be a reference to territory located in the west of Basse Terre, Guadeloupe's mountainous, western island. *The North American and the West Indian gazetteer*, 2nd ed. (London, 1778), unpaginated (entry for Guadeloupe); George Long (ed.), *The geography of America, and the West Indies* (London, 1841), p. 35. 16 Major-General Hugh Lyle Carmichael (1764–1813) had been commander-in-chief in Jamaica, but had left the island in 1809, following a dispute with its

heard a word from Graves since he has been in Jamaica, but I have reason to believe they are all well. It is possible Carmichael may have letters for me, but they have not yet reached me. The 18th were employed at the reduction of Santo Domingo and Graves was with them,[17] but he never wrote me from thence on the subject, though the opportunities between Santo Domingo and the Windward Islands are frequent, so far as St Thomas.[18]

You promised in your letters by Adele to send me on your return home an account of her expenses and of what I may remain in your debt. Pray don't delay sending it, for it's enough to be under the weight of such signal services as you have rendered me in the raising and improving my child without adding to it pecuniary ones.

The *Louisa* is sheeting home her topsails, I have not time to extend, but I entreat you will assure my good dear sisters, and their progeny of the tenderness of my affection for them and its inviolability, would to God I could have the happiness of telling them so in person.

My dear George, your ever loving brother

John

Pray who is Mrs Seton, a relation of our governor who Adele speaks of?

It will be good to wash the monkey throttles out, with a strong lixivium of lime to make them white and nice.

---

assembly. Carmichael had earlier served, close to Trinidad, on Tobago. He was governor of the island in 1802, and had been present in 1801, in which year he helped prevent a rebellion of the enslaved by staging executions. As Gertrude Carmichael relates: 'when he learned of the plot, [he] seized thirty of the ringleaders. One of these he ordered to be hanged on the signal staff and raised and lowered the body twenty-nine times. This sight, witnessed by the insurgents from a distance, decided them to surrender or disperse immediately.' In 1812, a year before his death, Carmichael was appointed lieutenant-governor of Demerara and Essequibo, former Dutch colonies which the British had taken in 1803; a memorial in Cathedral Church, George Town records that he 'departed this life during his government'. Henige, *Colonial governors*, pp 98, 179–80; Carmichael, *Trinidad and Tobago*, pp 308–9, 434; Roger N. Buckley, 'The admission of slave testimony at British military courts in the West Indies, 1800–1809' in David Barry Gaspar and David Patrick Geggus (eds), *A turbulent time: the French Revolution and the greater Caribbean* (Bloomington, IN, 1997), pp 226–50 at 229, 242; *Monumental inscriptions of the British West Indies from the earliest date … chiefly collected on the spot by Captain J.H. Lawrence-Archer* (London, 1875), pp 424–5. 17 The Spanish colony of Santo Domingo bordered French St Domingue/Haiti. During the early 1800s, conflict in Haiti spread to Santo Domingo, which was invaded by Haitian troops and subsequently occupied by French forces who stayed when finally driven out of Haiti in 1803. Spain recaptured the territory with British assistance in 1809; the 18th Royal Irish Regiment were deployed but saw little action, leading a later regiment historian to conclude that 'the expedition to San Domingo cannot be counted as a campaign'. Henige, *Colonial governors*, p. 336; Eakin, *Latin America*, pp 198–9; G. Le M. Gretton, *The campaigns and history of the Royal Irish Regiment from 1684 to 1902* (Edinburgh, 1911), pp 117–19. 18 St Thomas was a Danish colony held by Britain between 1801 and 1802, and between 1807 and 1815 – as were the other two Danish West Indian islands, St John and St Croix. Henige, *Colonial governors*, p. 10.

Letter Nineteen

Written on 10 January 1836, twenty-six years after letter eighteen, letter nineteen is one of two later surviving letters. Referring, as it does, to a previous letter received from George Black Jr, and to other family letters, which had been received by the December and January mails, it indicates that Black had remained in contact with his family during the period 1810–36. In terms of content, the letter is concerned chiefly with family affairs, with Black, now a grandfather, offering news of his daughters and grandchildren, and responding to the news he himself received of the wider Black family.

10 January 1836

My dear brother

The second January mail has brought me your agreeable letter of the 23rd of November. I have also letters from George[1] by her of the first of December. The report you make of your family with the exception of Mrs Black of whom you are silent is very acceptable, and I hope you will always be able to continue it; except the painful loss we sustained by the death of my grandson, we have had no alteration of late, that however was a very sensible one, he was a valuable young man and promised to be a great acquisition.[2] At present we are all well thank God. Mrs B carries her age in good health and spirits, notwithstanding our being reduced in number to three persons (Miss Stewart has been reared by us since her infancy and never knew any other parents) the rest except Adele being dispersed.[3]

We are now looking daily for Mr Shine,[4] the physicians had recommended him to come out to avoid the severity of the winter. I wish that may be the true cause; I suspect it is not and that, his complaint being out of their reach, they have prescribed his coming to this warm climate as his only physician. He must be now in the West India latitudes and we shall soon see him. Adele and the family are all perfectly well and a fine family they are. Cloe the second eldest is a young lady of fine figure, superior education and abilities. Jane the eldest is married[5] and now ready to lie in of her second child, George

1 Most likely George Macartney Black, son of George Black Jr. 2 The identity of the grandson referred to here is unknown. 3 i.e., the rest of his family. 4 John Shine (1777–1837). Originally from Cork, Shine had settled in Trinidad in 1804, and married Black's daughter Adele in February 1811. Letter twenty; appendix, letters one, two and four; Pocock, *Shadows*, pp 212, 215; [Anon.], 'Further extracts', 210. 5 Jane Shine's husband was Henry Murphy, 'a man devoted to commercial pursuits'. Like John Shine (see note 4), he was originally from Cork. Letter twenty; Carlos E. Finlay (ed. Morton C. Kahn), *Carlos*

and Adelina,[6] one of 10 the other 7 years, are as fine children as ever the sun shone upon and taking the whole together there cannot exist a finer family. I wish Shine may live to enjoy them.

We have not had for some time any letters from Philadelphia. My poor Esther Neilson has had another miscarriage and nearly lost her life, but by the latest advices she was in a fair way of recovery.[7] My Josefine fortunately was with her and I am not without hopes that William Neilson (who must be now convinced that the American climate will never agree with Esther) will decide upon removing to Trinidad and then at least I shall have the satisfaction of having a part of the family about me, especially Josefine whose absence gives her mother and me great concern. The report you give of the <u>plantation</u> (I will call it) of your family is very enticing, they are disseminated far and near, but with the exception of John a Bordeaux all within hail, they appear <u>all</u> to be happily situated and I hope will always be so.[8] As to John I [–] not his happiness but his enjoyments at Bordeaux. I have been there and experienced them and Mr Johnston[9] will be a second John Black (my honoured uncle)[10] to him. I wish you could procure me a detail of all the family, what is become of them and where they are. What family did Mrs Barton (Peggy) leave and what became of Betty, for I suppose she is dead long ago.[11] You should allow

Finlay and yellow fever (New York, 1940), p. 18. 6 Black's comments here suggest that Adelina shine (d. 1916) was born in 1829, but a later account, by her son, gives her date of birth as 8 February 1833. Like her mother, Adelina spent a part of her childhood in Ireland – though in Cork, rather than Belfast. There she was educated in the Ursuline convent, where, according to her son, she 'received an excellent literary education in English and French, both of which she spoke perfectly, and acquired a solid foundation in the tenets of the Catholic Church, of which she was a devout member.' She later lived with her sister Jane and her husband (see note 5), and in 1865 married the Cuban-born physician Carlos Finlay (1834–1915), who discovered that yellow fever was transmitted by mosquitos. Finlay (ed. Kahn), *Carlos Finlay*, pp 1, 14–15, 18–20, 37–8. 7 Esther Neilson née Lacoste, Black's granddaughter, was the daughter Josefine Lacoste née Black and Hugh Lacoste (see letter four, note 6). She is said to have married William Neilson in Philadelphia in 1830, Neilson most likely being a son of the Trinidad merchant Robert Neilson, who himself later settled in Philadelphia. 'Esther Lacoste F, #405426', available at http://www. thepeerage.com/p40543.htm#i405426 (accessed 15/8/2018); 'Robert Neilson: Profile and Legacies Summary', available at https://www.ucl.ac.uk/lbs/person/view/44571 (accessed 15/8/2018). 8 John Black, son of George Black Jr, had gone into business as a merchant in Bordeaux. Ward, 'Black family', 188; John Black to George Black Jr, 14 Dec. 1836 (PRONI, D1950/36). 9 Most likely a reference to Nathanial Weld Johnston, an Irish châteaux owner in Bordeaux. The Johnstons were an Ulster Scots family involved prominently in the Bordeaux wine trade. *DIB*, i, 358–9; Renagh Holohan, *The Irish Châteaux: in search of descendants of the wild geese* (Dublin, 1999), pp 61–2. 10 Black's uncle, John Black IV (1717–82), was a merchant in Bordeaux. Ward, 'Black family', 187; 'Black family tree' (PRONI, D4457/363). 11 'Peggy' was Margaret/Marguerite Barton née Black (d. 1821), wife of John Barton, a Bordeaux merchant originally from Co. Fermanagh. The Bartons had connections with the Johnstons (see note 9), and were, by the late-eighteenth century, a well-established presence in Bordeaux. Indeed, as Renagh Holohan notes, they had, by

Ellen[12] [to] pass some months at Bordeaux, it would improve [her] much to her advantage; you will be astonished to see John's wife,[13] should she return to Dublin on a visit, and Ellen would reap the same advantage. You have had a wet season, so have we and it is not yet quite over. I believe we shall have a short crop; not wishing to put you to the expense of unnecessary postage I will conclude by wishing you, your wife, your children etc. all manner of happiness with uninterrupted health and with Mrs Black's blessing [I] remain ever your brother

John Black

the mid-1770s, become 'the biggest buyers and shippers of fine clarets in the region'. Peggy Barton's father was John Black IV (see note 10) and 'Betty' was most likely Eliza Bagnall née Black (b. 1751), another of his daughters. 'Black family tree' (PRONI, D4457/363); Bertram Francis Barton, *Some account of the family of Barton* (Dublin, 1902), pp 44–8; *CJB*, ii, 1085–6, 1179–80, 1435; *DIB*, i, 358–9, 364–5; Holohan, *Irish Châteaux*, pp 53–8 (56 for quote); Cullen, 'Irish merchant communities of Bordeaux, La Rochelle and Cognac', p. 55. **12** i.e., his daughter (see letter sixteen, note 13). Ellen's date of birth is unknown, but she was old enough, in April 1838, to marry Edward Harris Clarke, a barrister. *BNL*, 13 Apr. 1838. **13** The wife of John Black, son of George Black Jr, was Mary Black née Lindsey (d. 1886). Ward, 'Black family', 188.

Letter Twenty

*As with letter nineteen, Black's last surviving letter is relatively short and is con-
cerned primarily with family news, though Black makes reference also to an
unnamed friend – a 'very particular friend' – who had spent time in Trinidad and
was resident in Newry: 'should he come in your way', Black instructs his brother,
'or if in your power to be civil to him or any of his family (who are all females
and very engaging) I request you to do so.' Thus, this final letter illustrates once
more the webs of connection binding the Atlantic world. In addition, Black makes
reference to his health. He does so phlegmatically, noting that 'I continue to enjoy
my health tolerably well for my age', but makes reference also to a derangement of
the head. The precise nature and seriousness of this ailment is unclear, but, whether
serious or not, Black died within four months of writing this letter, on 6 October
1836.*

Trinidad 5 June 1836

My dear brother

Our gazette of Friday informs me that a vessel for Belfast had sailed and
as she had no letter from me (from my not being informed of any vessel
lading for Belfast), and as it may have surprised you, I avail of myself of an
occasion for Dublin to repair the error.

I continue to enjoy my health tolerably well for my age. My head is the
only member deranged. I have not any pain in it but I feel it somewhat light
when I am on my feet, but perfectly well when I lie down. I sleep well, digest
well and do all my functions well, it is only when I am perpendicular that it
annoys me, and by what I now do you can perceive I am not much afflicted.
Mrs B is also in perfect health. I have not seen her so active and intelligent
for years and as my household is composed of us two and a Miss Stewart who
I took under my care when an orphan, and [who] is like one of the family, we
don't incur the expense of a physician.

Josefine has been some time at Philadelphia taking care of Esther Neilson,
whose health was for a length of time very precarious, but we have received
lately a very favourable account of her being completely restored by the reme-
dies of a German doctor lately arrived there, who carries his apothecaries shop
in a small box in his pocket, out of which he prescribes for all corporeal complaints and succeeds in an extraordinary style, and Esther writes me herself
that she is perfectly restored to the days of her youth.[1] Charly her son, a child

1 Possibly Thomas Dent Mütter (1811–59), a Virginian of German and Scottish ancestry,
who established himself as a surgeon in Philadelphia during the 1830s. A 'biographical

of extraordinary endearments, is also on foot and active. Such is William Neilson's account to me from Philadelphia.

Adele Shine and her family are all well; he[2] has been so ill that he bid us all *adieu*, and indeed I thought it impossible he would recover, but I at last discovered it was that change of constitution that attacks mankind in general at mid age. He had no malady. It was the effects of 50 years, and by good nourishment and Adele's attention he is now well and thoroughly recovered even to becoming more corpulent than he ever was and with an excellent appetite.[3] The children are all quite well and Jane the eldest who has been two years married to a Mr Murphy of Cork and has two fine children embarks tomorrow for Cork where she will spend some time.[4] I don't expect her here again for a couple of years. It is very possible she may take a trip to the northward.

George, from whom you hear frequently, has yet a long spell to serve at his studies.[5] If he does not return soon he may come too late, for we are both very old and although we enjoy our health tolerably well it would be easily deranged. The law has made the fortune of many men here and continues to be a profitable profession, but there will be too numerous a body. All our youths natives go to the law and George has a fellow lodger hence at his studies, who I don't expect will ever become a Cicero.[6] There is a very particular friend of mine now at Newry, who should he come in your way or if in your power to be civil to him or any of his family (who are all females and very engaging) I request you to do so. He is a thoroughbred Irishman and a very able physician; his family is from Nova Scotia where I received great civility from them. He had a very narrow escape here from fever during which I was

notice' published shortly after his death records that he 'achieved a high reputation as a practical surgeon, as attested by his large *clientelle* among the citizens of this place, and the strangers from various parts of this wide domain, who sought from his skill the relief their various sufferings demanded.' Samuel D. Gross, *Autobiography of Samuel D. Gross, M.D., D.C.L. Oxon., LL.D., Cantab., Edin., Jeff. Coll., Univ. Pa., emeritus professor of surgery in the Jefferson Medical College of Philadelphia. With sketches of his contemporaries. Edited by his son* (2 vols, Philadelphia, 1887), ii, 301–6; J.P. 'Biographical notice of Thomas Dent Mütter, M.D., LL.D.' in *Transactions of the Medical Society of the State of Pennsylvania*, new series, 5 (1860), 148–54 (esp. 152).   2 i.e., John Shine, husband of Black's daughter Adele.   3 John Shine in fact died less than a year after this letter was written, on 25 February 1837. [Anon.], 'Further extracts', 210.   4 See letter nineteen, note 5.   5 Most likely a son of Josefine Lacoste née Black, Black's daughter, and Hugh Lacoste. A letter George Black Jr received from his son John late in 1836 contains a reference to news received (concerning the death of Black) 'thro' G Lacostes', and a notice of the marriage of 'G. La Coste, of Trinidad, and Lincoln's Inn, Barrister-at-law, to Eliza Piggot, youngest dau. of J.C. Constable, esq.' appeared in the *Gentleman's Magazine* in 1839. John Black to George Black Jr, 14 Dec. 1836 (PRONI, D1950/36); *GM*, 12 (1839), 196.   6 Marcus Tullius Cicero, a Roman statesman and philosopher of the first century BC, was renowned for his eloquence. The identity of the Trinidadian youth unlikely to succeed in emulating him is unknown. Miriam Green, 'Cicero and Rome' in John Boardman, Jasper Griffin and Oswyn Murray (eds), *The Oxford history of the Classical world* (Oxford, 1991), pp 454–78 at 454–9.

his doctor; he lost his son here, a fine boy who lies interred in my family graveyard. Should you by any accident see them or any of them remember me kindly, nay affectionately, to them. What is become of Kitt Read and his brother?[7] They were Newry men bred at Ballydrain.

But I must conclude for this is Sunday and the church bell is ringing at 10 o'clock, so *adieu* my dear George for the present. Assure my sister of my tender regards and if you have any stock at home married or unmarried I embrace them.

John Black

7 Possibly Christopher and James Reid, residents of Newry during the 1780s. *DML*, i, 95, 145, 330–1.

Appendix: The Letters of Adele Shine

The sequence of five letters presented here were penned by Black's daughter, Adele Shine née Black, between March 1814 and July 1817: letters one to three were written in 1814, letter four in 1815 and letter five in 1817. Written to George Black Jr and Ellen Black, with whom Adele had lived during the period 1803–10, the letters reveal Adele's affection for, and close connections with, her Irish relatives. As might be expected, there is much family news. Adele, who had married in 1811, makes reference to her husband and children, discusses her sisters, asks after her Irish relatives, including her 'sisters and brother' – that is, the children of George Black Jr and Ellen Black – and gives news of her parents. Her references to her father indicate that Black had a troubled relationship with Trinidad's new governor, Ralph Woodford, and had given up on any hopes of revisiting Ireland.

Letter One

Port of Spain 18 March 1814

My dear dada and mamma[1]

This is the first opportunity since our arrival here we have had of writing to you. Mr Shine[2] wrote you a few lines from Barbados to inform you of our speedy voyage so far, we were obliged to stay there a week much against our inclination, but the fine passage we had from there made up for all our disappointments for we were only two days coming home. I am sure you will be happy to hear we found all our dear friends in good health and spirits, and as you may well suppose quite rejoiced to see us again. As for our good negroes, they began to sing and dance, and began to huzza so that it was enough to deafen any person.[3]

1 Adele Shine née Black, Black's daughter, is in fact writing here to her aunt and uncle, John Black Jr and Ellen Black née Stewart, with whom she had lived for several years between 1803 and 1810 (see letters eight to eighteen). That she refers to them here (and in the opening salutations of appendix, letters two, three, four and five) as 'dada' and 'mamma' testifies to the emotional bonds that had developed between them during this period.   2 i.e., John Shine, Adele's husband.   3 The Trinidad 'slave registers', first compiled in 1813, show Adele to have been the owner, the previous year, of four so-called 'personal slaves'. These were Clarice Stephens, a 25-year-old domestic, who had been born in the Gold Coast, and her two young daughters (one aged 3 and the other under 2 years old); and a 12-year-old, Trinidad-born domestic whose surname is given as Wilberforce, and who was no doubt named, with a degree of malice, after the prominent abolitionist. John

I am writing this epistle in Esther's room (for since our arrival we have been living at my mother's house until our house is painted), she is very happy and comfortable. I never saw any person in my life so much altered for the better as Mr P. He is a kind, fond husband, and does every thing in his power to make our dear Esther happy.[4] She in return is so doatingly fond of him that when he is out of her sight she is perfectly miserable. A few days before our arrival home there was a very odd circumstance happened. A whale of forty feet long swimming away from some enemies of its own species got ashore completely. The negroes immediately surrounded it and cut about 1 ton of flesh off it, it then made three movements and escaped from them all though they took to their boats with the intention of [striking] but its remaining fins moved so much faster than their oars it got away from [them], this is hardly to be credited but it is a fact.

Tell my dear brothers and sisters[5] that I am searching for all kinds of curiosities for them and am in hopes of being able to procure a pretty little collection, to send by the *John* if she goes in this fleet. Tell my Uncle and Aunt Younghusband[6] that [my] mother desires me to return [them] [–] many thanks for the butter [–] [–] etc., etc., they sent them, but between ourselves there was not one hamper of all those he sent for sale good, out of them all I picked half a hamper of good ones, that is to say they were passable. Tell George[7] that I must beg of him, if any vessel of the captain's coming are careful enough and will take charge of it, he must send me a lark and a thrush. I brought a little goldfinch with me, it sings so beautifully I am afraid my father won't let me take it away from his room where he has hung it. Mr

Shine possessed twelve 'personal slaves' in 1813: eight labourers, a house servant, a cook, a carpenter and a mason. All were male and all bar two were African-born, the exceptions being Joe Miller, an 'American from New York', and Billy Pitt, a 'Creole of Barbados'. 'Register of personal slaves', 1813 (TNA, T71/503 at 135 and 412/414), consulted online via the 'Slave Registers of former British Colonial Dependencies, 1813–1834' database, available at https://search.ancestry.co.uk/search/db.aspx?htx=List&dbid=1129&offerid=0%3a7858%3a0 (accessed 16/11/2018). **4** 'Mr P' was David Park, brother of James Park (see letter two, note 13), who had married Black's daughter Esther in 1813. The pair appear to have had at least two children, David Jr and James John. Park also had a family with a woman named Polly Wilson. His will contains provision for 'one thousand dollars … for the benefit of Polly Wilson during her natural life to descend on her demise to Pinkey and David Park my children by the said Polly Wilson and also that a sum of one thousand dollars, shall also be placed under the sanction of my Executors for the sole benefit of my two children, the said Pinkey and David Park.' The identity of Wilson is unknown. 'Will and probate of David Park', 6 Dec. 1820 (PRONI, D1905/7/27); Pocock, *Shadows*, p. 217. **5** i.e., her cousins, George Black Jr's children. **6** i.e., Letitia Younghusband née Black, Black's sister, and her husband John Younghusband. **7** George Macartney Black, Adele's cousin. Adele Black arrived in Belfast the year after George Macartney Black had been born (see letter sixteen, note 13) and it is clear from her comment at the end of this letter – 'tell George to write soon to me' – and those in subsequent letters that she had grown particularly fond of him during the time she spent with his family.

Shine's head is so bewildered today I am afraid he won't be able to write to you, yesterday was St Patrick's day and all the Irishmen gave [a] subscription dinner and as they generally have many toasts to drink their heads pay for it the next day.[8] As for my father he began this day by taking a large dose of magnesia to clear his head. My kindest and best love to all our dear friends and to my dear brothers and sisters and believe me dearest dada and mamma your affectionate

    A. Shine

    Tell George to write soon to me.[9]

---

8 St Patrick's Day dinners appear to have been an annual occurrence, Adele's father having made reference to a similarly drink-soaked occasion – 'many friends inebriated' – in his letter of 19 April 1800 (see letter three). 9 See note 7.

Letter Two

Ariapita[1] 24 June 1814

My dearest dada and mamma

Since the April fleet sailed from this I have never had an opportunity of writing to you but by packet and I wrote so many letters at that time that I thought it better to delay doing so until now, we are all here rejoicing at the fine news of peace and planning <u>our</u> departure from this for Belfast. I hope and trust we will not be disappointed in our calculations as we have both even been dreaming of the happy days we are to pass near you on some little farm of our own; I fear I can't say my father is of the same way of thinking, all we dreaded respecting some letters, which we mentioned to you, proved all but too true and it hurts me to say they have greatly injured him. Our new governor Sir Ralph Woodford is a very just and good man but very arbitrary and when once he takes a dislike to any individual he is very bitter against them, and I fear he <u>is not my</u> poor father's friend.[2] All these misfortunes have had [a] very bad effect on my mother's health. About a month ago we were very much afraid we would have lost her, but thank the Almighty she is much better and the doctors say that her complaint with care may be cured; it is what is called an inflammation on the liver and which nothing almost but change of climate ever cures. She wishes very much and seems determined to do so next year, but I fear when that time comes she will change her mind as my father won't be able to go with her, and though he was to remain with us during her absence she would never be satisfied altogether. You may perceive we are not quite as well contented with matters as we ought to be; as to us we are both getting so fat that we hardly know what to do with ourselves. As to me I am as <u>broad</u> as I am long and in reality if I continue to get so square I'll be a perfect curiosity. There is a gentleman of the [name] of Cacharde[3] who goes in this fleet to England and intends taking a tour through Ireland, I have

---

1 An estate named Ariapita is known to have been located on the outskirts of Port of Spain. According to Lionel Mordaunt Fraser it was, by 1816, 'a barren waste', and later provided a site for a courthouse and police barracks. Fraser, *Trinidad*, ii, 56.   2 Ralph Woodford (1784–1828) had become governor of Trinidad in 1813, and held the position until his death in 1828. During his first meeting with Trinidad's council (see letter four, note 28), Woodford raised questions over the expenditure of money to rebuild Port of Spain following the fire of 1808 (see letter eleven, note 4) and communicated the Prince Regent's decision that the current councillors' services were no longer required, owing to the 'want of temper, discretion and tact' they displayed, two years previously, during the dispute between Governor Hislop and Chief Justice Smith (see letter eighteen, note 4). These circumstances might account for Adele's assertion that Woodford was not her father's friend, not least as Black was chair of the building committee. Henige, *Colonial governors*, p. 182; Carmichael, *Trinidad and Tobago*, pp 105–7, 114, 151; Pocock, *Shadows*, pp 214–15.   3 Most likely Francis Cachard. See letter sixteen, note 2.

taken the liberty of giving a letter of introduction to you. He is an intimate of ours and his wife, an elegant woman,[4] remains in our neighbourhood until his return. He is a well informed man and I have no doubt that George[5] will be glad to see him as he will be able to give him a very correct account of all Europe. He intends going to France, Switzerland, Italy etc. etc. before he goes to your part of the world. Give a thousand embraces to my dear brothers and sisters and a thousand kind [reme]mbrances to all my dear friends, and believe me dear dada and mamma your ever

affectionate child

A. Shine

John[6] writes you himself therefore I won't say anything for him.

4 Most likely Caroline Cachard née Devenish. See letter sixteen, note 2.   5 i.e., George Macartney Black, Adele's cousin.   6 i.e., John Shine, Adele's husband.

Letter Three

Trinidad 8 September 1814

My dear mamma

Since the departure of the *John*[1] this is the first time I have addressed you. Mr S[2] wrote you a long letter a few packets ago, which I have no doubt you have received e'er this, not one line have we received from you since our arrival here, every packet I hope to get a letter but by each one am disappointed. To what to attribute your silence I am at a loss to conjecture, but I trust in God that it is only a little laziness. We had letters from Mariquite by the last packet.[3] She was in great spirits at the prospect of meeting with the colonel, she also informed us of the death of the poor old lady whom I sincerely lament, but it must be a great relief to them all as she had been so long suffering.[4] Mr Shine and I are every day proposing to ourselves the pleasure of meeting you all in the year 1816, the expectation of a little new comer among us seems rather to increase than abate his desire of settling in Ireland.[5] You cannot think how proud I am when I think of introducing a little creature to you, whom I am sure (that is to say I flatter myself) you and my dear dada will be fond of. <u>Somebody</u> is as proud as myself at the idea, but of course, would not own it.[6] I hope and trust it will be as deserving of our affections as your dear flock, I think of them every day and already try to recollect all your first lessons; you will I am afraid laugh at my nonsense, but it is my first and you must forgive my foolishness. My poor father's heart seems as much pleased as mine.

We are all here very dull, the bad prices of sugars after so fair a prospect and a very sickly season seems to have broken every person's spirits. Thank God we are all very well, except a little cold now and then. As for my John, and myself, we seem as if we had laid a wager to see which would be fattest and be in best health. I am actually ashamed in the morning at breakfast I eat so much. How has peace affected Belfast?[7] I hope there are a few more beaux and fewer belle's than there were before. Mr S often laughs at the story of

1 See appendix, letter one.   2 i.e., John Shine, Adele's husband.   3 i.e., Mariquite Graves née Black, Adele's sister.   4 James Graves, husband of Adele's sister Mariquite, had been promoted from lieutenant-colonel to colonel in June 1814, and had travelled to Europe on leave in July 1814. The 'poor old lady' referred to was his mother, Ann Graves née Dunlevie (1751–1814), who had died on 17 June 1814. *RMC*, iv, 162; Burke, *Landed gentry*, p. 275.   5 The child with whom Adele was, at this point, pregnant was Jane Shine. Letter nineteen; appendix, letter four.   6 i.e., Adele's husband, John Shine.   7 Napoleon had been defeated, and exiled to Elba, in April 1814. As is, of course, well known, he returned to the field in 1815 and was not finally overcome until the Battle of Waterloo in June of that year. In Belfast the initial peace of 1814 was celebrated with an illumination, during which 'the most perfect harmony and good humour prevailed', and a public dinner. *BNL*, 26 and 29 Apr. 1814; Uglow, *In these times*, pp 598–602, 615–20.

their never having been more than two beaux in Belfast, he says the next time he visits it he hopes the complaint will be reversed, and there will be more beaux than belles. We have done all in our power to get my father to go and pay you a visit but all to no effect. He thinks of going to Halifax next spring.[8] Our new governor is not at all his friend and we hope by his absenting himself for a while it [–] be the means of making the one forget his [–] and restore the other to his usual spirits.[9] How much better it would be if he would go and see his native place once more. I don't like to think of it, as it always puts me into bad spirits. How are all my dear sisters and brothers? We hope soon to have letters from them all, as Mr Park[10] tells us he expects a vessel called the *Atlantic* from your port. Don't let them forget me, I assure you Mr S and I talk of them every day and wish we were nearer them, a thousand kisses to them. My affectionate love to my dear dada and tell him to write soon to Mr S. My kindest love to Mrs W,[11] Alick and Mary,[12] Mrs Sturrock[13] and the girls, Mrs Clarke and the Clarkes[14] and all the Ballydrain family.[15] Mr Shine desires his love to you all, and believe me dear mamma your ever affectionate child.

    A. Shine

8 John Black had spent time in Halifax, Nova Scotia in 1799. Whether or not Black did return to Halifax is unclear, but in her subsequent, surviving letter, dated 9 February 1815, Adele notes that '[m]y Father who I wrote you some time ago had left us for his health returned the day before yesterday quite recovered'. See letters two, three, four, six and twenty and appendix, letter four. 9 See appendix, letter two, note 2. 10 i.e., David Park, husband of Adele's sister Esther. 11 Probably Mrs Wilson, who Adele refers to in her subsequent letter and who was, most likely, Jane Wilson née Stewart, the sister of Ellen Black née Stewart, Adele's aunt. Riddell, 'Great chemist', 67. 12 Most likely Mary Isabella Wilson (1799–1900), daughter of Jane Wilson née Stewart and Walter Wilson. The precise identity of Alick is unclear, though in addition to Mary Isabella, Walter and Jane Wilson had two sons. Riddell, 'Great chemist', 79. 13 'Mrs Sturrock' was Annabella Sturrock née Stewart, sister of Ellen Black née Stewart, Adele's aunt, and widow of the Revd James Trail Sturrock (*c.*1772–1803). *DML*, iii, 401; Riddell, 'Great chemist', 67. 14 i.e., the family of Mary Clarke née Stewart, sister of Adele's aunt, Ellen Black née Stewart. 15 Around 1805, Ballydrain was purchased from George Stewart, brother of Ellen Black née Stewart, Adele's aunt, by John Younghusband, the husband of Letitia Younghusband née Black, another of Adele's aunts. Younghusband retained the property until the mid-1830s and thus, when Adele wrote, the Younghusbands were the Ballydrain family. Benn, *Belfast from 1799 till 1810*, p. 166; Riddell, 'Great chemist', 71; Black, 'Ballydrain', 17.

Letter Four

Ariapita 9 February 1815

My dear mamma

A young man who leaves this for Belfast in a few days has promised to be the bearer of any letters we may wish to send, therefore I shall take the opportunity and write you a long letter. In the first place I must inform you of my happiness, on the 10 November I was blessed with a <u>beautiful</u> little daughter, of course the very image of Mr Shine, that is to say she has got his eyes, eyebrows, mouth, and chin, but my pug nose as completely as anything you ever saw. She is thank God a healthy child, small but very firm, and as lively as a little grig.[1] For 1 month she suffered a good deal with cholics (and like a great goose each time she had a little cholics I used to cry ready to break my heart). Since she made her appearance we have made fifty plans about taking her to dear Ireland but have been obliged to break them all again, and content ourselves with [the] idea of being able to take her there in a couple of years. I would be perfectly satisfied if I thought we could accomplish it in as short a time but when Mr S[2] says two I fear he means 2 x 2. My father who I wrote you some time ago had left us for his health returned the day before yesterday quite recovered. We have delayed christening little Jane Clotilda until his return. Without having asked your permission, I have appointed you one of her godmothers and my mother the other and my father godfather. She is to be christened on the 26th of this month, the anniversary of our marriage (what an old woman I am growing, 4 years married).[3] If it was 10 and all spent as happily as those four, how proud I would be, but I fear I will rebel as I can <u>never</u> content to bringing my little Jane up in this vile place.[4] We have always been very economical but were never so much so, as since her arrival. We try to save every <u>stampy</u> (I will enclose 1 that you may know what a small thing it is) to enable us to take her from here. Each day makes me hate this place more and more. We have news here that there is peace with America.[5] How true this is we are not yet certain, but if it is I trust my father (as he does not seem to have any idea of visiting Ireland) will go there, if not to settle to take a trip. Our governor is far, far from being his friend and it is greatly to be feared he will make his time most disagreeable to him, poor old man. How

1 A variant of 'merry as a grig', a phrase dating from at least the sixteenth century and denoting liveliness. John Ayto (ed.), *Oxford dictionary of English idioms*, 3rd ed. (Oxford, 2010), p. 156.   2 i.e., John Shine, Adele's husband.   3 In the original manuscript, the number four is underlined three times.   4 In the original manuscript the word never is underlined twice.   5 Britain and the United States of America had gone to war in 1812, in a conflict provoked, at least in part, by British violations of American maritime rights. A treaty formally ending the war was signed on 14 December 2014. Davis and Mintz, *Boisterous sea*, pp 304–15.

hard it is he cannot spend his latter days in peace and quietness, but must be tormented and teased by such a fellow; the merchants of late have refused paying some of the taxes laid by him on all mercantile produce brought here. He seems a little alarmed at it, which has given them still greater courage, as he pretended heretofore that it was by the Prince Regent's orders. I hope from my heart they may be able to make him quake a little as his tyranny was becoming so great that some [–] speak to him.[6] In fact we thought we were [going] to have a second Bonaparte here.

How do my dear sisters and brothers get on?[7] I long to hear from them. My mother received a letter from you by the packet which gave us the pleasant intelligence of your being all quite well. I heard there was a vessel expected from your port, I hope it is true as we shall have letters from both great and small. I wrote my little dear John a long letter enclosed to George by the *John* that went from this some time ago, did he ever receive it?[8] I had almost forgot to wish you joy on the business between my dear dada and Mr P being at an end. When I heard of it (which was from yourself) I absolutely cried with joy, I never was fond of <u>that</u> <u>uncle</u> but I'm sure I hate him now.

Mr S is so very busy with a vessel which he loads by this fleet that he will not be able to write himself but he desires me to say everything that is kind to you all for him and he will write you by the next fleet which goes in April. My very best love to my dear, dear dada, sisters and brothers and tell George[9] I am [–] angry with him for not writing to me; my love to my dear Mrs Wilson[10] and Mrs Sturrock[11] and the <u>children</u> (which are as big as myself in width but not in circumference for nursing agrees with me so well I am as big as a puncheon) and believe me dear mamma your ever affectionate child

A. Shine

My little Jane sends you a kiss each, her little kisses are so sweet I am all day tormenting with [–]

6 Gertrude Carmichael notes that governor Ralph Woodford, to whom Adele here refers, was said by some to be 'haughty and proud'. 'In private life', she writes, 'he was kind and friendly, but knew when to be severe. As governor of the colony he demanded to be treated with the dignity due to his office, and when this was forgotten he had no compunction in administering a stern rebuke.' Carmichael, *Trinidad and Tobago*, p. 152.   7 i.e., George Black Jr's children, Adele's cousins.   8 i.e., George Macartney Black and his younger brother John, sons of George Black Jr.   9 i.e., George Macartney Black.   10 Most likely Jane Wilson née Stewart, sister of Adele's aunt, Ellen Black née Stewart.   11 i.e., Annabella Sturrock née Stewart, sister of Adele's aunt, Ellen Black née Stewart.

Letter Five

Ariapita 9 July 1817

My dearest mamma

Our dear, dear Esther[1] leaves us tomorrow for Scotland from thence to Belfast where they mean to remain. Judge my dear mamma what are my feelings on the occasion. We have always been inseparable companions and since our return from Ireland the intimacy between Mr P and Mr S[2] has made us still more so. Esther's fine disposition and gentle manners will make any person love her. Do my dear mamma be kind to her for my sake, you will in a short time be so for herself. She is a pattern to all young wives and as a mother her little boy[3] will speak more forcibly than I can. Mr Park will improve more on acquaintance than you can imagine. He is one of the best and most generous hearted men I ever met. His temper is a little hasty, but has been greatly improved by Esther. He is much beloved by us all and I assure you deservedly so; he has been the kindest of sons to my father, without him he would have been a ruined man. He, poor man, feels their going away as much and perhaps more than any of us, but he bears it silently. My poor mother is inconsolable as she says she will never see Esther again. Since their departure has been fixed upon, she has been constantly fretting about it, which I am sorry to say has made a visible alteration in her. I trust after they are gone she will have fortitude to view Esther's going to so fine a country in a different way from what she does at present. Her constitution is not a very good one, which I hope the fine air of sweet little Ireland will do a great deal of good to, and I'm sure her poor little boy will escape many many complaints which our poor children in this country are subject to. I was much alarmed a few nights ago, by hearing a noise in my little Jane's bed and on going to see her I found her suffocating from worms coming into her throat. The doctor gave her some medicine which gave her great relief but she has [had] a [little] fever ever since. She is very [–]. Esther wished to take her with her, but she is too young to send her away from me yet. Your little name sake Ellen is a fine stumpy wee thing, all good humour and play, she puts me very much in mind of Mary[4] when her age. She was a year old on the 7th of this month, the doctor desired me to wean her but I cannot find it in my heart to do so, poor

---

1 i.e., Esther Park née Black, Adele's sister.   2 i.e., David Park and John Shine. That the two were on good terms is confirmed by Park's will, in which Shine is named as an executor. 'Will and probate of David Park', 6 Dec. 1820 (PRONI, D1905/7/27).   3 Most likely a reference to David Park Jr, son of David Park and Esther Park née Black.   4 Most likely a reference to Mary Isabella Black, eldest daughter of George Black Jr and Ellen Black née Stewart. While her date of birth is unknown, Mary Isabella was of marriageable age in 1825 and was therefore likely born during the years Adele had spent in Belfast. *BNL*, 7 Aug. 1825.

little thing she has only six teeth. Mr Shine still holds out the hope of going in a few years to Ireland. He has formed a partnership with Mr Paterson a relation of Mr Lindsay who you may have seen in Dublin.[5] He is a young man of great abilities and I hope will let us take a trip home in a year or two or perhaps to remain. Besides being a merchant Mr Shine is still (baker and butcher) contractor for beef and bread to the troops, he is working hard. God grant he may succeed, it would be a miserable thought indeed if our little children were to remain in this country. Dear mamma write to me soon and tell me all about yourselves, it is time out of mind since I have had a letter from any of you. God bless you all my dear mamma and grant we may soon meet. A thousand loves to my dear dada and believe me ever your affectionate child

    A. Shine

[5] Possibly a reference to the Dublin merchant John Lindsay. *DML*, ii, 14.

Index

reputation of, 15–16, 56–7, 61–2; requests goods be sent to Trinidad, 53, 91–2, 93, 94, 107; sends goods to Ireland, 80, 93–4, 99, 107, 116, 119, 148, 149–1; settles in Trinidad, 31–3; West Indies as home for, 40, 45, 62, 148, 151

Black I, John, 20

Black II, John (son of John Black I), 20

Black III, John (son of John Black II), 19, 20, 21, 22, 23, 24–5, 27, 30, 40, 69n13, 70, 72n26, 87n21, 90n40, 90n41

Black IV, John (son of John Black III), 20, 24, 86n21, 90n40, 91n45, 154, 154n10, 155n11

Black V, John (son of John Black IV), 20, 91n45

Black, John (son of George Black Jr), 144n12, 154, 154n8, 155, 155n13, 157n5, 167

Black, John Joseph (son of George Macartney Black), 117n7

Black, Josefine (daughter of John Black), 35, 40, 43, 64, 74n2, 75, 79, 82, 82n5, 95, 102, 108, 110n4, 117, 124, 129, 132, 154, 156, 157

Black, Joseph (son of John Black III), 15, 20, 28–9, 30, 52, 60, 72, 72n26, 73n29, 73n30, 78, 79, 79n4, 101, 101n22; will of, 30, 78, 79n5

Black, Julie (daughter of John Black), 35, 40n167, 43, 74n2, 78, 79, 85–6, 105, 124

Black, Katharine (daughter of John Black III), 21n40, 24, 43, 86, 86n21, 103, 122n19, 123, 130

Black, Letitia (sister of John Black), 16, 22, 25, 43, 61, 68, 72n24, 76, 77, 78, 80, 84, 94, 97, 104, 108, 109, 112, 114, 124, 136, 137, 140, 151, 160, 165n15

Black, Letitia (daughter of Letitia Black), 68n6

Black, Letitia Adelaide (daughter of George Black Jr), 144n13

Black, Margaret (wife of John Black III), 20, 72n26, 90n41

Black, Margaret (daughter of John Black III), 21n40

Black, Margaret (daughter of George Black), 21

Black, Margaret (daughter of Letitia Black), 68n6

Black, Margaret/Marguerite (daughter of John Black IV), 154, 154n11

Black, Mariquite (daughter of John Black), 35, 40, 41, 43, 64, 74n2, 78, 79, 85, 95, 106, 108, 115, 116, 117, 118, 129, 132, 138, 139, 140, 145, 164; departure from Trinidad, 43–4, 52, 105–6, 109–11, 113–14; marriage of, 41, 93, 95, 95n6, 97, 99

Black, Martha (daughter of Letitia Black), 68n6

Black, Mary (wife of John Black VI), 155, 155n13

Black, Mary Isabella (daughter of George Black Jr), 144n13, 168n4

Black, Matilda, 72n23

Black, Priscilla (daughter of John Black III), 21, 21n40

Black, Robert (son of John Black II), 20

Black, Robert (son of John Black III), 21, 21n40, 76n11, 77n13

Black, Robert (son of George Black), 21n47

Black, Samuel (son of John Black III), 21n40, 23, 103, 103n32

Black, Sarah Anne (wife of George Macartney Black), 117n7

Black, Thomas (son of John Black III), 21n40, 69n12, 90, 90n41, 113n2

Blackwood family, 89n35, 100

Blackwood, Dorcas (Baroness Dufferin and Clandeboye), 89n35

Blackwood, Frederick Temple Hamilton Temple (marquis of Dufferin and Ava), 89n35

Blackwood, James Stevenson (Baron Dufferin), 89, 89n37

Blackwood, John, 89n35, 90n39, 90n40

Blackwood, Leeson, 81, 89–90, 89n35, 95, 100

Blair, James, 26

Blair, Lambert, 26